Welcoming each wonder

Welcoming each wonder

More contemporary stories for reflection

Tom Gordon

WILD GOOSE PUBLICATIONS

First published 2010

Wild Goose Publications
4th Floor, Savoy House, 140 Sauchiehall Street, Glasgow G2 3DH, UK
www.ionabooks.com
Wild Goose Publications is the publishing division of the Iona Community.
Scottish Charity No. SC003794. Limited Company Reg. No. SC096243.

ISBN 978-1-84952-078-2

Cover photograph © Mary Gordon

A catalogue record for this book is available from the British Library.

Overseas distribution:
Australia: Willow Connection Pty Ltd, Unit 4A, 3-9 Kenneth Road,
Manly Vale, NSW 2093
New Zealand: Pleroma, Higginson Street, Otane 4170, Central Hawkes Bay
Canada: Novalis/Bayard Publishing & Distribution, 10 Lower Spadina Ave.,
Suite 400, Toronto, Ontario M5V 2Z2

Printed by Bell & Bain, Thornliebank, Glasgow

Mixed Sources
Product group from well-managed
forests and other controlled sources
www.fsc.org Cert no. TT-COC-002769
© 1996 Forest Stewardship Council
FSC

To

F J

a good friend,
fellow traveller
and sharer of stories.

Contents

Preface

I have to confess I've always been a fan of the Lectionary, the Calendar of Bible readings for the year. This way of charting a pilgrimage through the seasons is becoming more popular, reflected in the growing number of books on the subject. Some of these volumes give the impression that they have to be very earnest – which is odd, because the Bible isn't. Well, mercifully, neither is this book.

You will be delighted to discover stories that are funny, moving and fresh. They are so obviously written by someone who has wrestled with biblical texts week by week, but has also lived in the real world where people seldom discuss the Lectionary at the bus stop. You will encounter different ways to think about the signposts of the Christian Year. So Epiphany, Transfiguration and Advent are approached through tales of a singer's debut in a folk club, a choir with an attack of nerves, and the adventures of a dodgy goalkeeper.

The writer of this book was familiar with the wilderness from the beginning of his life. Tom Gordon was born and brought up in Fort William, surrounded by the peace and beauty of the lochs, coast and mountains of the West Highlands. He spent his formative years in the shadow of Ben Nevis, the highest mountain in the British Isles. The silence and aching beauty of the Highlands lingers around these pages like the smell of a peat fire.

Tom is also drenched in another aspect of the stillness of wilderness and mountains, having spent years as a Chaplain in a Hospice. He will have sat for hours at many a bedside, sharing the silence and listening passionately for that still, small voice. Those skills are glimpsed in these earthy prayers and gentle meditations. Only rarely are we given any personal background to the words on these pages. So watch out for the one story written in the first person, and for the poem written for a dying friend while Tom was on Sabbatical at the Church of the Saviour, in Washington DC.

It was in 1977 that I first met Tom Gordon. He was working as the Minister of the Old Kirk of Edinburgh. However, that rather grand title gives you no clue about the part of Edinburgh where he ministered. These days it's a different world, but back then the West Pilton housing scheme in Edinburgh was a neighbourhood at the top of all the league tables for poverty and multiple deprivation. Community groups from Soweto or East Berlin used to come on solidarity visits to Scotland and declare that they felt at home in West Pilton. This was not the Edinburgh that tourists saw during the Festival. The place was just down the road from Princes Street, but a million miles away.

However, if the neighbourhood was depressing, the neighbours were welcoming, and life was never dull. Against all the odds and despite the statistics to the contrary, the Old Kirk was a model of the Kingdom of God. Tom thrived in this environment and the people loved him – particularly those who never darkened the doors of the church building. So it's no surprise to read the story of Michelle, the prostitute, and Toni, whom she meets regularly in a dark, graffiti-covered stairwell in the most dangerous part of town. But the story is not what you expect.

I have a hunch that you will enjoy this pilgrimage, in the company of Farrin, the asylum-seeker from Iran, Alan, the one-legged footballer, Scooby the dog's mum, the girl who sent the text to Twisted Face, and all the other colourful characters who will go with you on this road to Emmaus.

The Very Reverend Alan McDonald

Introduction

We all need patterns and familiarity in our lives to help us make sense of the changes we have to cope with on life's journey. The sun sets in the evening and rises in the morning; the harshness of a winter follows the mellowness of an autumn; the warmth of a summer follows the freshness of a spring. And while the pattern of the seasons isn't rigid or always predictable, the framework of a year's journey remains pretty stable.

Our religious frameworks often embrace nature's patterns and follow natural themes. But where they don't, the patterns we create in our religious lives still seek to give us the stability and familiarity we crave.

For Jews, the Festival of Purim in February is followed a month or so later by the eight-day Festival of the Passover; Yom Kippur falls in September, with Chanukah (or Hanukkah) the eight-day Festival of Light, coming along in early December. These festivals and days of memorial recall historic events, and bid people reflect on important times for their community as well as their own journey of faith.

For Muslims, Milad-un-Nabi allows them to celebrate the birth of the prophet Muhammad in February or March, and Ramadan, the month of fasting, begins in mid-August; Ramadan ends with Eid-Ul-Fitr (Id) in mid-September, and Al-Hijira in early December marks the Islamic New Year. These are times of devotion, fasting and prayerfulness, familiar to individuals and Muslim communities at worship.

For Christians, Advent leads them into Christmas, and Epiphany closes the festive season; Lent prepares them for Easter, and the Ascension and Pentecost offer significant celebrations on the conclusion of Jesus's earthly life and the beginnings of the Christian Church. And, even in a secularised society, the Easter Bank Holiday, Christmas Day and even Whitsuntide are our markers in the unfolding of another year.

So patterns matter, not just because they are sometimes slavishly observed, but because they help us make sense of changes and movement, landmarks and celebrations, as nature progresses, as another year unfolds, and as our faith is restored, renewed and given meaning again.

The religious pattern I know best is the Christian one, and so this book – along with the other two books in the series – takes the cycle of the Christian Lectionary as its framework. But it is simply that, a framework, a pattern to follow, with my hope that it will be a pattern which will be helpful in all faith contexts and none.

There's a traditional Yorkshire carol called 'Candlemas Eve' which runs:

Down with the rosemary and bay, down with the mistletoe,
Instead of holly, now up-raise, the greener box to show,
The greener box to show.

>   *Thus times do shift, thus times do shift,*
>   *Each thing its time doth hold,*
>   *New things succeed, new things succeed,*
>   *As former things grow old.*

The holly hitherto did sway, let box now domineer,
Until the dancing Easter day, on Easter's eve appear,
On Easter's eve appear.

>   *Thus times do shift, thus times do shift,*
>   *Each thing its time doth hold,*
>   *New things succeed, new things succeed,*
>   *As former things grow old.*

The youthful box which now hath grace, your houses to renew,
Grown old, surrender must its place, unto the freshened yew,
Unto the freshened yew.

Thus times do shift, thus times do shift,
Each thing its time doth hold,
New things succeed, new things succeed,
As former things grow old.

When yew is out, then birch comes in, and many the flowers beside,
Both of a fresh and fragrant kin, to honour Whitsuntide,
To honour Whitsuntide.

Thus times do shift, thus times do shift,
Each thing its time doth hold,
New things succeed, new things succeed,
As former things grow old.

These traditional words reflect the changing seasons. And as the Christian year was traditionally tied to these changes, the growth of flowers, shrubs, trees and produce echoes the Christian journey. As nature moves from mistletoe and holly, through the growth of the yew tree, to the coming of the birch and summer flowers, so life and faith move inexorably from Christmas, through Easter, to Whitsun. And in this old carol, this movement and change is pondered on the eve of Candlemas in the middle of it all.

'Times do shift', the song says. And they do indeed. Nothing stands still. 'We go with the flow', as we would say in modern parlance. Everything has its time. 'To everything its season', as the writer of Ecclesiastes puts it. Former things grow old. Life moves on.

So, as another guide through these shifting times in nature, life and faith, this book follows the same pattern as the first, *A Blessing to Follow.* It provides more stories and reflections, this time for Year A of the Lectionary cycle, as another year passes.

People have asked me how I manage to come up with so many stories. The answer to that is, 'I don't know.' The stories are there. I just access them when I need to. I've stopped trying to work out 'why? or 'how?' I just hope you'll continue to enjoy the stories and find them helpful.

As before, each story concludes with a poem, reflection or prayer of my own. I hope these continue to be helpful too, as an adjunct to a story, an elaboration of an idea, or a stand-alone piece. This time I've included two pieces which aren't mine. 'The seed I have scattered' and 'The land o' the Leal' are two songs, from religious and secular contexts respectively, that have always meant a great deal to me.

John Bell and Graham Maule have another song called 'Enemy of Apathy', which gives the title to one of their compilations of new songs for worship published by the Iona Community in 1988. These are the words:

> *She sits like a bird, brooding on the waters*
> *Hovering on the chaos of the world's first day;*
> *She sighs and she sings, mothering creation,*
> *Waiting to give birth to all the Word will say.*
>
> *She wings over earth, resting where she wishes,*
> *Lighting close at hand or soaring through the skies;*
> *She nests in the womb, welcoming each wonder,*
> *Nourishing potential hidden to our eyes.*
>
> *She dances in fire, startling her spectators,*
> *Waking tongues of ecstasy where dumbness reigned;*
> *She weans and inspires all whose hearts are open,*
> *Nor can she be captured, silenced or restrained.*
>
> *For she is the Spirit, one with God in essence,*
> *Gifted by the Saviour in eternal love;*
> *She is the key opening the scriptures,*
> *Enemy of apathy and heavenly dove.*

So, if the Spirit which moves amongst us is really involved with welcoming each wonder, might we not do the same? I hope these stories will help you with your own welcoming and wondering as you journey through another year.

Once again, I am grateful to a number of people who have a hand in this book: my daughter, Kathryn, for her endless support and enthusiasm, and the insight she offers when children are part of a story; her sister and brother, Mairi and James, for their unfailing encouragement; my wife, Mary, for her helpful comments on stories and poems, and for the way that encourages me with future work; and of course thanks to her, once again, for the cover photograph; my sister, Margaret, who could double as my agent as she encourages people to read what I've written; Bob Glover for his permission to use one of his ideas as the basis for a story; Sandra and Neil and the other staff at Wild Goose Publications for all their good work; Grace and George at the Edinburgh Presbytery office for their practical support; the Very Rev. Alan McDonald for agreeing to write a preface and for such kind and generous words; the countless people who have given positive feedback and encouragement to continue this process of writing and reflecting; all those unnamed and unknown folk who have been the inspiration for many of these stories; and, of course, to my friend, Father John, the FJ to whom this book is dedicated, who is simply a very special person.

So *Welcoming Each Wonder* is now yours to enjoy, with my sincere hope that new wonders might be welcomed by you through the pages that follow.

1 Ready and standing guard

Micky was a goalkeeper. He wasn't a very good goalkeeper. But, then, he didn't play for a very good football team – so why should *he* be any different? Micky didn't enjoy being a goalkeeper and he doubted whether he would have enjoyed it even if he'd been any good. But being a rubbish goalkeeper in a rubbish team just wasn't a lot of fun.

He *had* to play – so his teacher said – because there were only thirteen boys in Primary 6 that year, so everyone had to play for the school team, eleven players and two subs – so his teacher said – and because girls couldn't play – so his teacher said – it had to be the boys, and the biggest one had to go in goal – so his teacher said – and that meant Micky. Huh! Micky had no choice – so his teacher said – and so he was a goalkeeper, even though he wasn't any good.

His dad, on the other hand, was *delighted* Micky was the goalkeeper in the school team. Micky's dad had great hopes for his goal-keeping son – 'He'll be a Gordon Banks one day,' Micky'd heard him say to a mate once – whoever Gordon Banks was – 'Play in the Premiership he will.' And he said things that Micky never understood, like, 'Always remember, you're the star man, son, the last line of defence. You're the custodian of the onion-bag, the guardian of the net.'

Micky reckoned his dad was deluded, or soft in the head, or deaf and blind. With scores in their last six games of 13-nil, 9-nil, 15-nil, 3-nil (that game was abandoned before half-time because of the rain ...), 10-nil and 16-1 (the opposing goalkeeper had slipped in the mud and dropped the ball into his own net ...) couldn't his dad see that it was all a waste of time? But what are dads like, eh? Full of hope that their rubbish goalkeeping son might one day make it big ... Ah well ... Back to being 'custodian of onion-bag' ...

Micky was in goal as usual on the town playing fields on a wet Saturday morning. It was nearing half-time – at least, he hoped it was, if the clock on the bandstand was right – and his team were already down 6-nil. Micky was wet, bored, cold, miserable, dirty and thoroughly fed up. His dad was there, of course, along with some of the other dads, shouting encouragement and offering regular advice on tactics and skills. (What *are* dads like, eh?) But it was when his team-mates were on one of their occasional forays up the other end of the pitch that Micky noticed that an old pensioner was in trouble.

He'd been keeping an eye on the old man on and off during the game, watching him shuffling into the park (1-nil), feeding the ducks by the pond (2-nil), settling down on the bench with his shopping at his feet (3-nil, Micky having gone the wrong way at a penalty and ending up *covered* in mud ...), lighting a cigarette (4-nil – 'Well off-side,' he'd heard his dad shout, though, it didn't matter much as the centre-forward would have scored anyway as the team's entire defence was posted missing ...), pouring himself a hot drink from his flask (5-nil, own-goal by the full-back ...) and opening his paper for a read (6-nil – centre-forward's hat-trick, so Micky calculated ...).

But now Micky reckoned something was wrong. The old chap had dropped his paper on the ground and it was blowing away in the wind. He'd spilled his tea, and the flask had fallen sideways onto the bench. And the man had fallen the other way and was slumped at an odd angle against the bench's arm. He didn't move. For a few moments Micky thought he was asleep. But it didn't look right.

He was so distracted that he didn't notice the marauding hordes of the opposition forward line descending *en masse* into his penalty box. 'Micky! MICKY! Concentrate. Micky! Dive, Micky! Save it! MICKY!' came the anguished cries of his team-mates and agitated dads. But it was no use. (7-nil – easy goal for the winger ...)

The recriminations were about to begin – big time – but Micky took no heed. By now he knew that something was *really* wrong with the old man. So he left his goal – and his bemused team-mates – and started to run towards the park bench were the old man lay. The shouts calling him back didn't last long as the grown-ups sussed in no time what was up. Things happened pretty quickly after that. Micky's dad used his mobile phone to call 999. Within minutes an ambulance and paramedics were on the scene. The old man was rushed to hospital.

There was a quick confab among the dads and the organisers of the two teams. It was decided the game should be abandoned. 7–nil it was. Game over. 'What a relief,' should have been Micky's reaction. But he was more worried about the welfare of an old man whose name he didn't know than he was about the rubbish football match.

'You did well today, son,' his dad told him on the way home from the game. Micky's dad *always* said something like that after a match, being his usual encouraging self. (What are dads like, eh?) Micky mumbled something about doing his best – as he always did. But his dad said, 'No, not just the game, son. You did well with the old guy. Who knows what would have happened if we hadn't got there that quickly. You did well son. I'm proud of you. You were ready when you needed to be, son. At the end of the day, it's that kind of standing guard that *really* matters. You're a star, right enough.'

Micky smiled. What are dads like, eh? But then, *he'd* always known that there were things to be ready for that were *much* more important than football.

On guard

Here I stand as I am bidden,
Waiting,
Watching,
Ready for anything.

Here I stand as is my duty,
Prepared,
Practised,
With a watchful eye.

Here I stand as I have responded,
Selfless,
Sensitive,
Aware of my tasks.

I pray I can wait with patience,
And always watch with diligence.

I hope I've prepared with thoroughness,
And I'm well practised in my skills.

I want to stay selfless, even when I'm tired,
And sensitive when it is needed most.

Ready,
Watchful,
Aware,
I stand on guard,
For all that I might find.

Because, that's what guardians do, eh?

First in Advent

Old Testament: Isaiah 2:1-5
Epistle: Romans 13:11-14
Gospel: Matthew 24:36-44

2 The Christmas project

Zac's dad had a shed. It sat at the bottom of the long back garden, partly out of sight behind the old apple tree. Zac had helped his dad build the shed during the school holidays in the summer. He'd been the one who did most of the painting too – at least as high as he could reach, for his dad had said it was too dangerous for a little boy to do painting from a ladder. So Zac's dad had painted the really high bits and put the felt on the roof – because it was Zac's dad's shed.

It wasn't that Zac hadn't been allowed into the shed – at least he had been at the start. He'd helped his dad put in a workbench and hooks on the walls for his dad's tools. He'd watched as his dad fitted a 'jig-saw' – whatever that was – though it didn't look anything like any jigsaw Zac had ever played with. He'd not been allowed to help with the big metal vice his dad had fixed to the workbench – 'too heavy and too dangerous', his dad had said – but he'd been amazed to see how tightly it gripped a piece of metal in its jaws when his dad had turned the handle really hard.

Zac had been chuffed when his dad had given him his whole box of tools and asked him to hang them on the hooks and holders on the wall beside the bench. Zac had great fun putting all the screw-drivers in a row, the little red one, the shabby blue one, the longer yellow one, and so on, till they were all in place – 'like soldiers on parade', his dad had said. And then there were the spanners, and pliers, and hammers, and funny tools with sharp ends which Zac didn't know the name of. And when he was done with arranging the tools, his dad was *very* pleased indeed.

But Zac hadn't really been in the shed much since then. It was his dad's shed, after all, and not for Zac to play in. It was locked when his dad wasn't there.

Zac's dad was in the shed a lot these days. As the summer moved into autumn, and autumn was taken over by the colder winter days, Zac's dad was in the shed more and more. When Zac was going to bed he could look out over the garden and just about see his dad moving around in the shed through the little window that faced the house, the lighted window now visible through the barer branches of the apple tree.

Zac had asked his dad what he was doing in the shed, and could he come and watch. 'Soon enough. You'll see soon enough,' was the gentle but dismissive response. He'd asked his mum if *she* knew what dad was up to in the shed. She replied that he should ask his dad. So he did – again – and was told, 'Soon enough, soon enough …' He'd asked his dad if he could help, just as he'd done with the painting and the tools. 'Not just now,' he was told. So Zac's dad spent a lot of time in the shed. And Zac wondered …

Four weeks before Christmas, the wondering was over. Zac had come home from school and, after his homework, he'd had supper with his mum and dad as usual. But before bedtime, instead of his usual milk and biscuits, Zac was in for a surprise when his dad sat him on his knee and announced, 'Would you like to come to see what's been happening in the shed?' 'Yes please!' said Zac excitedly. 'Can we go now?'

So with great ceremony and with Zac's mum and dad grinning from ear to ear and Zac about to explode with excitement, a procession to the bottom of the garden took place. The investigative party stopped at the door. 'Wait there,' dad instructed and, having unlocked the padlock, he slipped inside the shed and closed the door behind him. And after a few minutes that seemed like an eternity, the door opened slowly, and there, in a brightly lid shed, Zac was greeted with an incredible sight. For filling the whole of one end of the shed was the most amazing Nativity scene he'd ever set eyes on. There was a stable with a light shining on it from above. There was a Mary and a Joseph and a baby Jesus in a manger, and shepherds and sheep and kings and all the rest … It was *all* there, and more besides, just as Zac had learned about the Christmas story. And it was just beautiful …

But as the wide-eyed Zac moved closer to take in the details, he began to notice things he *thought* he'd seen before. He tried to work it out. Could the walls of the stable be the insides of the kitchen cabinets that he was sure had gone to the tip when the kitchen had been revamped back in the autumn? And that light that shone on the stable looked *remarkably* like the broken lamp that used to be in his bedroom. And was that manger really a margarine tub? And could the sheep have been made from his mum's fleecy slippers that she'd thrown out weeks ago?

Zac was amazed. There was so much to take in and it would take him several visits over the next few weeks, as well as detailed explanations from his dad, to believe that kings could start off as sauce-bottles, transformed with cloaks made from discarded curtains; a Joseph could have his beginnings in parts rescued from an old vacuum cleaner; and shepherds' crooks could be fashioned from garden stakes.

It was the best Christmas scene Zac could ever have imagined, and he took great delight in showing it all to his friends as Christmas approached – and auntie Gladys when she visited, and Mrs Tomlinson from next door, and the postman, and anyone else who came to the house – and excitedly explaining how the amazing Christmas scene had been put together. His dad was *so* clever in making all of this from things that had been thrown away.

And in a well-practised speech, Zac always added what his dad had told him when the Nativity display had first been unveiled: 'Things that are wasted can still be well used. There's a lot can be done with stuff other people just throw away. What's broken and useless can be made new again at Christmas.'

Broken

A broken world,
Picked up,
Examined,
Ready to be thrown away;
But taken,
And reformed,
And made whole again.

A broken hope,
Dismissed,
Cried over,
Ready to be cursed;
But taken,
And reclothed,
And offered a new beginning.

A broken soul,
Blackened,
Ruined,
Ready to be rejected;
But taken
And loved,
And nurtured into a new possibility.

A broken love,
Useless,
Failed,
Ready to be discarded;
But taken,
And restored,
And beautifully transformed.

Second in Advent

Old Testament: Isaiah 11:1-10
Epistle: Romans 15:4-13
Gospel: Matthew 3:1-12

3 A job for Billy

Timothy William Innes Tomkins — known affectionately as Billy — couldn't sing for toffee. In fact, he couldn't sing for *anything,* because if you were to promise Billy a million pounds to sing in tune, he just couldn't. He was what the school music teacher referred to as 'a groaner', and many a time she'd regaled her colleagues in the staffroom with yet another story of the excellent singing abilities of Class 6C, but how Billy Tomkins could sing so far out of tune it was almost in harmony.

Billy was nothing if not enthusiastic and would belt out his monotone with total commitment, to the extent that he would often drown out the other kids or put them off the tune completely. His music teacher would regularly find things for Billy to do during a singing lesson so that he didn't go on disrupting the class. 'Billy, would you pop along to the head teacher's office and ask her for a copy of today's register? There's a good lad.' And with a bit of luck, Billy the Groaner would be away for long enough to allow the rest of the class to enjoy singing in tune. The head teacher was, of course, familiar with the music teacher's dilemma, and would contrive to keep Billy busy – 'Just looking for the register, Billy … Won't be long …' for *much* longer than was really necessary.

It was a tradition in the school that some of the Primary 6 children took the lead role in the School Nativity Play. And this year — traditions being what traditions are — it was the turn of Class 6C. Just after the October mid-term break, the preparations for Christmas would begin. And, traditions being what traditions are, the music centred round much-loved Christmas carols. There was always 'Away in a Manger' for the birth of the baby Jesus, 'Silent Night' for the announcement of the angels, 'We Three Kings' for the arrival of the Wise Men with their gifts, 'Little Drummer Boy' sung *ensemble* towards the end, and much more besides. And, traditions being what traditions are, all the children were involved, especially in the singing. *All* the children ... and that also meant Timothy William Innes Tomkins.

Billy loved Christmas and he'd been looking forward for *ages* to the time when it was the turn of his class to do their bit for the School Nativity Play. He was enthusiastic. He knew all the stuff off by heart. He was ready to go, and at the first rehearsal he gave it all he'd got. *That's* why the music teacher was seen tearing her hair out in the staffroom later in the morning as she recounted her tale of woe, and how 'Still the Night' would have been much better if it hadn't been accompanied by a monotonic dirge, and how 'Away in a Manger' had been all but ruined by the equivalent of a mooing cow or a braying donkey.

What was to be done? There were only so many excuses which could be contrived to keep The Groaner out of the classroom at rehearsal times. And what of the performance itself? Billy would *have* to be there with the others, for his parents would be there to watch, and his Gran would expect her adored grandson to be on stage, and his big sisters would want to be proud of their little brother – traditions being what traditions are ...

It was the head teacher who had The Idea ... One day, during Class 6C's singing rehearsal, the practice was interrupted by a visit from her. There was a whispered conversation between the head and the music teacher, the result of which was an instruction to Billy Tomkins to accompany the head teacher out of the class and down to the staffroom. And in the weeks before Christmas that's what happened at every singing practice. Billy would be removed from the class; the children would rehearse their singing; the music teacher would beam with delight; the preparations for the School Nativity Play would be deemed to be successfully on track. Billy never attended another singing practice. The kids never asked him where he was during the lessons. Billy never told them. And when the costumes were being worked on, the positions on stage arranged, and the final rehearsals in the school hall sorted out, Billy Tomkins was nowhere to be seen.

So it came to the great day. The school hall was packed. The children of Class 6C were predictably excited. The music teacher was at the piano. Everyone was well rehearsed. The audience was in a state of great expectation. But there was no Billy … His parents and his Gran and his two sisters were right in the front row – but there was no Billy Tomkins.

Now – traditions being what traditions are – the School Nativity Play *always* began with a welcome from the head teacher, and, at the beginning of every scene, there was a word of introduction from someone as to what was to happen next. So when the house-lights went down, the curtains opened to reveal the rosy faces of Primary 6C's opening tableau – and a silence ensued. There were the beginnings of anxious murmurings among the audience. 'What's wrong?' 'Where's the Head?' 'What's happened to the introduction?' Until, that is, there was a loud chord on the piano, and in from the wings, prompted by a just-out-of-sight-and-no-more head teacher, came Timothy William Innes Tomkins, proudly carrying the biggest placard anyone had ever seen, boldly announcing in big letters, and clearly in a child's hand, 'WELCOME TO OUR NATIVITY PLAY.' Billy stood, centre stage, nodding his head to a silent count, and then, with a deft flick of his wrist, the placard was turned round to announce, 'SCENE 1. THE ANGEL'S MESSAGE'. And with another silent count that was long enough for the audience the get the idea, the messenger exited stage left with the placard under his arm. And so it continued, Billy the messenger, placard-carrier *extraordinaire*, silently announcing each event and item with another sign of his own – and a cunning head teacher's – making.

When it was all over, Billy came on to the stage with a final placard which boldly asked for APLAUSE. And when the thunderous applause had finally died down, the messenger, with impeccable timing and a – by now, well-practised – flick of the wrist, turned the placard around and offered to the people, on behalf of the whole of Primary 6C, a THANK YOU FOR COMING and a MERRY CHRISTMAS TO YOU ALL.

Traditions being what traditions are, that's why, every year when the school has its Nativity Play, there's a special part for a silent messenger, announcing every scene with home-made placards, and it's always known as the 'Billy Tomkins Role'.

The message

The messenger stood up in front of the crowd
And called for a silence from all those around.
They listened with dignity, some with heads bowed,
The day the messenger came.

His voice ever calm and his words always clear,
His message was simple, his meaning sincere.
They listened intently, and some shed a tear,
The day the messenger came.

No long explanations were needed; no pleas;
No forceful persuasion; the truth came with ease.
They listened in wonder; some fell to their knees,
The day the messenger came.

'Your Love is incarnate,' the message they heard.
'The Truth is amongst you, no longer deferred;
The Way is before you; I give you my Word.'
The day the messenger came.

The crowd stood and listened; and some felt a chill;
Some harboured suspicion; some plotted to kill;
Some scratched at their heads, and are wondering still,
The day the messenger came.

But some saw the spirit descend like a dove;
And some glimpsed the hope and the faith and the love;
And some knew this truth was their gift from above –
The day the messenger came.

Third in Advent

Old Testament: Isaiah 35:1-10
Epistle: James 5:7-10
Gospel: Matthew 11:2-11

4 The real meaning?

Mike had to admit it – he was the one to blame for the lack of chipo-lata sausages on Christmas morning. No, he hadn't eaten them all – it was just that he'd forgotten to buy them in the first place. Oh, he could give you loads of excuses – too much to do; a supermarket that was too busy; a freezer so full it was hard to know where anything was; not used to doing the Christmas shopping – but the fact remained, he'd forgotten to buy the chipolatas.

The dearth of mini-sausages wasn't discovered till late on Christmas Eve, when he and Mandy, his ever-tolerant and forgiving partner, were checking over the wherewithal for the family gathering the following day. There were to be fourteen for Christmas dinner, and the list of what was needed – who was to bring which accompa-niment; where the food preparation was to take place; what the best recipe was for turkey-stuffing; how the timings were going to work out; what the seating arrangements were to be; who was in charge of the drink; and much more besides – was extensive and detailed. The absence of chipolatas was met with a great deal of consternation and a little recrimination. Mandy eventually said it didn't matter. Mike insisted it did. It was his fault. He was consumed with guilt. Christmas dinner wouldn't be right without a plentiful supply of little sausages. His two strapping nephews would complain. There would be nothing to keep his grandkids happy if they didn't like turkey. There would be no extra sausages. And he was the one to blame.

Mike didn't sleep much on Christmas Eve. Not for him the excitement of a Santa visit, or the anticipation of the exchange of presents, or the prospect of a family gathering. He fell asleep thinking of chipolata sausages. He woke up thinking of chipolata sausages. He'd probably dreamt about them too, though he was grateful he couldn't remember. He was the first one up on Christmas morning. And there and then he made a decision – he was going on a chipolata sausage hunt.

It wasn't quite fully light when he left the house but, at just after nine on Christmas Day, he was grateful the roads were quiet. The shopping precinct was deserted. The big supermarket – boldly announcing 'Open 24/7' – was closed, though Mike was greatly irritated that there was no signage to inform him that it was 'Closed 24/1 for Christmas'. His heart sank. If this megastore was shut, that was likely to be the case for the other two supermarkets he had on his mental list. There was nothing else for it – he'd have to go into town and find a corner-grocer's that was open on Christmas morning.

And that's why, twenty minutes later, Mike was breathlessly enquiring of a bemused Asian shopkeeper in 'Ali's Food Emporium' as to whether he happened to have any sausages on sale. Now, it's possibly because Mike hadn't explained himself properly or because the nice man behind the counter hadn't grasped the urgency of the situation, but it was no help at all to Mike to hear, 'No, we have no sausage. We sell out yesterday. But we have bacon, very nice, several packets. And there is black pudding for fry-up. Mushroom too, very good, very good. And eggs … But regret, no sausage for breakfast today.'

Mike tried to envisage a plentiful supply of black pudding for Christmas dinner, but decided it wasn't worth the effort. So leaving his wide-eyed salesman with his thoughts of persuading his next customer to buy into the pleasures of a sausage-free fry-up for Christmas morning, Mike continued on his search for another corner-shop. He was delighted to find 'Fawaz Foodstore' open and welcoming for Christmas morning trade.

By now, Mike's desperation was hard to conceal. He found what he assumed to be Mr Fawaz replenishing the baked beans in the tinned-veg aisle. 'Excuse me,' Mike announced, 'I'm on a chipolata-sausage hunt. Can you help?' In the ten seconds it took Mr Fawaz to respond, Mike could see seventeen questions in the shopkeeper's eyes. They ranged from 'What strange food is this "chipolata" that I have never heard of before?' through 'Is this some kind of treasure-hunt where you have to collect various items on a list and bring them back to the final rendezvous?' to 'Might this be a strange part of Christian culture I am still to understand, like Father Christmas and Yule logs and carol singers?'

But whatever questions might have been on Mr Fawaz's mind, his ten-second-delayed response simply consisted of 'What you need, my friend?' 'Sausages,' the desperate customer replied, 'sausages. I need sausages. Do you have any?' 'Ah, you seek sausage. Yes, I have sausage. Over here. Beside bacon and black-pudding for fry-up. How much sausage you want?' Mike looked at the six packets of skinless sausages on the shelf. He tried to do a calculation in his head that each of the long sausages could be halved and made to look like chipolatas, and if there were four per person, and there were to be lots left over for the kids, and if people wanted seconds … But he went brain-dead. 'I'll take them all,' he announced, and sweeping all the sausages from the shelf, accompanied a bemused Mr Fawaz to the check-out counter.

He had no idea how much the sausages cost. He was just relieved that his chipolata hunt had been successful. Christmas just wouldn't have been Christmas without the accompaniment of mini-sausages.

Mike had no more idea than Mr Fawaz as to why this should be so … So he decided on the way home that, after Christmas, he would try to find out why. And if he did work it out, he might even go back one day and explain to the helpful Muslim shopkeeper, who was his saviour on Christmas morning, what the real meaning of Christmas actually was.

The search

There was once a man who went on a search
for the meaning of life.
He travelled far and wide, covered many miles,
and looked in many places.

He gained wealth, status and fame.
'I will find meaning here,' he said.
But wealth gave no purpose,
and status no peace,
and fame was an illusion of worth.

He found ritual and tradition.
'I will find meaning here,' he said.
But ritual became empty,
and tradition became a dull set of routines,
devoid of substance.

He met saints and heroes.
'They will give me meaning,' he said.
But though he copied their ways
and sought to emulate their living,
he felt no fulfilment of his own.

He saw sights and wonders.
'They will give me meaning,' he said.
But though he marvelled at mystery
and delighted in beauty,
he was not changed.

So he abandoned his travels
and gave up his search for meaning.
He came home to what was familiar,
where he knew what to expect.

He lived simply,
for he needed no wealth.

He reflected deeply,
for he had no ritual to use.

He communed with his own soul,
for he had no other companion.

He found mystery in the silence,
and guidance in his dreams.

There was once a man who went on a search
for the meaning of life,
but discovered it only when he came home
and found himself.

Fourth in Advent

Old Testament: Isaiah 7:10–16
Epistle: Romans 1:1–7
Gospel: Matthew 1:18–25

5 The word on the streets

The word on the streets was that Norrie Brentwood was in trouble. He'd been 'lifted' by the local boys in blue the night before Christmas Eve for being drunk and disorderly outside the Highwayman bar. It wasn't the first time Norrie had been drunk and disorderly, or spent a night in the cells, for that matter. For Norrie Brentwood had been on a downward slide for a long time. But it was Christmas, and despite there being little sympathy locally for Norrie's drinking and anti-social behaviour, no one wanted to see the poor guy inside over the festive season.

But the word on the streets was that this was the way it was going to be. Christmas being on the Sunday, what self-respecting court was going to sit on a Christmas Eve Saturday to dispose of the flotsam and jetsam of the town's pre-Christmas revelry? So the word on the streets was that Norrie Brentwood was going to be banged up over Christmas.

Kirsty didn't always believe the word on the streets ... There were always rumours about this and that. The area seemed to thrive on gossip, a precious piece of juicy knowledge being an effective trading commodity that everyone valued. But the rumours weren't always accurate. Like the one about the local primary school closing down, just because one of the local shops was planning a 'closing down' sale in the school hall, and someone overhead it wrongly and, two and two making five, the rumour spread like wildfire that the school was for the chop.

So Kirsty didn't always take the word on the streets at face value. But she wasn't sure about this one. It sounded true enough. Norrie Brentwood was probably in trouble.

Kirsty shouldn't have been around the area on Christmas Eve at all. But who else was going to do the last charity run taking toys and food around the poorer families of the district? It's what Community Workers get paid for. Well, actually, you don't get paid for working a Saturday, even if it's Christmas Eve. So it's what Community Workers *do,* would be a more accurate way of putting it. But she was around the area on Christmas Eve, and that was that. And the quicker she got the last charity run completed, the sooner she'd get home to her own Christmas preparations.

She was surprised, therefore, as she turned the Transit van into the Community Centre car park late on Christmas Eve afternoon to see Norrie Brentwood slumped against the Centre's front door. Swinging the van into its designated space and making sure it was all locked and secure, she wandered over to the seated figure, expecting to find a drunk Norrie Brentwood, the worse for celebrating his escape from the clutches of the law. She was surprised, therefore, when, as she approached, Norrie lifted his head from his hands and said, 'Hello Kirsty,' and promptly burst into tears.

In an instant Kirsty was on the ground beside the weeping figure. She put her arm round his shoulders and felt the regular shudder of Norrie's sobbing shake through her own body. She sat with him for ages until the tears began to subside. And then, offering the forlorn figure a tissue to wipe his eyes, she asked him gently what was up.

Norrie spoke slowly and deliberately. 'Last night,' he said, 'was the final straw. Ah was in the Highwayman wi' ma brother an' his missus and ma maw. She was naggin' me somethin' rotten. An' ah was legless as usual. An' wi her naggin' on and on and on, somethin' just snapped. An' ah picked up a bottle from the table an' ah held it above ma head tae smash it doon on her face. An' ma brother went mental, an' dived across the table, an' heaved me right out the door. An' the barman must have called the bizzies, for the next ah knew, ah was in the cells.'

Kirsty had nothing to say. So she reckoned it was best that she said nothing, hoping her silence might encourage Norrie to continue. It did. 'A night in the cells sobered me up, right enough. So ah got bailed this mornin'. Nae mair trouble, or else, the polis said. So there it is, lassie. Nae mair trouble.'

He paused. He turned and looked Kirsty straight in the eye. He began to cry again. 'It's gone far enough,' he sobbed. 'Look at me, and on Christmas Eve tae. Ah need help, lassie. It's the drink that's got a grip o' me. Ah need help. An' ah need it now. Nae mair trouble … Nae mair trouble …'

As Norrie's voice tailed away, Kirsty was pondering the options. There weren't many. In fact, they were very limited indeed, what with all the Social Services being closed for Christmas, and the like. And she didn't want her *own* Christmas to be ruined.

There was only one possibility. Fumbling around in her rucksack, she unearthed her purse and pulled out a little scrap of paper. Handing it to Norrie, she said, 'Phone this number. You have to want to, and you have to believe it will make a difference. But it's all I can suggest.' Norrie took the paper and read it aloud. 'AA helpline. 24/7. Ask for Joe.'

'Who's Joe, an' why would he want tae be bothered wi' me on Christmas Eve, eh?'

Kirsty squeezed Norrie's hand. 'I don't know who he is, Norrie. I've never met him. But if it says 24/7, I reckon that includes Christmas Eve. So, if you're up for it, if you really mean it, it might be worth it, eh?'

When Kirsty and Norrie parted on the steps of the Community Centre on Christmas Eve, she had no idea what kind of Christmas Norrie Brentwood was going to have. But she knew he wasn't going to be far from her thoughts through her own Christmas celebrations …

When Kirsty got back to work after the Christmas and New Year break, the word on the streets was that Norrie had had an OK Christmas. The word on the streets was that Joe had come right away, and had spent Christmas Day with Norrie. The word on the streets was that Joe had taken Norrie to an AA meeting every day over the holidays. The word on the streets was that Norrie was hanging in there …

Kirsty didn't always believe the word on the streets. But she wasn't sure about this one. It sounded true enough – at least she hoped so …

The Word

What is the Word today?

It comes to me in the words I read –
from my newspaper's comment
to my Bible stories;
from my magazine's trivia
to my prayer book's depth;
that I might know the Word
in all its present fullness for me, today.

Does the Word speak today?

It comes to me in the words I hear –
from the kindness of a friend
to reports on the news;
from morning worship
to the laughter of children;
that I might hear the Word
in all its living fullness for me, today.

Where is the Word found today?

It comes to me in the streets of my living –
from the wisdom of the prophets
to the instructions of a teacher;
from the admonition of a parent
to the writings of the Saints;
that I might live the Word
in its eternal fullness for me, today.

Christmas Day

Old Testament: Isaiah 52:7-10
Epistle: Hebrews 1:1-12
Gospel: John 1:1-5, 9-14, 16-18

6 The age of innocence

As the new policeman on the estate, PC Eddie Harrower was spending time getting the feel of the place, and found himself down at the local football pitch watching some of the boys having a kick-around. One athletic-looking lad seemed to be running kind of awkwardly as if he was carrying an injury. 'Enjoying himself too much to come off,' Eddie thought. Just then, the limping footballer was tackled ferociously by a flying winger. Both fell in a heap. There was much writhing about and exchanging of oaths. The big lad was first to his feet. 'B★★★★r me,' he shouted. 'You damn near broke ma leg. See'f it's knackered, you're fur it, nae messin'!'

With that he rolled up the bottom of his denims to examine the injured leg for damage. Eddie expected to see severe bruising, if not an ugly, bleeding gash. What he saw, to his absolute surprise, was a flesh-coloured, shiny, artificial leg. The irate centre-half rubbed the prosthesis lovingly, the way anyone would massage a damaged limb. He looked down at his still-writhing opponent and broke into a broad grin. 'Yer aff the hook, wee man. It's no' even scratched. Jist as weel, eh?' And with his trouser leg rolled back down, he swivelled on his bad leg, called his troops back to action, and limped off into the fray once more.

The one-legged football player turned out to be Alan Morton McInnes (for ever carrying the names of the legendary Glasgow Rangers winger of the 1920s – Alan Morton, one of the 'Wembley Wizards', the 'Wee Blue Devil' himself …), a young leader in the local YMCA youth club. Over the months Eddie got to know Alan – or Ally, as he was better known – very well indeed and came to admire him a great deal. It turned out that Ally'd had a leg amputated when he was five-years old. He'd been messing about behind an ice-cream van and it had reversed over him. He was lucky to survive, but his leg couldn't be saved. So, from then on, he'd had a succession of artificial limbs, and now in adult life, at the ripe old age of nineteen, it didn't seem to bother him at all.

You should have seen the looks on the faces of opposition football teams when Ally and his lads from the youth club ran out for a game, with Ally's prosthesis now unhidden behind faded denims but pro-truding boldly beneath his tight, white shorts! Surprise would turn to derision. But derision always turned to respect – especially when they saw him play, and even more when they clattered into his bad leg and regularly came off worse. And Ally would often regale Eddie with stories of the time when he worked in a local factory and would regularly purloin goodies from the production line and hide them inside his artificial leg, all to escape the scrutiny of the security guards on the way out! And Eddie pretended he didn't hear …

But most of all, Eddie quickly became aware that Ally was brilliant with kids. He would be seen regularly at the after-school-club with a bunch of wee ones, sitting on the floor of the club-room, telling them fantastic stories. One week it would be about him losing his leg in a battle with a sword-wielding giant in a far-off, exotic land. The next, it would be how he used his artificial leg to ward off a roaring lion who'd found his way into his tenement kitchen. And another week, he would be singing a made-up song:

> *I'm Ally, and I have to hop.*
> *You know I can't possibly stop.*
> *I wear this false leg,*
> *Like a giant clothes–peg*
> *Which I got from a novelty shop.*
> *Boom! Boom!*

The kids loved it. Singing and story-telling time with one-legged Ally was always the highlight of the week.

And it always seemed to be the most difficult kids, the most dam-aged ones, who related to Ally the most. He would spend hour after hour with kids who'd worn out the patience of the most tolerant of youth leaders – and of the best of local policemen – in three-and-a-half-minutes flat. But that's because Ally seemed to have endless patience. Nothing seemed to faze him. He gave the most trouble-some of youngsters all the time they needed.

In a rare quiet moment with Ally, when he had one of his occasional pauses for breath between his stories and his messing about, Eddie asked him why it was the hardest kids, the most difficult ones, that mattered most to him. He thought for a moment and, with an unusually serious look on his face, he replied, 'It's no' me that looks for them, Eddie. They aye seem tae come ower tae me.'

'So why you?' Eddie asked. There was another long pause and an even more serious frown.

'Weel, ah lost ma innocence early on, ken? The leg, see? An' ah had tae grow up affae quick, or else the ither kids would hae made mince-meat o' me. These kids have lost their innocence tae, no' wi' losin' a leg, ken, but wi' losin' ither things, like their childhood, faimlie-life, parents, freens. They've had mair chopped aff than ah ever had. They've lost mair than wan leg, they kids. Maybe they'll no' survive. But they huv tae huv a decent crack at it, eh? Maybe seein' how ah've coped can gie them anither chance.'

Alan Morton McInnes broke into a wide grin. Being serious was obviously over for now. 'Did ah ever tell ye the time ah used ma gammy leg as a plant-stand fur ma granny's aspidistra?'

Based on a story first published in 'Going home another way' (ed. Neil Paynter, published by Wild Goose Publications, www.ionabooks.com)

Innocence

In innocence I was born,
not knowing,
not wanting to know
what this innocence meant,
and whether it was all there was.

In innocence I was broken,
not knowing,
not trying to know
where this innocence went,
and whether it would ever return.

In innocence I was destroyed,
not knowing,
not willing to know
when this innocence died,
and whether it had gone for good.

In innocence I was loved,
not knowing,
not able to know
what this innocence deserved,
and whether love would make a difference.

In innocence I was held,
not knowing,
not seeking to know
how this innocence could matter,
and whether it was worth the effort.

In innocence I was healed,
not knowing,

not asking to know
how this innocence could be restored,
and whether wholeness was possible.

In innocence I was me,
not knowing,
not daring to know
how this innocence had been redeemed
and whether I was the 'me' I was meant to be.

In innocence I had hope,
not knowing,
not needing to know
how this innocence had found comfort,
and why it kept my voice from weeping.

In innocence I had a future,
not knowing,
not searching to know
what this innocence might face,
and when it would bring me home.

First after Christmas

Old Testament: Isaiah 63:7-9
Epistle: Hebrews 2:10-18
Gospel: Matthew 2:13-23

7 Advance planning

It was January 12th. Andrea had the date firmly fixed in her mind. The event had such an effect on her that it wasn't surprising the date wouldn't be forgotten.

The Christmas and New Year celebrations were long past. The early-year snow and ice had made memories of the festive and holiday season dissipate more quickly than usual this year. It had been a struggle to get around for a week or so, and that, on top of getting back to work after the break, had made the start of the year a real chore. The Christmas lights in the town square were already a distant memory. And now that the decorations were down at home and in the office, things had lost their colour and sense of fun. Life had returned to a dull, grey kind of grind. 'January?' Andrea thought. 'Who needs it?'

Andrea worked on the front desk at the Council offices. It was a job she enjoyed and, despite the January drabness, she had begun to be cheered up by the usual variety of people who came and went through the Council's front foyer.

Candidates for a job interview: 'Just take a seat for a moment, and I'll inform HR you're here … That's fine. You can go through now. Down the corridor. Miss Cunningham will meet you there …'

Councillors come to meet with departmental officials: 'Good morning, Councillor Edwards. Just go on up. You know where to go. Mr Gallagher's expecting you …'

People in overalls arriving to repair this or deliver that: 'Photocopier to be repaired? Finance department? I'll just check … That's OK. They're delighted *you're* here! Just sign the book. Here's a visitor's badge. Someone will be down for you in a moment …'

The man who arrived first thing on the morning of January 12th was in no way out of the ordinary. A suited, business type, carrying an attaché-case and with a laptop bag over his arm, he was no more or less than a run-of-the-mill visitor to the Council offices. 'Good morning. Can I help you?' Andrea enquired. 'Thank you, yes,' replied the suit. 'I have an appointment. With Mrs Illingworth ...' He paused, set down his attaché-case on the floor, unearthed a small, slimline diary from the inside pocket of his jacket, and announced, 'Mrs Illingworth. Admin. 9.30. Yes. I've to see Mrs Illingworth at 9.30. I'm a minute or two early. I do hope that's OK. Can you tell her I'm here?' 'Certainly, Mr ... I'm sorry. Whom shall I say?' 'Oh, sorry ... Kennedy. Martin Kennedy. From Quentin Oswald's. Tell her Mr Kennedy from Quentin Oswald's is here as arranged ...' 'That's fine, Mr Kennedy. If you just take a seat, I'll tell Mrs Illingworth you've arrived.'

'Mrs Illingworth?' *Head of admin ... Nice lady ... Cheery ... Always says hello ...* 'Mrs Illingworth, your 9.30 appointment is here.' *Early start for her today ... Unusual ...* 'He's from Quentin Oswald's.' *Now, that's a new one on me ... New stationery supplier, perhaps?* 'Shall I send him up? OK, I'll tell him you'll come down.' *Something private going on upstairs, then ... Doesn't want anyone to know she's meeting the suit ... Mmmm ... I wonder ...* 'OK. Bye ...' Andrea called to the waiting visitor at the side of the foyer. 'Mrs Illingworth will be down in a moment, Mr Kennedy.' 'Thank you very much,' came the reply.

The receptionist returned to her duties but was surprised to see the visitor setting up his laptop on the foyer's coffee-table and opening up what looked like a full attaché-case. He was *just* too far away for Andrea to make out what was on the laptop screen or in the case. *'Rep, of some sort,'* she mused, convincing herself that it was nothing more exciting than a stationery salesman after all. The head of admin breezed into the foyer. 'Thanks, Andrea,' she chirped and, heading across the foyer, greeted the visitor like a long-lost brother. 'Martin,' she said, shaking him warmly by the hand. 'Good to see you again. Early as usual.' 'Vera. Good to see you again too. All well I hope.' 'Just fine. Just fine.' And Vera − *didn't know that before,* thought

Andrea – Illingworth settled at the coffee-table beside the animated businessman. 'Now, what have you got for me?' she enquired brightly.

The visitor turned his laptop round so that Mrs Illingworth could see the screen and informed her, 'It's all there. This is the stock for this year. Some of it you'll know. But there are some new lines. They've got the red star at the side. Some quite tasteful ones too, as you'll see.' Mrs Illingworth was obviously well familiar with the presentation. There were occasional pauses at particular images. There was a regular exchange of *sotto voce* comments. There was the occasional scribbled note on Martin Kennedy's pad.

Now, it's not that Andrea was *nosey*. It's just that she was … well … interested … *What on earth are they looking at that's so important – and so secret?* she wondered. There was nothing else for it. She would *have* to find out. So, abandoning her station, she slipped across the foyer to where Mr Kennedy from Quentin Oswald's and Mrs Illingworth, head of Admin, were now deep in conversation. 'Andrea?' Mrs Illingworth said as the receptionist approached. 'Sorry, Mrs Illingworth. I was wondering if you and Mr Kennedy would like a cup of tea or coff …'

And it was then that Andrea saw it on the screen. The rep was showing Mrs Illingworth a range of Christmas cards and calendars. The head of the Council's Department of Administration was buying – from Quentin Oswald's, as it would appear – the Council's Christmas cards and the like for the end of this year.

Two cups of coffee having duly been provided for the foyer's occupants, Andrea was back at her desk. She could *not* believe it. She looked at her desk-top calendar as a way of pinching herself out of a dream. But it was no dream. On January 12th the head of Admin was choosing that year's Council Christmas cards! And a young Council receptionist – who couldn't plan for the weekend, far less for Christmas, eleven-and-a-half months away – was absolutely flabbergasted! *'Now that's what I call advance planning,'* she mused.

It was January 12th. Andrea had the date firmly fixed in her mind. The event had such an effect on her that it wasn't surprising the date wouldn't be forgotten.

Gifts

What gifts can I bring you?

To look ahead, and walk with you
towards whatever comes?
This I know I have.
This I bring.
This I offer now.

To listen, and to talk with you
about your hopes and dreams?
This I know I own.
This I bring.
This I'll always share.

To promise, and to keep my word to you,
that I'll be there, whatever happens?
This I'm glad I have.
This I bring.
This you'll never lose.

To forgive what comes from you
through brokenness and pain?
This I need to show.
This I bring.
This, to heal and save.

To hold what sadness dwells with you
and share the burden for a while?
This gift I've been given.
This I bring.
This comfort, this healing for you.

What gifts can I bring you?

I have no wealth or fame,
no gold,
no treasure-trove,
no grand ideas.
And so I offer what I have,
to walk with you and listen,
to promise and forgive,
to comfort and console;
On this day,
I bring you what I know I have,
and offer all of me
to mark this day of giving.

Epiphany

Old Testament: Isaiah 60:1-6
Epistle: Ephesians 3:1-12
Gospel: Matthew 2:1-12

8 Marty's baptism

The baptism wasn't supposed to be like this. Marty simply wasn't ready. And it had all been sprung on him without proper preparation.

Marty was eighteen and it was Freshers' week at the University, an introductory week before classes began in earnest. He'd enjoyed the stimulation of all the new things that were available. This was what Uni was about – lots of things to try, people to meet, pubs to explore, and eventually, when there was time, the odd lecture or tutorial to attend … Not surprisingly, for Marty, Freshers' week was a ball!

The culmination of it all was the Friday night visit to the University Folk Club. Marty was a folk-singer. Well, in the late 1960s, in the midst of the 'folk revival', everyone, it seemed, was a folk-singer of sorts. The Dylan, Seeger, Baez, Guthrie, Paxton generation had folk-singing in their blood. Songs of protest, peace anthems, sing-along songs, old ballads, even the odd self-penned ditty, were all grist to the mill for budding talent. And there was no doubt about it, Marty was a budding talent.

At least that's what he thought. And the people who knew his singing style thought so too – his Gran, who was always good for a 'Sing us one of your songs, Marty …' with Marty only too happy to oblige; a string of girlfriends who had fallen under the young troubadour's spell; and, of course, the school folk-club … no wonder Marty reckoned he was pretty good.

He'd been playing guitar for a few years now, and could pretty well copy the style of most of his musician heroes. All in all, Marty had a pretty high opinion of his budding folk-singing talent.

It was no wonder, then, that the University Folk Club was a *must* in Freshers' week for Marty. And that's why he found himself well positioned near the podium in the smoky cellar of a pub round the corner from the Uni's main square well in time for the start of the

Friday evening event. Marty was not to be disappointed. It was all he could have hoped for. He sang along with familiar ballads; he joined in with gusto with the new choruses he picked up from singers who encouraged participation; he laughed loudly at the funny stuff, old and new, offered to the crowd; he cheered to the echo the headline act that closed the first half. Fabulous stuff!

Fortified by a couple of pints in the break, Marty settled down for more of the same in the second half. But this time the set-up was different. It was what the front-man had described as an 'open mike session'. The fact that there was no actual microphone to be seen didn't seem to deter people, as a string of budding folk-singers took to the stage to do their thing. Some were OK; there was one guy who was rubbish – and too drunk to notice; and two women singing unaccompanied American ballads were just terrific. It didn't seem to matter if you didn't have an instrument with you. You either sang without one or you borrowed a guitar from one of the resident musicians.

Marty loved it. And before long he had a voice in his head saying, 'You could do that,' quickly followed by his own rational voice saying, 'Don't be so stupid. You couldn't handle this …' He'd sing along some more and still hear, 'You could do that …'; he'd listen to someone struggling to get it right and hear, 'You could do that …' and all the time he tried not to listen.

Why, then, he stepped up to the stage when the front-man asked one last time for volunteers, Marty will never know. But there he was, hanging a borrowed guitar round his neck, turning towards a drink-fuelled audience, and hoping to announce that he would sing the sure-fire winner, Tom Paxton's 'Last thing on my mind …' He *hoped* he could announce … *Hoped* … But when he opened his mouth, not one word came out.

Marty had no idea how long he stood there. It might have been a few seconds; it could have been a few hours. Time simply stood still for a budding folk-singer who couldn't even announce his song. And now the voice in his head was shouting, 'What on EARTH are you doing here?'

It was then that the miracle happened. Marty strummed a chord on the guitar and just started to sing. Not boldly, not with much style, but he just started to sing. The familiar chords and the well known tune did the rest. Soon people were humming along with the verses and joining in with the chorus. Marty felt his confidence grow. He was doing his thing. He was giving it all he had. The song came to an end all too soon. The applause was warm, not great, but good enough. Marty resumed his seat while the resident crew closed the proceedings with one last sing-along. Marty's maiden outing as a folk-singer was done – and he had survived.

On the way out he met one of the resident singers, guitar case in hand, heading for the door. 'Well done, son. No' bad, no' bad at all. First time, eh? Some baptism, so it was. But you'll remember tonight for as long as you live, so you will. Aye, well done, son. You've done good.' And as Marty stepped into the night, he reckoned *that* comment was worth more than all the applause a budding folk-singer would ever hear.

Don't

Don't ask me to stand in front of the crowd …
I'll have nothing to say;
and, even if I do,
they won't like it anyway.

Go on.
Give it a go.
Put your toe in the water.
I believe in you.

Don't ask me to perform miracles …
That's not my style;

and, even if it was,
it wouldn't make any difference anyway.

Come on.
You can do it.
You've got more to offer than you'll ever know.
I believe in you.

Don't ask me to do clever things …
That's not me;
and, even if it was,
it wouldn't be as good as the others anyway.

Carry on.
You can do it.
Just be yourself.
I believe in you.

Don't ask me to carry huge expectations …
The load's not light enough for me;
and, even if it was,
I'm not sure I want this burden anyway.

Sign on.
You can do it.
You've got the strength you need.
I believe in you.

Don't ask …

I will.

Don't expect …

I will.

Don't believe …

I will.
For you are my beloved;
in you, I am well pleased.
This is your baptism …
Come on!
I believe in you.

Baptism of our Lord

Old Testament: Isaiah 42:1-9
Epistle: Acts 10:34-43
Gospel: Matthew 3:13-17

9 Forgiveness

Mrs Rennie and Mrs Davy were inseparable. Despite the fact that Mrs Rennie was ten years older than her best friend, the two ladies had been constant companions for as long as anyone could remember. Well, when you're in your mid-eighties and your friend is in her mid-seventies, the age gap isn't that important. Mrs Rennie and Mrs Davy were both widows and neither of them had any close family. So their enduring friendship had become the mainstay of their lives as the later – and frailer – years of life had come along.

So Mrs Rennie and Mrs Davy were inseparable. They sat beside each other in their usual pew in church every Sunday, having been picked up for church, and later to be delivered home safely, by one of a team of volunteer drivers. They both lived in sheltered housing, though in different complexes a quarter of a mile apart. No longer able to socialise under their own steam, they enjoyed the two days a week they spent at the Day Centre where, of course, they sat together, ate together, squeezed up next to each other when the Centre took the folk on a trip to the country, and were a more than passable double-act when they sang together at the Christmas party.

Walter had got to know Mrs Rennie and Mrs Davy very well indeed in recent months. As driver of the Centre's minibus on both of the days when the two friends attended, it was Walter's job to collect them from home in the morning and take them back in the afternoon. They were his first two passengers to be picked up and they were the last two to be dropped off. Walter never failed to be touched by the two friends' welcome of each other and their farewells at the end of the day. Clearly this was a special friendship, obvious for all to see and admire.

Mrs Rennie and Mrs Davy were inseparable – until Mrs Rennie died. She wasn't supposed to die. The spell in hospital had been announced as 'routine', with some planned tests on a heart problem. But a massive heart attack had been the devastating news. Mrs Rennie's death was unavoidable.

The funeral service at the church was as full and as moving as anyone could remember. The talk on the day and for weeks afterwards was the effect of the loss on Mrs Davy. She looked broken at the funeral. She declined the offer to be picked up for church on Sundays. She said that coming to the Day Centre just wouldn't be the same any more. Mrs Rennie and Mrs Davy had been inseparable. Death had changed that. Mrs Davy was left on her own.

Walter was worried. He was grieving too, of course, because Mrs Rennie was one of his favourite people. And he'd had no real experience of what the effect of the loss of a much-loved person could have on a community of friends, such as the folk who attended the Day Centre. But he had enough insight into the human condition to know that, whatever he or anyone else felt, Mrs Davy must have been struggling big time – and more than most.

Three weeks went by before Walter plucked up the courage to go round to visit. He was understandably anxious. He wasn't sure he was doing the right thing, and he had no idea what he was going to say. This was way out of his comfort zone. What if he messed up? What if he made it worse? What if …?

He sat in his car outside Mrs Davy's house rehearsing his words, turning various scenarios over in his mind and working out how long he should stay. 'Hello, Mrs Davy, how are you?' 'Not to worry, Mrs Davy, we're still here for you.' 'It takes time, Mrs Davy.' 'Anything we can do for you, Mrs Davy, you only have to ask.'

After a while, calmer and a bit more confident, Walter locked up his car and walked the few steps up Mrs Davy's path to her front door. He rang the doorbell, and a minute or so after the chimes had sounded inside there was the sound of a steady shuffling of feet and the rattling of a key in the lock. After a while Mrs Davy's front door slowly swung open to reveal a frail, elderly woman leaning heavily on a walking frame, standing in the doorway. 'Walter,' she said, 'how nice of you to call.' Walter's smile was one of relief, and relaxing somewhat he announced, 'Hello Mrs Rennie, I've just popped over to see …'

The cry of distress could be heard at the end of the street. 'Ohhh,' Mrs Davy wailed, 'you've just called me by the name of my dead friend. Why did you do that? Ohhhhh! And she's gone. My best friend … Oh, it's so terrible, terrible. I miss her so much …'

Walter remembers little of the aftermath of the disastrous start to his caring visit. He recalls that he helped the wailing woman back into the house. He has a dim recollection of not being able to get her to stop crying. He knows he didn't stay long. But what he remembers well, for it will never leave him, is that he'd blown it! His honest but insensitive mistake was unforgivable. He was an idiot, plain and simple.

Walter never told the folk in the Day Centre the story of his stupidity. They would either have laughed at his misfortune or criticised him for his uselessness. Neither would have helped. Walter decided it was enough that he – and a distressed Mrs Davy – knew what a failure he was. He'd like to tell you that Mrs Davy came back to church and told him not to worry, that it was an honest mistake. But she didn't – not yet, anyway. He'd like to report that he'd got a nice letter from the offended party telling him she was better now. But he didn't – not yet, anyway. He'd like to say that he'd forgiven himself and that he'd eradicated all the pain of the disaster from his mind. But he hasn't – not yet, anyway.

But what he *will* tell you is that he will never, ever make the same mistake again! That much he *does* know – and that will just have to be forgiveness enough for now …

Redeemed

Fashioned and made with real beauty and form;
Cherished and loved since the day I was born;
Broken and lost, now a victim of shame;
Tarnished and spoiled, I'm thrown out of the game;

Far from a home of true welcome and peace;
Tortured by doubt, with no blessèd release;
Outside the walls of calm shelter and rest;
Missing the times when the loved ones are blessed.

Where is my home now, my purpose, my worth?
Where is the meaning I've craved since my birth?
Where is the rescue, the word from above?
Where is the faith, or the hope, or the love?

Come now my child, for I know who you are;
Come now in brokenness; come from afar;
Come with your questions, your sins and your shame;
Come from your wilderness; rejoin the game;

Come with your fears and your worries and grief;
Come with your doubts and your lack of belief;
Come, though you've plotted and selfishly schemed;
Come! You're forgiven. Now, you're redeemed.

Second after Epiphany

Old Testament: Isaiah 49:1-7
Epistle: 1 Corinthians 1:1-9
Gospel: John 1:29-42

10 Rory's wall

Rory was fascinated by the workmen building the wall. Living on the farm as he did, he was well used to things being repaired – old huts to be made wind- and water-tight; new storage sheds to be built; rusty corrugated-iron to be removed and replaced with fibreglass sheeting; and broken-down walls to be restored. Rory liked to get involved and feel grown-up with his father and elder brother. He loved all the building work – 'You'll be an engineer one day and not a farmer, lad,' his father had often said.

But when it came to the rebuilding of the end wall of the old barn, well, that was quite out of Rory's league. The old barn was one of a series of ramshackle outhouses at the back of the farmhouse which had never really been needed. But with the expansion of the farm and the increasing need for storage (especially safe storage for the various new pieces of farm machinery) Rory's father had decided the barn needed to be rebuilt.

It would have been easy enough to demolish the three remaining walls of the roofless barn and start again with some prefabricated structure of wood and metal. But Rory's father had decided that it would be a great shame to waste the good stone of what had been a solid and dependable structure in its day. So a firm of stonemasons had been brought in to restore the barn by rebuilding the end wall in the same style as the three remaining walls. Putting the roof on would be relatively easy once the four walls were in place, so Rory had heard his father say. But the stonemasons needed to do a good job before that happened, to make sure the walls were strong enough to take a solid roof and make the old barn what it once was.

There was no shortage of good stones around the farmyard and in the fields beyond, scattered there from the fallen walls of the old barn and several of the other dilapidated outhouses. Some of these stones had already been used to repair broken dykes or to mark off farm-tracks as the need had arisen. So before they were ready to do anything else, the stonemasons had collected suitable stones of all shapes and sizes from near and far and made a great pile of them in the corner of the farmyard nearest to the barn.

Then their job was to ensure that the bottom part of the ruined end wall was solid. First, they stripped out all the loose stonework, with the discarded stones being thrown onto the pile to be used later. Then slowly, to Rory's constant fascination, the wall began to grow.

Pretty soon the wall was higher than he was, and within days it was over the workmen's heads. So scaffolding had to be erected, with a platform running the whole length of the wall, to take the building work on to its next stage. A pulley was rigged up to allow the bigger stones to be hauled up onto the platform ready for their place in the wall, with the smaller stones being carried up in buckets either by the workmen or by using the pulley.

The biggest stones needed two workmen to lift them, and Rory would watch as they heaved a big boulder into its place. Sometimes it would nearly fit, and with great exertion the men would move it this way and that to try to make it fit better. Often it didn't fit at all, and it was decided that this wasn't the right stone for this part of the wall. But the workmen never threw an ill-fitting stone back down again. That would have been a waste of the effort to get it up onto the platform in the first place. Instead, they would drag it along to the end of the platform and leave it there with several other discarded stones, ready to be used in another part of the wall when the time and the space were right.

Rory was fascinated by the workmen building the wall. But what fascinated him even more than the big stones being heaved about was how the masons used all the little stones that had been brought up onto the platform, fitting them carefully between one big stone and another. Every stone, it seemed, had its place in the wall – the big ones, of course, but also the misshapen ones that you wouldn't have thought would have been any use at all; ones with jagged edges that just seemed to be the very stone to grip on to the stones on either side; little ones that could be jammed in between the others to make sure none of the stones could move or fall.

As the wall rose, so the pile of stones in the corner of the farmyard went down. There didn't seem to be a stone that wasn't of use. Soon the wall was finished, its pointed top giving the gable-end of the barn the correct shape for the fitting of the roof when the time came. Finally the last part of the pointing was done, cement squeezed into all the cracks and spaces, so that all the big stones and little stones could bind together. And, with the wall completed, the pile of stones in the yard had all but disappeared.

Rory was fascinated by the workmen building the wall, how every big stone had somewhere to fit, and how they weren't any use on their own, and how the wall was made strong when all the little stones were fitted into the spaces. Every stone had its place, or else there would have been no wall and no barn in the corner of the yard.

This prayer was first used in worship in Iona Abbey, but was later adapted for use in Chalmers Memorial Church, Port Seton. It is a prayer which is applicable in many different settings.

Stones

God of this place,
there are big stones in these walls
solid, dependable stones,
hauled up onto scaffolding by pulleys and ropes,
heaved into place by skilled masons,
and holding these walls in place,
for centuries, for decades, for now,
so that we can use this place
for our worship and rest.

God of this place, thank you for these big stones,
for their strength and purpose,
and for their enduring ability
to make this place what it needs to be.

God of this place
there are little stones in these walls,
fitted in, banged into place,
to fill the gaps, to bind with other stones
to make these walls complete;
misshapen stones,
all with an appropriate space for their shape alone;
once discarded stones, discarded no longer;
odd stones, each one with its special place.

God of this place, thank you for the little stones,
for their unobtrusive, necessary part,
strengthening these walls for us,
making this place what it needs to be.

God of our lives,
thank you for the big people,
in our churches, in our communities, in our world,
carrying responsibilities,
carved out for important roles,
people we rely on, people who are our role models,
people we trust, people who make our lives,
our church, our world worthwhile.

God of our lives,
help the big people to hang in there,
because we need them so much,
to keep the whole thing going,
making our world what it needs to be.

And if I'm one of those big stones,
help me not to crumble with the weight of it all.

God of our lives,
help us not to forget the little people,
those seemingly insignificant, misshapen people,
the ones who don't get much thought
or much recognition,
who're often rejected as being useless;
the shy people;
the different people;
the gentle people;
the low-self-esteem people;
the diffident people;
the not-so-sure-I'm-really-any-good people.
Fit them into your walls
to make the church, our communities, our world
what they were meant to be.
And help us to see that without them
churches crumble, communities perish,
the walls of our world fall down.

God of our lives,
hooray for the little people!
Three cheers for the little stones!
Thank God they're there.

And if I'm a misshapen, ordinary stone,
minding my own business,
just doing my bit
of filling my place in the wall,
just being me,
thank you for putting me here.

Thank you for believing in me,
and building me into your walls.
Amen.

Third after Epiphany

Old Testament: Isaiah 9:1-4
Epistle: 1 Corinthians 1:10-18
Gospel: Matthew 4:12-23

11 Blessed

When George Campbell walked to the lectern to read the Gospel lesson for that Sunday, his heart wasn't in it. He'd had a busy week, and hadn't had his usual time to familiarise himself with the content of the reading – so that he wasn't caught out by awkward words like Melchizedek and Pamphylia and Nebuchadnezzar. But when he checked the details, he was much relieved to find that he was well familiar with the passage. Indeed, it was a reading he'd learned as a child, and while the version he was to read from today was different from the King James' version of his youth, he reckoned it would hold no worries for him. He could pretty well have recited it off by heart. He would give it his best shot, of course. Reading the Gospel lesson wasn't to be taken lightly. But, if he was to be honest, his heart wasn't really in it.

So George Campbell began … 'Hear now from the Holy Gospel of St Matthew, chapter 5, and reading from verse 1. Listen now for the Word of God.' And after an appropriate pause to allow those in the congregation who had pew bibles to look up the passage, George continued:

> 'Now when he saw the crowds, he went up on a mountainside and sat down. His disciples came to him, and he began to teach them saying: "Blessed are the poor in spirit, for theirs is the kingdom of heaven."'

That was all Jeanie Cunningham heard of the reading. She doesn't know why, but as soon as George Campbell started, the Littlejohn family popped into her mind. They were a sad lot, never seeming able to get on top of things. Jeanie helped as best she could, of course, and so did lots of the neighbours. But it was a real struggle. 'Poor in spirit' was only the half of it. Poor in opportunity too, Jeanie thought; poor in decision-making as well; poor in budgeting; poor in … well, just about everything. 'The Kingdom of Heaven for them?' Jeanie pondered. She wasn't so sure what that meant. But it didn't matter anyway. All she knew was that she was still thinking about the poor Littlejohn family all through the reading and by the time the vicar announced the next hymn …

   '*"Blessed are those who mourn, for they shall be comforted."*'

That was as far as the vicar got with the reading. She'd had three funerals that week, each one more distressing than the last. The culmination had been the young lad's funeral service in the church on the Friday, one of the bikers she'd married only six months before. He'd taken a corner too fast, and that was it. Twenty-two he was. And she couldn't get out of her mind the pathetic figure of his young wife in the wheelchair at the front of the church. Too much mourning for one week. And the comfort? Where was the comfort for her – or for a struggling vicar for that matter?

   '*"Blessed are the meek, for they shall inherit the earth."*'

That was Margaret's trigger. 'Meek,' she thought, 'that'll be Janice Channing, then.' And her mind went to the quietest, most timid and shy kid in her second-year geography class. 'I wonder what she'll make of the world when she leaves school,' Margaret thought. 'And I wonder what the world will do to her? Will she make it? Can she survive? But then, maybe there's more to little Janice than meets the eye,' she pondered. 'I wonder …'

   '*"Blessed are those who hunger and thirst for righteousness, for they shall be filled."*'

David was still thinking about the agenda for the meeting on Wednesday night. It was the beginning of the planning for Christian Aid week, and he'd been reading over some of the material that had come out from Central Office. It was good, as it always was, and brought home not only the poverty that needed to be tackled but the injustices and the fear and the lack of opportunity and the oppression that needed to be dealt with too. He hoped he could get the message over and help people grasp the urgency …

‘ *"Blessed are the merciful, for they shall be shown mercy."* ’

It was at the 'merciful' bit that John's mind drifted away. He'd had a punishment exercise to do over the weekend. Well, it was justified a bit, he reckoned. What else was the headmaster to do when he'd come into the hall at the end of the exam and found John and three of his mates playing football with a pencil in and out of the desks? A week's detention and a 2000-word essay on the 'Laws of Association Football' were the result. Where was the mercy in that? And what would John have done if the decision had been his?

‘ *"Blessed are the pure in heart, for they shall see God."* ’

Maureen was sitting next to Grace as she always did. 'Grace by name and grace by nature,' she'd said often enough. For Grace Cameron was one of the loveliest people Maureen had ever met. There was a holiness about Grace that Maureen could only wonder at, a serenity that simply shone from her face. Maureen had no doubt where it came from, for Grace was one of the most devout people she knew. 'Pure in heart, right enough,' thought Maureen as she glanced across at her companion. And there Grace Cameron sat, eyes tightly closed, absorbing every syllable of the Gospel lesson.

‘ *"Blessed are the peacemakers, for they shall be called sons of God."* ’

Edward was always thinking about his grandson in Afghanistan, and today was no different. Peter was on his second tour, and loved being in the army. There could be no prouder family than Peter's. My God, were they proud of their boy? But there was always the worry. And when news of another death by a roadside bomb or a stray bullet came on the news, Edward's blood ran cold. He didn't want the boys to be there. Surely peace could be found in other ways. 'Peacemakers,' the lesson said, as tears, once again, ran down Edward's cheeks.

'And here ends the Gospel lesson,' George Campbell was saying, 'and may God bless us in the hearing of his Word.'

When George Campbell walked back from the lectern after reading the Gospel lesson for that Sunday, he knew his heart hadn't been in it. But then, he wasn't to know about the hearts of Jeanie and Margaret, and David and John, and Maureen and Edward, and the vicar too, for that matter, now was he?

Blessed again

Now when he saw the crowds, he went up on a mountainside and sat down. His disciples came to him, and he began to teach them saying:

"Blessed …"

Blessed are the tolerant,
for they shall help people to understand
what tolerance means.

Blessed are the quiet ones,
for they shall be praised for speaking
only when they have something worth saying.

Blessed are the thoughtful,
for they shall be known as people worth relying on.

Blessed are the loving,
for they shall celebrate love where they find it.

Blessed are the welcoming
for they shall not judge people
by the colour of their skin
or the words of their creed
or their sexual orientation.

Blessed are the humble,
for, in time, their humility will shame the arrogant.

Blessed are those whose minds wander away sometimes,
for they're likely to be thinking
of the right things.

Blessed are those whose prayers are constant,
for they shall know that others pray for them.

Blessed are those who don't even know they're blessed,
for they are being blessed anyway.

Fourth after Epiphany

Old Testament: Micah 6:1–8
Epistle: 1 Corinthians 1:18–31
Gospel: Matthew 5:1–13

12 Let it shine!

No one bothered too much about the abandoned lighthouse. Ever since Trinity House had begun the process of moving towards automated lights, it was inevitable that the lighthouse on The Point would become surplus to requirements. It had done its job for over a century, and since it was built in 1871 it had been a guiding light for many a young sailor at sea on many a dangerous voyage round The Point and along the rocky coast.

Several possibilities for the abandoned tower and its outbuildings had been mooted since its closure. There was talk of a lighthouse museum, but the location was considered too remote to attract enough visitors to make such an enterprise viable. At one time there had been plans to convert it into an up-market 'restaurant with rooms', but the recession had hit the financial backers and the scheme was abandoned. Rumour had it that someone had bought the site and was going to convert it into luxury flats. But that remained no more than a rumour as the buildings continued to lie unused.

No one bothered too much. The lighthouse was simply a feature of the coastline, as if it had been there for ever, part of the fabric and the beauty of the area. Whether it was the stark white against the grey background of a bleak winter day, or the glint of morning sunshine on its glass dome at a spring sunrise, the solid nature of the structure as a bastion against fierce autumn winds, or a landmark for summer sailors returning to the bay from the open sea, the lighthouse still mattered. So no one bothered too much about what it might be used for or what its future might be.

No one bothered too much … apart from Tam McCarthy. Tam McCarthy had plans. Not for him a fancy restaurant or luxury homes, a folk museum or a feature landmark. Tam McCarthy had plans … and he was determined they would succeed.

Tam was a local man who'd begun his life – as was the case with most of the local lads – at the fishing, a crew member on his uncle Jim's trawler, fishing for herring off the coast. Tam had moved on from the fishing and away from the town long before the decline had begun. He could see the start of it, mind, though that wasn't the reason he'd left.

It was Tam's passion for painting that had taken him away from home. A recognisable young talent in Art College, Tam had no difficulty moving into teaching, and in a few short years he'd become head of art in a major city high school. But that was never going to be enough, and after years of exhibiting his work Tam hit the jackpot. It was his painting of seascapes and ships that had been the key. He'd been in the right place, at the right time, with the right style. A couple of celebrities had bought his paintings; he'd had a write-up in the weekend supplement of a national newspaper; he'd been the subject of a feature on TV. People talked excitedly about his use of colour, his capturing of light, his attention to detail, his sense of drama. Whatever it was, Tam's career as an artist took off. His rise was meteoric. His output was prodigious. His exhibitions were many and spectacular. Tam McCarthy, artist *extraordinaire,* became a star.

But he never lost his local roots or his passion for his home town. The sea and its traffic were still inspirations for him. His mother still lived down by the bay. He was still a local lad at heart. And, through it all, he never lost his awareness of the needs of the local people, affected as they were by the decline of the fishing. And in particular he was well aware of the local kids who, unlike himself in his younger years, had little prospect of work and plenty of opportunity for getting into trouble.

Quietly, and without any publicity, Tam had pumped money into the local youth club. He kept in touch with the club leaders, and as a result had his ear to the ground regarding local needs and possibilities. And that's where the idea for the lighthouse first came up …

If you were to ask Tam McCarthy now who first had the notion of converting the lighthouse into a climbing centre, he wouldn't be able to tell you. But what he would be sure of is that, like his own career, once the idea took hold, there was no stopping it. Within months the buildings had been bought and work had begun. The road to the site was resurfaced and properly fenced. The accommodation blocks were refurbished into dormitories and store-rooms. With the advice of world-renowned climbers, an artificial climbing wall was prepared on the landward side of the lighthouse tower.

The internals of the lighthouse were spectacularly renovated, the windows at different levels being opened up to become the culmination point for the novice, intermediate and specialist routes. The pinnacle of achievement was climbing to the top of the tower, all one hundred and seventy-five feet of it. No one got to see the full extent of the view from the top of the lighthouse unless they'd achieved the ultimate climb.

The climbing centre was an amazing success. It became a magnet for the whole area, and within a few years it was reckoned to be one of the best climbing schools in the whole country.

No one had bothered much about the abandoned lighthouse, apart from Tam McCarthy, whose vision was worthy of the lighthouse's original purpose – a light that was a guide for many a person in danger. No one much bothered – apart from the local folk coming to know that, every now and again when darkness fell, the light at the top of the lighthouse on The Point would be lit, and they would smile and say, 'That's another youngster made it to the top ...' or 'That's Tam McCarthy helping some kid let their light shine.'

A little light

See this little light of mine, I have to let it shine,
Not so that others hear me say, 'The best one is always mine' …
But it's because I'm worried that its brightness will decline –
So it's mine, and by design I let it shine.

Can this little light of mine encourage yours to shine?
Where's your achievement, gift or skill that's worthy of a sign?
Even the small successes which are hardest to define –
Shout 'They're mine!' – so, that's fine, let them shine.

See these little lights that shine – yours, and theirs, and mine?
Look at the brightness that's around when every light can shine …
Banishing darkness, chasing fears, as lives are redesigned …
Love divine? Unconfined? Let it shine!

Fifth after Epiphany

Old Testament: Isaiah 58:1-12
Epistle: 1 Corinthians 2:1-16
Gospel: Matthew 5:13-20

13 Mr Symington's conversion

Mr Symington didn't much like the man who lived next door. For a start, he wasn't as nice as the Donaldsons who'd moved out earlier in the year. The Symingtons and the Donaldsons had moved into the street at the same time over forty years ago, newly married couples in their first homes, in a quiet cul-de-sac in a new estate.

It had been five years since Mr Symington's wife had died, and now that the Donaldsons had moved into sheltered housing, he felt more isolated than ever. And look at what had moved in next door … One of those 'biker' types, a big, hairy guy with a leather jacket and a union-jack bandana round his head, and, worst of all, with a huge motorbike parked halfway up the garden path. The racket it made when biker-man drove away in the morning, and the racket it made when he came back at night, was enough to waken the dead.

Mr Symington had never spoken to biker-man, and he wasn't about to lose any sleep over that. In fact, he didn't even know his neighbour's name. He just hated the idea of what had become of his lovely street, epitomised by hairy biker-man and his loud machine.

And that's the way things were … until the Home Help forgot to bring in Mr Symington's wheelie-bin from the street. She was always forgetting things. Mr Symington reckoned she'd forget her head one day if it wasn't fixed to her shoulders. So when Mr Symington had his bag of rubbish to put out as he always did at the end of the day, he had no bin close to his front door to put it in. He cursed his forgetful Home Help under his breath. He resolved – for the umpteenth time – to write to the Council and complain about Home Helps who would forget their heads if they weren't fixed to their shoulders. And he headed out the front door and down the garden path to retrieve the forgotten wheelie-bin.

It must have been a combination of Mr Symington rushing when he shouldn't have been, still wearing his carpet slippers, the gathering gloom of an autumn evening, and that awkward crack in one of the slabs, but Mr Symington fell his length on the path. He came down with a right clatter and knocked himself out cold. He lay there for what must have been ages. When he came round it was pitch dark, he was very cold, and he didn't know where he was. He tried to get up, but the pain in his hip was too much to bear.

When he heard some folk coming along the street, young voices, giggling and laughing, he tried to call out, but he didn't have the energy and he was too sore. And anyway, the big hedge at the foot of the garden hid him from view. He saw a bedroom light come on across the road. 'Maybe they'll come to help,' he thought. But it was too dark, and with no light cast over his garden no one could see he was there. Mr Symington closed his eyes and drifted into sleep. 'Is this what it's like to die?'

It was a loud roaring noise that roused him. He was shaking uncontrollably. He'd never been so cold. A piercing light swept across him and stayed, so that he remained lit up by the spotlight. But, try as he might, he just couldn't keep himself awake. He drifted back into sleep.

The next he knew, a big man, silhouetted in the light, was standing over him. Mr Symington had no idea who it was and, in and out of consciousness, he couldn't concentrate anyway. Once more, the grip of sleep dragged him away from the reality of his fate.

Things were a blur from then on, and when he was able to focus once more and orientate himself to his surroundings, he realised he was in a hospital bed. He was wrapped in a flimsy foil blanket. He had a drip fixed to his arm. A nurse was holding his hand, taking his pulse. She reassured him things were OK and told him that he was in hospital, that he was suffering from hypothermia, and that he'd broken his hip in a fall in his garden. 'And your friend's stayed with you since he came with you in the ambulance. If it hadn't been for him, who knows what might have happened?' She smiled reassuringly and squeezed his hand. 'Now, you just rest up for a while, and we'll have you right as rain in no time.'

'Hospital', 'broken hip', hypothermia', 'friend' were all swirling round in Mr Symington's head as he tried to take in his surroundings. And, as he did, he discovered that there, at the other side of the bed, sat a big, hairy guy wearing a leather biker-jacket and with a union-jack bandana round his head. 'Hi,' the man said. 'You back in the land of the living then, old codger?' He smiled, and rising from his seat, he came over to where Mr Symington lay in his bed and announced, 'I'm John, your next-door neighbour. How're you doin'?'

To judge

You know, it's a funny thing …

I was watching a TV drama the other night,
based in a courtroom,
and there was this judge,
with his red robes and his fancy wig,
up there on the bench,
in charge of it all.

It was great …

He could interrupt when he wanted to,
and tell people off when they went off track;
he could ask his own questions,
and insist that people answer him;
he could make sure he had proper respect,
and give people a hard time
if they didn't bow or call him 'M'lud';
and, in the end, he could decide,

who was right and who was wrong,
who were the good guys and who weren't ...

It was great ...

And I got to thinking ...
'What would it be like to have that kind of power?'

Then I got to thinking some more ...

Actually, that's what I do a lot of the time already ...
I sit on my bench, and I judge!
Oh, I know I don't wear red robes and a wig
and have people call me 'M'lud.'
But I judge, none the less, don't I?

That one's good, and that one isn't;
that lady on the bus is doing well with her child,
and that one's motherhood skills fall short;
that young girl with the pretty hair is OK,
and that one with the piercings and tattoos just isn't acceptable;
that man is reading the wrong kind of newspaper,
not as balanced as mine;
that precocious child ...
that guy with the turban ...
that woman who smells ...
that old man who shakes ...
that woman who mutters to herself ...
that lad with the dreadlocks ...
that girl with the torn jeans ...
that woman who's mutton dressed as lamb ...
that weird guy with the Mohican haircut ...

I sit with my superior gaze,
bedecked in my wig of authority,
wearing my red cloak of prejudice,
behind my bench of power,
in the courtroom of my decisions –
and I judge.

Great?

That's when I got to thinking some more ...

Sixth after Epiphany

Old Testament: Deuteronomy 30:15-20
Epistle: 1 Corinthians 3:1-9
Gospel: Matthew 5:21-37

14 Tit-for-tat

Jack's uncle Ken was taking him to the park. Jack liked his uncle Ken, and he liked going to the park. So today was going to be an interesting day.

Jack had put on his coat as instructed and had pulled on his woolly balaclava as a barrier against the cold. Uncle Ken had just finished his coffee in the kitchen and was sorting out his own warm jacket, when he called out to the waiting Jack. 'Ready, young man?' 'Ready to go, Uncle Ken.' 'Warm enough?' 'Warm as toast, Uncle Ken.' 'Well, best bring me my titfer so that I can be warm enough too.'

Jack didn't reply – simply because he had no idea what his uncle Ken was on about. But the voice came again. 'Jack! You gone deaf? Go and fetch my titfer, there's a good lad.'

Titfer? Well, Jack had obviously heard OK the first time. But what on *earth* was a 'titfer'? There was nothing for it – he'd have to ask. Jack wandered into the kitchen. 'Where's my titfer?' enquired his uncle. 'No idea,' replied Jack, 'because I've haven't got a clue what it is …'

Uncle Ken laughed. 'Sorry, son. You're right. I never thought. It's rhyming slang. "Titfer" is short for "tit-for-tat", and that rhymes with hat. So it's tit-for-tat – hat. Titfer … Got it?' 'Oh yes.' Jack nodded in response, though he still had no real idea what his uncle Ken was on about. But what he *did* know now was that his uncle wanted his hat – *why didn't he make that clear in the first place?* – and so he went to fetch it from the coat-rack in the hall. When Jack returned, hat in hand, Uncle Ken was about ready. 'Thanks, son,' he offered as he pulled on his battered baseball cap. 'Ready for anything now …'

On their way to the park Jack and his uncle chatted animatedly as usual. Just as they were turning through the park gates, though, Jack had to get something that was bothering him off his chest. 'Uncle Ken,' he began, 'what's "tit-for-tat" mean?'

'Tit-for-tat? Oh, from "titfer". Oh, yes. Well, tit-for-tat means ... I suppose ... let me think now ... well ... it's about getting your own back, revenge, doing something not very nice to someone who's not been nice to you, one bad turn deserves another, that kind of thing. OK?'

'I think so,' said Jack. 'But why would you want to do something bad to someone in return ...?'

'OK,' Uncle Ken continued, 'well ... let me see ... OK, let me tell you a story.' He beckoned his young charge over to a park bench and the two companions sat down together. Jack was all ears. He liked his uncle Ken's stories. So now that they were sitting comfortably, Uncle Ken began.

Once upon a time, in the warm days of spring, Sammy Sparrow was building his nest. He did this every year, because he and his mate, Suzie, needed a new home for their family. This year they'd chosen a new site for their nest – a little hole in the brickwork, right under the eaves of an old barn – and, slowly and carefully, Sammy and Suzie Sparrow filled the hole with a jumble of bits of rubbish, straw and feathers. Their new home was taking shape nicely. But Sammy wasn't happy. He was uneasy about the shape of his nest. So he thought of a plan. If he couldn't find enough stuff on his own, he would steal stuff from another nest.

Sparky Sparrow and his mate, Stella, were working hard on their nest too, tucked behind the ivy on the barn wall, and they were doing pretty well. Imagine their surprise when they got home one day to find Sammy stealing some feathers from their nest and flying away to his own nest under the eaves. Sparky was furious. So he waited till Sammy and Suzie had left the eaves to search for more feathers, and sneaked in and pulled out the big twigs that held Sammy's nest in place. When

Sammy got back, his nest was in a shambles, and he knew who was to blame. And he couldn't wait to raid Sparky's nest and pull it to bits.

And so it went on – Sammy getting his own back on Sparky, and Sparky getting his own back on Sammy, tit-for-tat, tit-for-tat. And do you know what happened in the end? Sammy and Suzie, and Sparky and Stella ended up with no nests at all for any of them, and no home for their families for the spring. Tit-for-tat, tit-for-tat had just made things worse.

'But what could Sparky have done, Uncle Ken?' Jack enquired when the story was done. 'He needed to build his nest, didn't he? And Sammy had spoiled it, hadn't he?'

Uncle Ken smiled. 'Uh huh,' he responded. 'But maybe if he'd got on with his own nest and not tried to get his own back, he and Sammy might both have had homes for their families in the spring. Tit-for-tat didn't work, did it?'

Jack thought he just about understood. A couple of sparrows were playing around the rubbish bin beside the bench. 'Well,' mused Jack, 'Sammy and Sparky seem to be getting on well enough *now* … No tit-for-tat for today, anyway.' And, as he watched them, he was remembering Lenny Billington pinching his crisps from his lunchbox in the school playground only last Friday and how he'd been planning revenge all weekend. And he wondered if 'tit-for-tat' might be something *he* needed to get out of his mind as well.

Right enough – today *was* turning out to be an interesting day.

Revenge

I'm plotting; I'm scheming; I'm working things out;
I'm seething; I'm boiling with rage;
I'm hacked-off; I'm angry; I'm wanting revenge;

I'm planning my hurt to assuage.

I'm patient; I'm calm; look, I'm turning my cheek;
I'm easy; I'm letting it go;
I'm tolerant, sensitive, quick to forgive;
I'm happy to go with the flow.

I'm driven by feelings of making it worse;
My motto's 'an eye for an eye';
I'm nursing my wrath, and I'm desperate to win;
I've bid toleration goodbye.

It's not 'tit-for-tat' that will motivate me;
My motto is 'live and let live';
I'm holding a hand out; I'm offering peace;
I'm trying my best to forgive.

So which one is me, and which life-stance will win?
And which one will fail in the end?
And will I do right, and rise up to the heights,
Or into despair still descend?

I wish it were easy to follow the way
that tells me forgiveness is right.
I'm trying; I'm pleading; I'm praying once more –
'Please help me to give up the fight.'

Seventh after Epiphany

Old Testament: Leviticus 19:1-2, 9-18
Epistle: 1 Corinthians 3:10-11, 16-23
Gospel: Matthew 5:38-48

15 A wee prezzie for Tracy

Freddy Aitcheson, out in the open, with a clearly visible brown paper parcel under his arm and with a grin as wide as a river estuary, was, to say the least, an intriguing sight. For a man who normally skulked in the shadows to avoid the searching eyes of the local constabulary to be seen stepping out so boldly in the broad light of day wasn't the usual way of things. He greeted Tim Gregory, one of the local Community Workers, like a long-lost brother.

'How's it goin', Tim?' he enquired chirpily.

'Not too bad, Freddy,' Tim replied, 'and it looks as though things are going pretty well for you too.'

'Aye, right enough. It's been a rerr day. Two winners on the gee-gees – at long odds too – an' a couple o' places. I took the bookie fur a fair bundle. An' noo it's hame tae ma darlin' Tracy and the bairns – wi' a wee surprise for her!'

'Surprise?' Tim responded, thinking it would be surprising enough for Tracy and the kids to see an errant husband and dad at home midway through the afternoon with the bookies still open and plenty of drinking time left at the local pub. 'Surprise?' Tim repeated. 'What surprise?'

'Ah've only gone an' bought a wee prezzie fur Tracy!'

Freddy beamed from ear to ear, mirroring the width of an estuary once again, and with a deft flick of his right wrist skilfully whisked the mysterious brown-paper parcel from under his arm and held it boldly in front of him.

'*Wee* present, Freddy?' Tim exclaimed. 'It looks a fair size to me.'

'Aye. It wis the biggest wan in the shop. D'ye want tae see it?'

And before Tim Gregory had a chance to reply with a 'yes' or 'no' or even a sceptical 'maybe', the precious present was being extricated from its brown-paper wrapping in front of his very eyes. Then, with commendable pride, and with the brown paper and what seemed like acres of bubble-wrap now around his feet, Freddy held in his hands the object of his pleasure, his wee prezzie for Tracy – a large, garish, brightly coloured, three-feet-long glass fish!

'It's what Tracy's aye wanted,' he crowed, raising the fish up to eye level in what was almost a sacramental gesture, 'an' it's the biggest wan there is. She'll be that chuffed, eh?' There was simply no answer to that. And anyway, by now Tim's lower jaw had dropped onto his chest thus rendering him temporarily speechless.

But Freddy was clearly in no mood to wait for his silent companion to make any comment on the quality or style of his 'wee' prezzie. So, not hanging about for any more conversation, he spun on his heel and headed down the street, veritably skipping like a child in a state of unbridled excitement. With the no-longer-needed brown paper and bubble-wrap already blowing decorously down the street, the precious glass fish was carried carefully in both hands as Freddy rushed home.

Later that week Tim had cause to visit the Aitcheson household to enquire after the welfare of the children. It wasn't an essential visit, but Tim's curiosity had got the better of him. He'd been wondering about the wee prezzie … When he got there, Tracy couldn't wait to usher him into the front room. 'Look,' she said excitedly, 'look whit ma man's bought me.' And she pointed to a large, garish, three-feet-long, brightly coloured glass fish, which now had pride of place on top of the TV.

'See yon?' she continued. 'Yon fish is what ah've aye wanted. An' it's the first prezzie ma man's brought me that didnae fa' off the back o' a lorry.' Tracy laughed uproariously at the amusing picture she'd obviously created in her mind. 'God, an' if it had fa'en aff a lorry, there'd no' be much o' *that* glass fish left, eh?' And she laughed loudly once more.

'Ach,' she continued when her laughter had subsided – and obviously now in more philosophical mode – 'you know that me an' Freddy huv had oor troubles. He's aye at the bookie's, ken? An' it's no' the furst time me an' the bairns huv had tae go hungry, just 'cause a wee waster has pit a' his cash in the bookie's pocket. An' he'll tell ye himsel' that ah've pit him oot often enough an' told him tae tak' a hike if he wisnae goanae get himsel' sorted.'

Tracy paused in her musings, smiled, and once again turned adoringly to the object of her undoubted pleasure. 'But ach, ye ken, whit wid ah dae wi'oot him. An' look at that prezzie. Whit can ah dae wi' Freddy when he gies me somethin' like yon, eh? Aye, he's no' that bad, no' bad at a' ...'

Tim Gregory smiled in agreement and joined Tracy in momentary worship of Freddy Aitcheson's wee prezzie for his wife ... And as he smiled and wondered if 'Solomon in all his glory was yet arrayed like one of these ...', Tim could swear that a large, garish, three-feet-long, brightly coloured glass fish on top of the TV in the Aitcheson household actually smiled back!

Consider

Consider the lilies of the fields ...

Consider the bunch of flowers
bought in the petrol-station
because someone forgot it was Valentine's Day ...
Is there not a little love
even in the wilting petals and the dripping cellophane?

Was not Solomon in all his glory ...?

Consider the sparrows under a park bench,
searching for crusts
or the crumbs of the crisps someone's dropped ...

Can't you see a little beauty
even in the drabness of their plumage on a grey day?

Was not Solomon in all his glory …?

Consider a glass fish on top of a TV,
the best gift in the world,
even though there's someone else who doesn't really think so …
Might you find a little wonder
even in the things that are hard to understand?

Was not Solomon in all his glory …?

Consider what you look at in your mirror,
with your wrinkles and your worried frown,
thinking, 'There's not much there that's worth looking at ..'.
Maybe you'll discover a little self-belief
even when your own worth and value are hard to see.

Was not Solomon in all his glory …?

Eighth after Epiphany

Old Testament: Isaiah 48:8–16a
Epistle: 1 Corinthians 4:1–5
Gospel: Matthew 6:24–34

16 I want to stay!

There was no doubt about it – it had been a real struggle. The rehearsals hadn't gone well at all. In fact, there had been talk of the performance being cancelled altogether. But then, the town hall was booked, the orchestra was arranged, the posters were around the town, the adverts had been placed and the pre-ordered tickets had already been sent out. Cancellation would have been a disaster, unthinkable – and yet the thinking was understandable enough.

The problems had started when the choir's conductor had got the flu. At a crucial time, several rehearsals had been missed. Oh, the choir had got together right enough. After all, the regular Tuesday night gatherings were in everyone's diary. Bobby from the tenors had taken charge as best he could, but he was no great shakes as a musical director, and some of the singers left the rehearsals more confused than they had been at the start.

The fall-out among the altos didn't help. They'd never been the most co-operative bunch, and now that two new people had joined this year there were more splits and factions than usual. Artistic temperament ruled – and not to the choir's overall benefit.

The final straw was Alfie's wife's death. Alfie was one of the choir's stalwarts, whose rich bass voice had held together the choir's lower tones for many years. How were the basses to survive without their mainstay?

The week before the choir's annual performance of *Messiah* was as bad as anyone could remember. It had been a huge mountain to climb, and there was still a long way to go, and so little time to make it to the top. They tried their best, of course. What else was there for them to do? The soloists, brought in for the occasion, were steady enough, and everyone was thankful for that. The conductor, pretty well fully restored to health but clearly under stress, was his usual encouraging self. 'You can do it! Don't panic! It'll be all right on the night!' he would intone, while his face betrayed his own panic and the belief that it would be far from 'all right'.

There was no doubt about it — it had been a *real* struggle. And Morag hadn't really enjoyed it at all. This was her second *Messiah,* the first being the previous year in her final year in high school. That had been fantastic, and though she was now in college, she'd committed herself to the regular Tuesday evenings for another year. She wished she hadn't, for she'd got little enjoyment out of the rehearsals this time round. Balancing college work and leisure pursuits was one thing. Coming home every Tuesday for a rehearsal that was seldom pleasurable was quite another. 'A mountain to climb?' she pondered, when she felt that the choir was still in the foothills.

The night of the performance, no one spoke much. Some of the choir members sat quietly sipping from their water bottles. A few of the sopranos were huddled in a corner going over a tricky section. Two of the basses had gone outside for a smoke. When the dreaded moment arrived and the choir took their places on the stage, Morag realised she was relieved when the house-lights went down, so that no one could see the worried frowns on most of the choir members' faces.

She needn't have worried … For on that night, the town's choir scaled a mountain-top, and a performance was transformed. To this day Morag doesn't know why. Some said it was because, when they walked on stage, they could see Alfie sitting in the front row. Others suggested that the quality of the soloists had pulled up the standard of the choir's performance. Morag knew that she'd never concentrated on anything so hard in all her life, and perhaps the others were doing the same. Whatever it was, something happened in the town hall that night. *Messiah* was as good as it had ever been.

The chorus singing 'Glory to God' was greeted with spontaneous applause — unheard of in the middle of a piece. The alto solo of 'He was despised' was as moving as anyone could remember. The soprano's singing of 'I know that my Redeemer liveth' was quite incredible. 'The Halleluiah Chorus' was a triumph. And all through the final chorus of 'Worthy is the Lamb', Morag was struggling to hold back her tears.

The conclusion was rapturous applause, as loud and sustained as anything Morag could remember. It was quite wonderful – what their conductor described later in his usual flamboyant way as 'a veritable thing of beauty'.

Morag was one of the last to leave that night. She was sitting in the dressing-room behind the stage with her water-bottle in her hand and her music-case at her feet, staring into space. 'You staying the night?' one of the tenors asked. Jolted out of her reverie, Morag turned to her enquirer. 'No. But I want to. I don't want to go home. I'd like to stay here, to hold on to this feeling for as long as possible. This is too good to let go.'

Her singing companion smiled. 'Aye, lass, it was good right enough. But you can't stay here for ever – none of us can. We'll remember tonight for sure, and we'll get a buzz out of our memories when we think back. But it's time to go now. And there'll always be another year.'

Morag rose to leave and took the arm of an old man she hardly knew. And as they left the town hall together, they saw that Alfie was still sitting in the front row.

Stay

> Lord, it is good to be here.
> Let me build shelters for you and me,
> and all the others too,
> so that we can stay here,
> and hold the moment for ever.

> OK. I understand.
> It's been good, that's for sure.
> Build your shelters if you like.

But I won't be here for long.
It's time for moving on.

But why? What's the hurry?
Can't we wait a little longer,
savour the moment,
enjoy all the feelings of wonder?
Why can't we stay?

OK. I appreciate that.
It's been amazing, I know that too.
Moments of mystery don't happen often, I know.
But it's time to go,
This is no place to stay.

But I'm not sure I'm ready.
And I don't fancy what's to come –
the ordinary, the routine,
the drab and the boring.
That's no life compared to this.

OK. I can relate to that,
though who can ever tell you
what awaits you, out there?
But I reckon that, one day,
there might be another mountain-top to climb …

Another time like this?

OK … OK?

Transfiguration

Old Testament: Exodus 24:12-18
Epistle: 2 Peter 1:16-21
Gospel: Matthew 17:1-9

17 Ashes to ashes

No one was very sure where The Idea came from or who came up with it first. Not that it mattered anyway, for, at the end of a stressful day, it was the disastrous outcome that mattered and not where the whole sorry event had begun.

The Idea had taken hold not long after Christmas. The congregation returned to church after the Christmas festivities, and of course till the 'twelve days of Christmas' had run their course, the decorations and the coloured lights had to stay in place. No one really understood why, and the whole Epiphany business was lost on most folk. It was just a tradition, and even though Christmas and the beginning of the year had come and gone, the decorations stayed.

And that, of course, meant that the massive Christmas tree at the front of the church was still the dominant feature when the parishioners gathered for the service on the first Sunday of the New Year. But there would soon be an end to it, and by the next Sunday, all the Christmas stuff would have gone and things would be back to normal.

So when the work-party gathered on the Monday to do what was necessary to restore the church to its pre-Christmas condition, there was a massive Christmas tree to dispose of. Soon enough, though, the tree was stripped of its lights, tinsel and baubles, and the decorations were stored carefully in their boxes. And when all that was done, a bare, unattractive, well-past-its-sell-by-date Christmas tree was ready for removal. And that's when The Idea was first mentioned. To this day no one will own up to making the suggestion. But pretty soon The Idea had been accepted with enthusiasm by all and sundry as the best and most meaningful way to dispose of a used Christmas tree – it was to be ceremonially burned in the car-park at the back of the church.

Those involved will argue that this was no simple convenience or an opportunity to relieve a work party of making arrangements for the tree to go to the town dump. It was all based on what appeared to be good, sound, acceptable theological and liturgical principles – or so someone said at the time. The tree would be burned as a visible symbol that Christmas was over. But the charred trunk of the tree would be kept and stored away till Easter time. Then it would be cut in two and formed into a cross, and would be placed in centre-stage at the Holy Week and Easter events. A direct link between Christmas and Easter … hope out of the ashes – or something like that.

Whatever the motivation, The Idea was agreed. It all sounded so right. The work party was excited. The minister was hurriedly called in to offer some extempore prayer to make the thing holy enough to be completely acceptable. The makeshift congregation carried the tree into the car-park and gathered round it with solemn ceremony. The clergyman intoned suitably prayerful words. And, in a holy silence, one of the men leaned forward and lit the topmost branch of the huge tree with his disposable lighter. It was all so right …

Now, the truth is … no one expected the tree to catch alight as quickly as it did. If they'd *thought* about it, someone might have suggested that a twelve-foot Scots pine which had been in a centrally heated building for three and a half weeks and which still had some of its needles attached would be kind of dry – tinder dry – catches-alight-more-quickly-than-anyone-expects kind of dry – and that's very, *very* dry indeed. The truth is … no one expected the enormous conflagration.

In an instant the entire tree was ablaze – with an audible 'whoosh'. Members of the work-party jumped back in fright. The horrified minister wasn't quick enough. His discarded anorak, which he'd carefully placed at his feet before he'd offered his prayers, caught alight. The briefcase lying beside it started to melt. A stray spark from what was now a raging inferno blew onto the hedge that bounded the car-park. It was winter and the hedge burned easily, far too easily for anyone to stop it taking hold.

The silver birch tree in the Sandersons' garden beyond the hedge was the next to go. Mr Sanderson's garden shed was in deep trouble. Panic ensued …

As it turned out, some sharp-witted neighbour had called the Fire Brigade, and within minutes the able men and women of the Fire Service were doing the necessary to extinguish the post-Christmas inferno. Thankfully, no one was injured by the blaze. The Sandersons' shed escaped destruction – which is more than can be said for their silver birch, the car-park boundary hedge, the minister's anorak and the exterior of his briefcase.

And the tree, and the clever theological idea of retaining its charred trunk for Easter usage? No chance, for all that was left of a once-magnificent Scots pine was some soggy ashes in the car-park at the back of the church.

There was a new minister in the church the following Christmas. When he was helping to take down the Christmas tree at the turn of the year he casually suggested, 'Don't you think it would be a good idea …' and was very surprised that, even before he'd finished his sentence, he was met, from the whole company, with a resounding, 'NO!'

The ashes

The ashes of my hopes and dreams,
the charred remains of my undying commitment,
the remnants of my broken promises
lie scattered at my feet,
dreadful reminders of what went up in smoke,
the destruction of all that was right and good.

So, as I gaze around me,
standing now in the remains of what once I was;
and I repent of my complicity

in the conflagration of my failure;
I offer my regret for the ways I've broken my life,
and the lives of others, and what I ought to be.

Restore my hopes and my dreams;
gather up the charred remains;
cleanse them with your grace;
make sense of the remnants;
heal the brokenness;
set my feet once more on holy ground;
offer me a new beginning
re-create out of what you hold
what is right and good again.

Ash Wednesday

Old Testament: Joel 2:1-2, 12-17
Epistle: 2 Corinthians 5:20b-6:10
Gospel: Matthew 6:1-6, 16-21

18 Temptations

Farrin Ghatary was sorely tempted. It wasn't for herself in any way. It was always the little ones who were uppermost in her mind. Her heart broke for them. What kind of mother was she who could not provide for her children?

Life as an asylum-seeker in Glasgow had never been easy. With all the dispersed asylum-seekers housed in deprived areas of the city, there had been tensions and resentment among the local communities right from the start. But, in that regard at least, things had improved. Charities which campaigned for better conditions for asylum-seekers and refugees had been an important support. The work of the Scottish Refugee Council and Glasgow's City Council had improved their lot. Local churches provided much needed immediate care, drop-in centres, English-language tutoring and cross-cultural events. It all helped, of course. But it didn't stop the temptations.

The first winter was the worst. The flat was never warm enough. The children's clothes didn't completely combat the bitter cold on some of the worst of days. And there was never enough food. So it was in the supermarket when she was taking time over the buying of her meagre family rations that the temptations were at their strongest. 'Who would miss a packet of biscuits?' the voices in her head would say. 'You need bread for your children. Why not provide them with a few things they need? Go on … No one will see you … It's easy when you know how …'

Farrin Ghatary was sorely tempted. It wasn't for herself in any way. It was always the little ones who were uppermost in her mind. Her heart broke for them. What kind of mother was she who could not provide for her children?

★★★

Mansoor Ghatary was sorely tempted. It wasn't for himself in any way. It was always his wife who was uppermost in his mind. His heart broke for her. What kind of husband was he who had put his wife and family in a situation like this?

Life since Mansoor had taken his family out of Iran had never been easy. His involvement with opposition politics had made life in his homeland intolerable and dangerous for him and his family. So they had fled. Why they had ended up in Glasgow, Mansoor never really understood. He hoped that one day they would all be able to go home, so that he could continue his work as a lawyer and provide stability for his family.

He had, of course, submitted his formal application for asylum, though he was sure the system was designed to make it as hard as possible for people to understand and make use of. The waiting seemed to be for ever. There was seldom any feedback, little word of progress. He had to report to a police-station once a week to be finger-printed – 'Like a criminal …' he always thought. And there were the financial restrictions. There was never enough money even for the basics. He often went without himself so that his wife and children could eat. He'd considered suicide several times. It was mental tor-ture. And there were the temptations …

There was money around if you needed it, but it was always on the wrong side of the law. He knew he could get money-in-hand as a labourer with a local 'cowboy builder'. He knew he could get ready cash as a 'runner' for the local drug-dealers. He knew he could 'earn' a bit by allowing his flat to store stolen property while 'the heat died down'. He knew all of this, because people talked, and stories were passed on, and offers were made … And money, and status, and com-fort, and improving his circumstances were always on his mind.

Mansoor Ghatary was sorely tempted. It wasn't for himself in any way. It was always his wife who was uppermost in his mind. His heart broke for her. What kind of husband was he who had put his wife and family in a situation like this?

★★★

Afsar Ghatary was sorely tempted. It wasn't for herself in any way. It was always her parents and her little brother and sister who were uppermost in her mind. Her heart broke for them. What kind of daughter was she who could do nothing to help her family in their dire circumstances?

The eldest of the three Ghatary children, Afsar had been eighteen when she'd arrived in Glasgow with her family. She'd had little English then, though she'd picked up a fair bit in recent times. She had to. How else was she to communicate? How was she to know what people were saying to her or about her when the language was beyond her?

It was the abuse that was the hardest to cope with. When she learned what the comments people made at the beginning really were, Afsar was horrified. She had done nothing wrong. She was not their enemy. She was not the cause of their troubles. So why did they hate her like this?

But it was the temptations that were the absolute worst. They were too horrible even to speak of. No one knew. She hated herself for even thinking about it. She felt dirty inside. She often cried herself to sleep. But ever since one of the other young refugee women had hinted at the possibility of prostitution, the temptations would not go away. To raise the family up above the gutter? To give them hope? To help them see the way ahead? Might it not be …?

Afsar Ghatary was sorely tempted. It wasn't for herself in any way. It was always her parents and her little brother and sister who were uppermost in her mind. Her heart broke for them. What kind of daughter was she who could do nothing to help her family in their dire circumstances?

★★★

Farrin, Mansoor and Afsar Ghatary were sorely tempted. It wasn't for themselves in any way. It was always the others who were uppermost in their minds. They never knew about each other's temptations. And none of them ever gave in.

Tempted

If I could turn stones into bread,
I think I probably would,
and then, what a difference I could make
for the poor of the world.

But I can't.
So I won't.
But, if I could …?

If I was in charge of the United Nations and could do anything,
I probably would,
and then, what a difference I could make
to the peace of the world.

But I can't.
So I won't.
But if I could …?

If I could be a superhero and pull off amazing stunts,
I probably would,
and then, what a difference I could make
to the troubles of the world.

But I can't.
So I won't.
But if I could …?

So, when I'm tempted to ignore the poor
because I can't make stones into bread,
sort me out,
and help me overcome that temptation.

And when I'm tempted to ignore injustice and inhumanity
because I'm too ineffective to create world peace,
stop me short,
and help me overcome that temptation.

And when I'm tempted to give up on being a hero
because I'm too small to make a difference,
stand with me,
and help me overcome that temptation.

Because I can.
And I will.
And I should ...

First in Lent

Old Testament: Genesis 2:15-17
Epistle: Romans 5:12-19
Gospel: Matthew 4:1-11

19 A new beginning

It had been a quiet evening for Father Lenny Stephens. He hadn't had many quiet evenings since moving to his new parish, such was the nature of things. Not that he'd expected anything else, for an inner-city parish – and a down-at-heel one at that – was bound to bring its own busyness. So Lenny valued this rare quiet evening and had spent a couple of hours catching up with paperwork and dipping into books he'd been meaning to read for a while – until the doorbell rang.

Lenny had a part-time housekeeper, but he was expected to fend for himself in the evenings. Callers were many and varied, and there was no telling who would be waiting on the doorstep. Lenny wasn't usually irritated by such passing trade – it was part of the job – but tonight, in relaxed mode, he wasn't best pleased with the untimely interruption.

He was even less pleased to find Valerie on his doorstep. Valerie was the oldest of a large family with whom Lenny had already become acquainted, oldest of twelve, he'd been told, though he'd not had the pleasure of meeting Valerie herself. But now was obviously the time, for facing him was a somewhat bedraggled woman in her late teens carrying an equally bedraggled small bundle.

'Hello, Father,' chirped the stranger, 'I'm Val Underwood. Ma mum and dad told me they'd met you. "Nice new priest," ma mum said. So I came to ask when you can do the baby.'

Lenny wasn't often lost for words, but he opened his mouth and nothing came out. Val picked up on the uncertain response.

'The baby, Father, the baby … the baby needs doin'. Mum said I should get it sorted. So, here I am, wi' the baby, to see when she can be done.'

Pulling himself together as best as he was able and, fortunately, regaining his power of speech, Lenny invited Val and her offspring inside and clarified the story. Valerie Underwood, just turned nineteen, had fallen pregnant. The baby – Madonna Cheryl – had been born three weeks early, two weekends ago. One more mouth to feed in the Underwood household didn't appear to be a problem, but Val's mum had clearly insisted that she 'do the right thing' and 'have the baby done' – christened, baptised – 'for if she's no' done, she'll no go to heaven', Val reported.

Lenny got all the details, or as much as he could really understand. 'Madonna's father?' he tentatively enquired.

'No idea,' was the unembarrassed reply. 'Whoever he is'll do nothin' anyway. So no point in tryin' to find out. Baby'll just be part o' the family, so ma mum says.'

Lenny hoped his furrowed brow didn't display too much anxiety. 'Who can come with you to church and stand with you,' he enquired, 'if there's no father for the baby?'

'Oh, that's no bother,' Val responded. 'Ah'll tell ma dad to come.'

So that's why Father Lenny Stephens found himself being introduced to Madonna Cheryl Underwood's grandfather at the church door the following Sunday morning. Wally Underwood was a remarkable sight. He'd obviously made an effort, but Lenny wondered what the head of the Underwood family would have been like if *no* special effort had been made. He had several days' patchy growth on his chin; his hair had been mostly plastered down with gel, but several stray chunks had obviously been missed; he wore horn-rimmed glasses with the archetypal piece of sticking plaster holding one of the legs together; and he was bedecked in the most crumpled suit Lenny had ever seen. The shiny-grey suit looked as if it had probably spent long months hidden from view, crushed into a plastic bag and stuffed deep in the recesses of a cupboard, to be unearthed, with much relish no doubt, for an auspicious occasion – such as attending church with his daughter as a forerunner to his first grandchild's baptism.

Wally Underwood fell asleep through every sermon Lenny ever

preached – though, graciously, he managed to waken up in time for the offering. He stood up and sat down at the wrong times – until he got used to the system. But the church folk were patient with him and were always welcoming and supportive. So, in time, Wally stood proudly beside his eldest daughter on the day Madonna Cheryl Underwood was finally 'done' as per the family protocol.

Valerie Underwood and her offspring never came back to church. Such was the way of things. Wally, on the other hand, came back the Sunday after the baptism even when he didn't have to – unshaven, crumpled suit, almost slicked hair, and all – and kept coming, Sunday by Sunday by Sunday. Eventually Wally actually stayed awake during a sermon. He joined the parish men's group Bowling Club. He came on the annual parish retreat – another outing for the crumpled suit. Wally had become part of the church community.

★★★

It had been a rare quiet evening for Father Lenny Stephens. He'd had hardly any quiet evenings recently, and he was tired and needed some space to himself. So he'd spent a couple of hours catching up with paperwork and dipping into books he'd been meaning to read for a while – until the doorbell rang. More than irritated, and determined to get rid of the random caller as quickly as possible, Lenny was surprised to find Wally Underwood on his doorstep.

'Wally,' Lenny offered, 'what brings you here? Everything all right?'

'Sure. Everythin's sorted, Father. It's just that I needed to ask you something.'

'Ask away,' Lenny responded. 'Want to come in?'

'No, it's OK here,' grinned Wally.

'Well?' Lenny prompted encouragingly after a while.

'Well, it's like this,' Wally continued. 'I heard you say in church on Sunday that there was to be a Confirmation Class soon, and I wondered if it would be OK to come along.'

My beloved

My beloved,
yes,
you ...
uh huh,
you,
with the scruffy suit
and the gelled hair.
Yes ...
you ...
who else could I be talking to
when you're the only one there?
Yes,
you ...
Don't look so surprised.
You,
you, with the worried frown
and the sceptical look ...
No use hiding that from me!
Yes,
you ...
Listen up ...
I've got a job for you to do ...

Second in Lent

Old Testament: Genesis 12:1-4a
Epistle: Romans 4:1-5, 13-17
Gospel: John 3:1-17

20 The meeting

It was the only place Toni and Michelle could meet without being found out. That's why one of the many dark stairwells in the West Mountfield estate had become their regular meeting place. West Mountfield – a complicated conglomeration of stairs, ramps, walk-ways, railings, flats, pensioners' houses and maisonettes – which, though it had won a design award when it was at the planning stage and had been trumpeted by the Council as 'the way forward for the public-housing sector', was now one of the most depressing – and dangerous – parts of the town. The whole of the Mountfield estate was bad. West Mountfield was the pits.

There were countless dark corners in West Mountfield that any self-respecting citizen would avoid like the plague. Graffiti-covered walls, dog-excrement on the walkways, discarded syringes on stair-landings, the detritus of fast-food outlets, and the all-pervading stench of urine and filth made West Mountfield a no-go area.

Michelle had no choice. She lived there. Toni had every choice. But she chose to visit her friend as regularly as she was able.

Toni and Michelle had first met down at the city docks. Michelle was a prostitute, plying her trade for the crews of the container ships which were the docks' stock-in-trade. And Michelle's stock-in-trade was prostitution. Her pimp's trade was Michelle – and several other girls. The trade for the heroin dealers was all of them.

Toni worked for a prostitute support project. With a supply of condoms and health advice, clean needles and emergency phone numbers, Toni and her colleagues were around the docks regularly. There was no judgement in it. The project was simply there to help.

Lately, the girls' pimp had been playing it rough. Toni had been warned off for being a 'bad influence' (now, there's an irony ...) because every time she was seen with one of the girls it scared the punters away – and no punters meant no work, and no work meant no profit, and no profit meant no deals … So Toni had taken to meeting Michelle in their chosen stairwell, the foot of a carefully selected, secluded, seldom-frequented stair at the far edge of West Mountfield. There was no way Toni would have been welcome at Michelle's flat – too risky by far. So they met at their secret place, when no one else was around, and no one else could know.

Michelle was HIV positive. Not surprising, really. The punters paid more for unprotected sex. Michelle knew the risks. But she had to turn a profit. And HIV was the result.

Toni could never tell you why she and Michelle had become friends. Maybe it was because Toni understood something of Michelle's vulnerability. She too had her story to tell. 'There but for the grace of God,' she often thought. Or maybe it was because Toni knew that Michelle had no one else, no one else with whom to have a normal conversation, share a cigarette or experience a hug. Or maybe it wasn't worth analysing and it was enough that Toni just liked her. But no matter – meeting Michelle served a purpose for both of them.

Michelle would often appear with a can of Special Brew – extra-strong lager – working on the principle that anything that dulled the mind – before or after a fix, before or after work – was worth it. Toni would be offered a swig. She never said no. Maybe she should have. Maybe the risks were too great. But then, who else would accept Michelle's small gesture of friendship without condition?

Sometimes Toni would talk with Michelle about her 'lifestyle' (that's what the books called it …) or how she 'was surviving' (which was more accurate …) and Michelle would talk. 'How come you can get me to talk about things I don't want to talk about?' she would ask on the better nights. 'How come you seem to know what's happening to me?' she would stumble in a sadder mood. 'Why the f**k d'you bother wi' me?' she would blurt out at the worst of times.

Toni never tried to answer. But she was happy with the talk and the shared lager and the smokes and the hugs and the friendship. She hoped it mattered to Michelle. All that was in her believed it did.

The last time Toni had been to their meeting place was the previous day when she'd met Michelle just before midnight. The two friends had parted with a cursory hug just before one in the morning. Michelle wasn't in great shape that last time … And, on her way for tonight's rendezvous, Toni was very fearful about how Michelle might be now …

You come

I hate being here;
I hate what I must do,
what I have become;
I hate the secrecy
the shame,
the dirtiness
of what I know I am.

And I so I hide;
I skulk in shadows;
I lurk in dark corners
where I can't be seen
or known for what I am.

I hate the self that only I can know,
that not one other self-respecting, living soul
would wish to learn about.

And you come
and know more than I would have you know;
you come,
into this place where hate is all-pervading;
you come,
into darkness, filth and deep despair;
you come,
where no one else would dare to dwell;
you come;
you stay;
you listen;
and you come again,
and again,
and again;
and that, for now,
seems to be enough ...

Third in Lent

Old Testament: Exodus 17:1-7
Epistle: Romans 5:1-11
Gospel: John 4:5-42

21 To see what you see

Timothy had to admit it as he looked out of his front-room window
– he was bored … Not mind-numbingly, this-is-the-worst-day-of-
my-life, nobody-could-ever-have-been-as-bored-as-this-in-the-
whole-history-of-the-universe kind of bored. Just bored, the kind of
bored that comes along when you've tried everything else – like your
computer games and puzzle books and a host of other things – and
you're not sure what to put your mind to next. This kind of bored
would pass – Timothy knew that – but for now, in that gap between
doing stuff that was interesting and doing some more stuff that was
interesting, boredom was the name of the game.

Having Gramps around helped, of course – or, at least, it had
helped up till now. On a mid-term long weekend break from school,
and with Timothy's parents both committed to work on the Monday,
Gramps was the childcare provision. Timothy didn't much like the
idea of childcare – after all, he wasn't a child (Well, you're not when
you're nine-and-three-quarters, are you?), and he didn't reckon he
needed *that* much caring for. But 'rules are rules', as his mum often
put it, so Gramps was the childcare for the day. But if Timothy didn't
much like the idea of childcare, he very *much* liked the times he had
with Gamps.

Gramps and Timothy were best mates, and there were lots of
things Timothy had learned from his gramps that he would have had
no chance of learning from anyone else. Timothy had perfected the
'broken-match-in-the-handkerchief trick (too complicated *and* secret
to explain …) – and he'd got that from his gramps. Timothy knew all
the books of the Bible (all sixty-six of them …) and could even recite
them backwards – and he'd got that from his gramps. Timothy could
write with both hands (*and* do mirror-writing with his left …) – and
he'd got that from his gramps. Timothy knew a song about 'Dan-

gerous Dan McGrew' (though nobody was *ever* to know that he knew *that* kind of song …) – and he'd got that from his gramps. *That's* why Timothy and Gramps were best mates …

Timothy's boredom was interrupted with an awareness that Gramps had appeared at his side.

'You look bored,' said Gramps.

'Yeah, kind of,' said Timothy, continuing to stare out of the window. It had been raining hard all day. Any chance of Gramps taking him to the park had disappeared ages ago. A very wet day and periods of boredom always went together.

Gramps went silent, joining Timothy in his bored quietness. Then after a while Gramps said, 'What do you see out of the window?'

'Same as you see, Gramps,' replied Timothy, somewhat puzzled by the question.

'Well, what's that?' Gramps continued. Timothy decided to go along with the questioning. He knew Gramps was onto something. He didn't know what, not yet anyway. But Gramps always had an angle …

'Well,' Timothy began, stating the obvious, 'for starters I can see the trees at the bottom of the garden.'

'Good,' responded Gramps. 'But what do you see?'

'I see the trees moving about in the wind, just like they've been doing all morning.'

'Good. Moving trees … good,' Gramps went on. 'But what do you *see*?' Timothy was puzzled (not that unusual a feeling when Gramps was onto something). But he decided to have a try.

'Well, I see trees moving in the wind … the branches going one way and then the other … all together … like … as if they were … waving their arms …'

There was a smile in Gramps' voice now. 'Good! Good! So you see trees, with branches moving all together, like people waving their arms, first one way then the other. Good. So what do you see now?' Timothy realised he was smiling too.

'Well, Gramps, they're kind of like … dancers.'

'Excellent!' said Gramps. 'And if they're *dancers,* there must be …'

'Music,' Timothy exclaimed, 'music that only the trees can hear.'

'Well done!' But Timothy was deaf to the praise. He was on a roll!

'Yes, Gramps, music, tree-music, special music for trees. See, the branches are nearly still, just moving a tad, look, hardly shaking. That's the quiet music, *really* quiet. That's why they've stopped moving.' Then, a sudden gust of wind shook the trees violently from their reverie, and the branches swung wildly again. 'There, gramps!' shouted Timothy, excitedly. 'Look at that. The music's gone *very* loud now! Oh wow! There must be cymbals crashing and loud drums banging. Amazing! Some of the branches are finding it awfully hard to keep up. They must be exhausted!'

'So, what do you see, young man?' enquired Gramps, during an appropriate pause in Timothy's effervescent explanation of the drama taking place at the bottom of his garden. Timothy turned to his gramps and beamed widely.

'I see trees, Gramps … I see dancing trees … I see dancing trees waving their arms together … I see musical, dancing trees, swaying back and forwards, side to side, to music only they can hear. It's amazing music, eh Gramps? D'you think if we listened *really* hard we might be able to hear the music too, eh Gramps?'

'Yup, I reckon we might be able to do just that …'

Gramps returned to his chair by the fire. Timothy continued to watch the dancing trees. He wasn't bored any more, and he was moving his head from side to side in rhythm with the dancers … And then Timothy started to hum a little tune. And as he did, he noticed out of the corner of his eye that Gramps was tapping his hand on the arm of his chair in time to the music …

To see

To look and see,
and enjoy the seeing,
and marvel at the beauty.

To look and see,
and enjoy the imagining,
and marvel at the mystery.

To look and see,
and enjoy more than the seeing,
and marvel at unfolding pictures.

To look and see,
and the enjoy the imagining,
and wonder why that couldn't be seen before.

To look and see,
and enjoy the seeing,
and marvel at the unfathomable beauty.

Fourth in Lent

Old Testament: 1 Samuel 16:1-13
Epistle: Ephesians 5:8-14
Gospel: John 9:1-41

22 Connections

This is the only contribution to this book that's written in the first person, because it's the only story that's autobiographical. I tried to change it, to make it relate to someone else. But it didn't work. It's my story, and I hope it might allow you to tell yours.

I didn't much like my grandpa. He shook a lot (Parkinson's disease, I discovered later) and that was scary for a wee boy. He drank too much beer – or so my granny always said – and with that and the reek of stale tobacco from his horrible pipe, he didn't smell too good either. He was way too grumpy for my liking. I don't remember him smiling much. He snored like a warthog. (I always shared a room with him and my dad when we stayed on holiday and I *detested* his snoring!) And my granny and my mum kept telling strange stories about his antics when he was a young farm-hand, all about drink and shouting and threatening behaviour. I'm not sure I ever grasped the details, but it didn't sound like living with him had been a bundle of laughs for my granny and my mum. So, I didn't much like my grandpa.

But mostly, we never spoke. He didn't say anything to me, anyway. Oh, he'd say plenty *about* me, like how I was too cheeky for my age and that I wasn't learning much about good behaviour from the Boys Brigade, and that I should leave things alone that weren't mine, and stuff like that. And for my part, I didn't say anything to him. There wasn't much I *could* say really, apart from calling him a smelly old man and asking him why he was always shaking like that. But I was too scared to be as cheeky as *that*! So we never spoke. We just watched each other, and kept our distance, and remained suspicious.

I wonder now what we would have said if we'd tried to speak. And I wonder if *he* ever wondered what I'd say to him if we'd ever conversed. And I wonder what he was really, *really* like, this grandpa of mine. But my grandpa died before we ever got to know each other, before either of us ever really bothered to get to know each other. The gulf was too wide and the differences too vast.

So I remember my grandpa as a man that I didn't really like much. Perhaps it's my granny's oft-used description of him that stays with me most. 'A bad old bugger,' she'd call him – and sometimes to his face … (Brave lady!)

One thing always intrigued me about my grandpa, though. It's a simple fact that I must have picked up at a very early age. He'd been brought up in an orphanage – Quarriers Homes in Bridge of Weir in Scotland. Not a particularly world-shattering piece of information, but an intriguing one just the same. And, years later, it was this single piece of information that changed my mind about my grandpa, and gave me a connection with him I'd never had before.

Some years after my own parents had died I spent some time researching my family tree on the internet. One day I keyed in my grandpa's name – and there it was! A little research unearthed the information that one year's census showed him in a family home as a one-year-old with his mother and his brother, and the next, ten years later, saw him listed among the boys in the orphanage. I was full of questions … What had happened? What had caused this dramatic change? What was the true story? So I tried to find out about his parents. His father was untraceable. And his mother? Well, I found her, sure enough. And I was horrified to discover that her death certificate read, 'Died as the result of a house fire' – when my grandpa would have been just over two years old.

'Died as the result of a house fire' – the death of a young mother, a single parent, in a tragic accident. 'Died as the result of a house fire' … And in an instant a horrible, unlikeable old man became a frightened, lonely child. A shaky, cantankerous grandpa became a disorientated wee boy, bereft of his mother, devoid of a home and family love. A smelly, argumentative figure to be reviled and suspicious of became an orphan, a tragic victim of hurt and poverty and a terrible trauma.

Whatever had happened in the unfolding of his years to make this child the grandfather I knew I shall never find out. But what I *do* know now is this – added to the ending of a man's life there was now this life's beginning. The old man and the broken child were one and the same. I now had a connection with a different grandpa.

I didn't much like my grandpa. I still don't. I didn't much care for the old man he'd become. But now I cried for the child he had been, and I wanted to hold him and comfort him and take him in and give him a home. So now my grandpa isn't just my grandpa. He's more than that. I don't know how, but he's more of a person than he was. And I'm still connected to him, and his old bones are alive for me in a new way.

I didn't much like my grandpa, but then I've begun to realise that he wasn't always a grandpa, was he?

Revised from a story first published in 'Holy Ground' (Wild Goose Publications) Eds Neil Paynter & Helen Boothroyd, 2005

Labels

It wasn't hard for Judas to betray Jesus.
For what he saw and what he knew
he'd labelled as 'dangerous' and 'renegade' –
a threat to stability,
a challenge to authority,
a disturbance of the peace of his faith.
So he betrayed what he saw.
He wanted rid of what he knew.
It wasn't hard for Judas to betray Jesus,
because he believed the label said it all.

It would have been harder for Judas to get to know Jesus.
For what he would have seen and known
was much, much more than the label –
a love that was all-encompassing,
a compassion that was life-giving,

a redemption for those rejected.
He would have been changed by what he then saw,
transformed by what he'd come to know.
If he'd worked harder at getting to know Jesus,
the label would never have been enough.

It isn't hard to understand people
when what we see and what we know
means that we label them all too easily –
because they threaten our stability,
and get in the way of our authority,
and disturb our peace.
So we reject what we see,
and want to get rid of what we know.
It isn't hard for us to understand people,
because we believe our labels say it all.

Maybe we should try harder to get to know people,
to see and to know much more than we did before,
and find that our labels aren't enough.
What about love that we've never seen at work,
and compassion that is self-giving,
and a redemption that they too might offer?
We could be changed by what we see,
transformed by what we come to know,
if we worked harder at getting to know people –
like the ones we and Judas betray
when we use our labels.

Fifth in Lent

Old Testament: Isaiah 50:4–9*a*
Epistle: Hebrews 12:1–3
Gospel: John 13:21–32

23 The parade

Brenda was very proud of the basket on her bike. It wasn't by any means a *new* basket. She'd been given it by her nan, who'd been given it by her next-door neighbour, who'd rescued it from his daughter's old bike that was going to the skip since she'd got a new one for her Christmas. But an old basket went well with an old bike – and Brenda's bike was certainly old!

It was what she'd heard called a 'hand-me-down', and having come down to her through the several hands – and some pretty severe usage – of a succession of older brothers and sisters before it got to Brenda, there was no doubt that the bike had seen better days. But with a coat of shiny, black paint, and with a few stickers of her favourite pop-stars on the frame, Brenda was happy enough with her old bike. Maybe she'd get a new one some day …

The basket was just what she'd needed to make her bike special. Like the bike itself, the basket had seen better days too. It had been bashed around a fair bit and the canes at one corner were in danger of coming apart. But the two leather straps were still sound, holding the basket firmly to the bike's handlebars, and so Brenda was dead chuffed. She used her basket to carry her ballet shoes when she went to her dancing lessons in the church hall. It was just the thing to hold the shopping her mum sometimes asked her to collect from the village store. She popped her granddad's Sunday papers in it when she took them round after church each week. And it would be just the ticket for her own paper-round when she was old enough. Yes indeed, Brenda was very proud of the basket on her bike.

When she joined the parade on a Spring Sunday afternoon, Brenda, like several of the other kids, took her bike along. Actually, it wasn't much of a show, because the village wasn't really big enough for a proper parade. But when the school football team wins a cup for the first time in years, well … you have to do something. So the instruction was to assemble just before two o'clock in the school playground, and the 'parade' would leave from there and make its way to the church hall – about ten minutes away! School to church – about a quarter of a mile. But, still, it was something. And when the school football team wins a cup … well …

When Brenda got to the school gates she saw that Bill Jenkins, one of the local farmers, was there with a tractor and trailer. Liberally bedecked in the school colours of gold and black, and with straw bales on the back as makeshift seats, the trailer was soon the means of transport for the whole school team, all kitted out in brand new football tops. Some of the parents had their cars, with balloons (in gold and black, of course) tied to their roof-racks and aerials. The headmaster was in the back of an open Land Rover with the team captain beside him carrying the cup. Parents, teachers, a couple of photographers, kids in buggies and a fair number of local people followed behind. And with Brenda and other kids on their bikes, the parade was complete.

On the stroke of two the entourage began to make its way out of the schoolyard and down the village street. More local people filled the pavements, stood in doorways and hung from first-floor windows. They clapped and cheered. It wasn't a great parade, but when the school football team wins … well …

Brenda was just about to mount her bike and join the others at the back of the procession when she saw Mrs Stewart running towards the gate. Mrs Stewart was Brenda's class-teacher, and Brenda had never seen her so hot and bothered before. She almost skidded to a stop right beside Brenda and, quite out of breath, spluttered, 'Brenda. Be a good girl and run into the school to our classroom and fetch the white poly-bag that's on my desk. Quickly, because I need it now.' 'But, Miss,' Brenda protested, 'I'll miss the parade.' 'It won't take you long if you're quick.' 'But, Miss,' the reluctant Brenda continued, 'the janitor won't …' 'Don't worry. Just tell him you're doing an errand for me.' 'But, Miss,' Brenda tried again, 'what if ...' But she never had the chance to finish. 'Go, now! Go! Quickly! The poly-bag. Bring it to me. I have to catch up with the ...' And in an instant the harassed Mrs Stewart was off to join the parade, leaving a bewildered Brenda to be about Mrs Stewart's business.

So, leaning her bike against the railings, she went in search of the white poly-bag. She had to get past the inquisitorial janitor. 'Why?' 'A message for Mrs Stewart ...' 'Who?' 'Brenda Smith, one of her class ...' 'What?' 'A white poly-bag ...' 'Where?' 'On her desk, in her classroom ...' 'When?' 'Now ...?' 'Why?' 'Don't know ...' 'What's in ...?' 'Don't know ...' 'What's so important ...?' Silence. 'What if ...' Silence. 'OK, but quickly, 'cause I should be locking up now.'

Brenda was indeed quick, and within moments the object of her quest had been discovered – just as she'd been told – and she was back in the playground ready to return the mysterious white poly-bag to the agitated Mrs Stewart. But the parade had gone. 'Oh, bother,' Brenda muttered to herself, 'and I was *so* looking forward ...' There was nothing else for it. She would just have to catch up. So with her precious cargo dropped deftly into her bike-basket, Brenda was up and on board and pedalling off down the village street as fast as she could go.

By the time she'd caught up with the parade it was over, and the whole crowd was milling about outside the church hall. 'Strange,' thought Brenda, dismounting at the back of the gathering, 'I thought they were all going inside for ...' But her musings were interrupted by the shrill, instantly recognisable voice of Mrs Stewart. 'Brenda! Brenda! Did you find it?' Brenda gave a thumbs-up. 'Well then, child, don't just hang around at the back. Come down here and give me the bag.' Within moments a still bemused Brenda was handing over a white poly-bag to a clearly relieved Mrs Stewart who immediately delved inside it, obviously looking for something important. And triumphantly she unearthed – a large, black key. Turning to the assembled company she announced, 'Here it is folks. The hall key! We'll be inside in no time.'

And in no time, that's just what happened. With the hall door now opened – courtesy of a Mrs Stewart with a key from the bottom of a white poly-bag – the crowd streamed inside to begin the end-of-parade festivities. A still bewildered Brenda was the last one to join the party. And as she laid her old bike beside the other bikes against the church wall, she found it hard to believe that she and her bike's basket had been carrying the key to the celebrations all the time and she'd never even known …

But …

I was asked to go.
The instructions were clear;
the command was compelling;
it appeared I had no choice.
And I kept thinking, 'But …'

I returned as I was bid.
The duties had been completed;
diligence was duly reported;
everyone was pleased.
And I was still thinking, 'But …'

I joined in with the crowd.
The gathering moved on;
the preparations had worked;
my part had been important.
And I still dwelt on the 'But …'

I was told there would be more –
instructions to follow;

duties to fulfil;
obedience to offer.
And always the 'But …'

I'm still on the go.
I'm playing my part;
I'm doing my bit.
I'm offering myself –
including the 'But …'
that never goes away.

Passion/Palm Sunday

Old Testament: Isaiah 50:4-9a
Epistle: Philippians 2:5-11
Gospel: Matthew 26:14-27:66

24 The uninvited guest

No one expected Patsy Gallagher to turn up at the show of presents. No one expected her because, for one thing, she hadn't been invited, and for another, it wasn't likely to be her scene anyway.

Patsy Gallagher was an outsider. It hadn't always been like that, because, as Veronica knew well, there was a time when Patsy had been one of the crowd, and her presence at something like a 'show of presents' would not only have been expected, it would have been positively welcomed. But that was then, and this was now. So no one expected Patsy Gallagher to turn up.

It was Veronica's do. Back in the 1970s, before 'hen nights' with their trips to Prague or Dublin or New York came into vogue, there was always a 'show of presents' a couple of weeks before a wedding. It was a way a grateful bride could say 'thank you' to generous people, and at the same time show off the nice things she'd been given to offer a good start to married life. All the goodies would be on display in her mum's front room, sometimes spilling over into the hall or a bedroom. And, if you were well enough organised, all the presents would be labelled, and if not actually labelled, then explained by a beaming bride-to-be or her proud mum.

'And these are the bath towels from my auntie Vi ... And here we have the canteen of cutlery from Jim's parents ... And this catalogue has a picture in it of the fridge Gran's getting us ...' and so on. It was the expected way of things. And the women who came to the show of presents – for it was *always* the women; men wouldn't be seen dead at such a do! – would murmur appreciation, drink sweet sherry or port and lemon, drink endless cups of tea and gratefully consume cakes specially made for the occasion, and of course chatter endlessly and have a thoroughly good time.

All the people that mattered were at Veronica's do. The show of presents had been weeks in the planning. It was turning out to be a great success. That is, until Patsy Gallagher arrived …

Patsy and Veronica had been in school together, all through Primary and the four years of Junior Secondary before they left school at sixteen and entered the world of employment. It would be too much to say that Patsy and Veronica had been best mates. There was a whole bunch of them who'd hung around together. All the rest of the gang had been invited to Veronica's do. All, that is, apart from Patsy. Patsy had changed. In fact, she'd started to change before she'd left school. 'Getting in with a bad crowd,' had been Veronica's mum's explanation. But whatever it was, Patsy drifted away from her friends and, more accurately, her friends were having less and less to do with her.

When Patsy fell pregnant, two months after her sixteenth birthday, that was pretty well the end of things. The social stigma of a teenage pregnancy was too much for a group of respectable young women to cope with. There were rumours of 'doesn't know who the father is' because of multiple partners and of an increasingly promiscuous lifestyle.

Patsy had moved away. No one held out much hope for her. The last people knew was that she was living with a pretty dubious character in a squat in town. The kids – three of them now – were in care. And no one bothered too much.

It was Veronica's sister who answered the door. And there in the stairwell stood Patsy Gallagher. The young lass didn't know what to do. So, leaving the door half ajar, she rushed into the living room and sought out her sister.

'Veronica, Patsy Gallagher's here,' she whispered.

'What?' asked a startled Veronica. 'Here? Who invited her? Where is she?'

'She's at the front door.' Veronica and her sister's attempt at a whispered conversation had failed. For now they realised that the whole room had gone quiet and that everyone knew what they were talking about.

'You can't let her in,' someone said. 'Who does she think she is?' offered another. 'Bloody cheek.' And, within moments, the chatter was loud and animated – and it was all about Patsy Gallagher.

Veronica slipped from the living room and into the hallway. What was she to do? She didn't want the show of presents to be ruined. And she wouldn't have anything to say to her former friend anyway. She was confused. And then the front door slowly swung open, gently pushed by the uninvited guest in the stairwell, and there Veronica saw Patsy Gallagher for the first time in ten years. She'd obviously made an effort, but she was still in pretty poor shape.

Picking up on Veronica's obvious uncertainty the bedraggled figure said, 'Hello, Veronica. Long time, eh? Hope you don't mind. But I couldn't let it go by, eh?' Veronica had nothing to say and just stood in the hallway and stared. She needn't have worried. 'I'll not come in,' Patsy said. 'But I wanted to give you this.' And with that she unearthed a small, rather grubby parcel, no bigger than a cassette-tape box, and held it out to Veronica. 'It's all I've got that's worth anything. I got it from my gran. I hope you like it.'

Veronica moved forward uncertainly. When she was close enough, Patsy placed the gift in her hand and said, 'I'll not stay. I'll just spoil things. But ... anyway ... all the best.' And she was gone, leaving a bewildered Veronica staring at an open door and an empty stairwell.

When Veronica returned to her friends in the front room, there was much relief that she'd managed to 'get rid of that toe-rag' and that the assembled company could get 'back to the fun'. Veronica just smiled. She never mentioned the contents of the grubby parcel. It was never put on display with the other presents.

But now, thirty years later, sitting on her dressing table in a non-descript cardboard box, no bigger than a cassette-tape, is a delicate silk handkerchief, with coloured lace edges, and bearing in bright yellow stitching the initial 'P'. Veronica's daughter asked her once where she'd got the handkerchief from, and why she kept it on display like that and never used it … And Veronica replied that it was too good to use, and that it had been given to her by an old and very generous friend.

Out of place

It was awkward when she arrived.
She looked out of place.
The clothes weren't right.
There was a strange smell.
She wore thick make-up
that didn't improve her looks much.
There were things she didn't do right.
She felt like an awkward, unwelcome stranger –
the wrong person,
in the wrong place,
at the wrong time.

The others weren't awkward when she arrived.
They gave a stranger her place.
No one mentioned her clothes.
They coped with the smell.
And they smiled in welcome,
and the heavily made-up face cracked into a smile too.
Not everyone got it right,
and some felt strange and awkward
with the wrong person,
in the wrong place,
at the right time.

She wasn't awkward when she left.
She'd had her place.
Maybe she had no other clothes,
and always smelled.
And the thick make-up was an attempt
to show she'd made some kind of effort
to do it right,
despite her awkward strangeness,
as the wrong person,
in the right place,
at the right time.

The others weren't awkward when they left.
They'd once been strangers in the place too,
worrying whether they were dressed properly,
and hoping they didn't smell.
But the smile of welcome
from all the made-up faces
had made them feel at home.
So they hoped they'd done it right,
and made the awkward stranger feel welcome,
and that she was the right person,
in the right place,
at the right time.

Monday of Holy Week

Old Testament: Isaiah 42:1-9
Epistle: Hebrews 9:11-15
Gospel: John 12:1-11

25 How did you know?

Alfie was having a bad day, and it being a Sunday, the day when Alfie was expected to be on top of his game, made it all the worse. Two of his kids had been up half the night with their coughing. Alfie was convinced he was coming down with flu. It was bucketing with rain when he left the house and walked to the church. And he knew that he was far from adequately prepared for the Sunday service.

In truth, Alfie was having a bad week. As minister in the local church he'd had one of those weeks which every minister dreads. There had been three funerals to prepare and conduct, and the death of one of his best church members made at least one of the losses all too personal.

There had been a difficult church meeting on the Wednesday when Alfie had to cope with bickering and tensions as decisions had to be made about the redevelopment of the church hall and meeting rooms. It had become a veritable battleground between the traditionalists and the modernists, with Alfie, as usual, in the middle.

And he'd had a letter of criticism about the choice of his hymns the previous Sunday – a 'what-happened-to-all-the-good-old-hymns' kind of letter.

All of which meant that, in terms of preparation for the Sunday morning service, Alfie was far from being on top of his game. He usually gave a lot of time to his preparation – 'It's not just a case of turning up and spouting forth, you know,' he was tired of reminding people. And as far as the regular jibes about it being 'a one day a week job …', well, enough said. But this week, he was ill-prepared – and he knew it.

He was relieved, however, that he had some ready-made material to work with. It was World AIDS Day, and, mercifully, the Church Education Board had prepared some useful worship material in a new resource pack. There were specially written prayers, suggestions about choice of Bible readings, words for a new hymn, notes for other items of praise, and – best of all – the bones of an appropriate sermon. Alfie had intended to adapt the sermon and put things in his own words. But, as a stressed-out minister at the end of a bad week, he had been reduced to trusting the material in the resource pack and offering it largely as it was.

Alfie had high standards and he knew he was falling short of his own expectations. And so, when eventually he was leading the worship, his inadequate preparation made him feel worse and worse as the service went on. In addition, he just *knew* that some of the material in the resource pack sermon wasn't going to go down well with the 'traditionalists' in the congregation.

As he talked forcibly of the scourge of HIV and AIDS in Africa; as he explained how the retroviral drugs had little chance of working unless people were adequately fed; as he suggested that our complacency had to be challenged – he just *knew* that there would be those who would complain about 'all this social justice stuff' that they'd heard more than enough of already.

As he encouraged people not to be judgemental of those who contracted HIV through the sharing of dirty needles in an all-too-familiar drug culture; as he shared insights into the care needed for HIV babies born to parents with AIDS and how these innocent little ones had to be given every chance – he just *knew* there would be mutterings about 'pandering to people who'd caused their own problems'.

As he called for the Church to be inclusive and for people to think of the damage done to those in the Gay community who felt rejected by the Church's stance on same-sex relationships; as he pleaded for compassionate church folk not to believe that AIDS was God's punishment for an 'abnormal' sexual orientation – he just *knew* that someone, even now, would be forming a letter of complaint about the Church abandoning the True Gospel.

By the time the worship was over, Alfie felt terrible. And as he smiled at people and shook hands with them as they left, he could just *feel* members of the congregation ready to add to his misery. It had been a bad service, on a bad day, at the end of a bad week.

When Alfie went back into the church after people had gone he noticed Mrs Henderson still in her place in the back row. Mrs Henderson was a quiet-spoken lady who came to church every Sunday. Alfie didn't know her too well. But, as he came closer to her, he saw that she had her head in her hands and that her eyes were closed. Alfie reckoned that it was better not to disturb her, and chose to slip past her quietly down the side aisle. It didn't work. As he was passing, Mrs Henderson lifted her head.

'Alfie,' she said, 'have you got a minute?' Alfie stopped, his heart sinking with the expectation that even a mousy person like Mrs Henderson was going to give him a hard time for his sermon content or his lack of preparation.

'Yes?' Alfie responded, turning round to the seated figure. Mrs Henderson looked him straight in the eye.

'I just wanted to say ...' she began. She paused. Alfie braced himself for the diatribe. It never came. 'I just wanted to say ... thank you for today. We heard this week that my son, Ian, has AIDS. He got it from a contaminated blood-transfusion for his haemophilia. We've been in tears all week. I didn't know whether I should come today. I felt dirty. The stigma of it all ... that stuff you read about God's punishment and things like that. It isn't Ian's fault, but it's just been terrible.' Mrs Henderson stopped and looked up at Alfie. She had tears in her eyes. 'How did you know?' she whispered. 'How did you know? It's as if what you shared today was just for me – and Ian too. Now I know that Ian can still belong here, and me too. But how did you know? How did you know?'

Mrs Henderson was now weeping openly. Alfie slipped in beside her and put an arm round her shoulder. 'How did you know?' she sobbed. Alfie didn't bother replying. There was nothing he could say.

So he just cried along with Mrs Henderson. And he knew that a bad feeling and a bad day and a bad week had just got considerably better.

Thanks

I was once thanked by a lady
for being kind to her when she was distressed,
and saying, 'Just the right thing.'
And, for the life of me,
I can't remember meeting the lady at all,
or what she was like,
or what I said that was so good.
But she remembered –
and that was enough.

I once thanked a friend
for her kindness when I was struggling,
and turning up out of the blue,
just for me, like a visiting angel.
But, you know, she just couldn't remember why she'd come,
or what I was like,
or how her kindness had been shown.
But I remembered –
and that was enough.

Once in a while I thank my God
for a sign of hopefulness on a bad day,
and tapping me on the shoulder,
just when I needed it.
And, if you were to ask me to analyse it now,
I'd tell you I can't remember the circumstances,
or what God was like,

or why he chose that moment.
But he remembered –
and that was enough.

Tuesday of Holy Week

Old Testament: Isaiah 49:1-7
Epistle: 1 Corinthians 1:18-31
Gospel: John 12:20-36

26 Badly betrayed

Ahmed stood in the doorway of his shop. It was raining. He'd only had one customer all morning. He felt as miserable as the slate-grey sky. Business had fallen off dramatically. And it was all because of the betrayal.

Kahn's All-Day Store had been a feature of the Brydon Road community for many years. Originally a small plumber's storeroom, it had been bought over and renovated by Ahmed's uncle in the 1970s and now, as the Kahn portfolio of corner-grocers had expanded, Ahmed had been running the Brydon Road shop for almost ten years. His uncle demanded high standards and would call in from time to time – usually unannounced – to make sure that all was in order. And it always was, for Ahmed had high standards too. He ran a successful and popular shop.

He was – as he'd overheard one of his regulars remark to another customer – unfailingly polite, 'The kind of gentleman you used to find around here all the time,' was the way she'd put it. Ahmed liked that. Courtesy was part of who he was. Respect, politeness, dignity and manners were all character traits he'd learned as a boy. They were integral to the religion of his adult years. And, of course, they cost nothing and were always good for business.

So Kahn's All-Day Store had thrived under Ahmed's care. If a customer asked for something and he didn't have it, you could be sure it would be on the shelf next day. If there was a regular item a customer expected, there would always be some in stock. And there was always the politeness, the cheery smile and the welcoming greeting.

The betrayal had changed all of that. Three of the young lads from the area being detained on terrorism charges was the start of it. It was a major sensation, all over the national news. One of the boys was married to Ahmed's second cousin. He knew the other two from the

Mosque. One of them had a flat at the top end of Brydon Road and all three of the lads were regular customers at Kahn's All-Day Store. The Brydon Road flat was raided. Nothing incriminating was found. Despite the three suspects being held in custody for a long time, no formal charges were ever brought. They were released after a lengthy investigation.

That should have been the end of it. But it was only the beginning. Mud sticks. And a lot of mud stuck to Kahn's All-Day Store. And some of the mud stuck to Ahmed Kahn.

Not long before the story died down the local newspaper, trying, no doubt, to fan the flames again and boost its circulation, published a front page story under the headline 'Brydon Road shop linked to terrorism suspects.' The story was innocuous enough and contained no more of the truth than that one of the arrested men was related to Ahmed, and that all three were known to be regular visitors to his shop. But comments such as '… sometimes leaving carrying suspicious-looking packages …', '… in secretive conversation …' and '… shop lights burning after closing time …' added colour to the otherwise bland story. And all the quotes were attributed to 'a local source'.

But who? Who was the betrayer? A disgruntled customer? Surely not. A rival shopkeeper? Inconceivable. Someone harbouring racist tendencies? Probably. But whoever it was, whatever the identity of the 'local source', Ahmed knew that he had been badly betrayed and that the betrayal was costing him and his shop. The unfounded bad publicity was having its inevitable effect. Business had plummeted. Loyal customers had abandoned a branded man. Ahmed Kahn had to suffer the consequences, and there was absolutely nothing he could do about it.

He wondered if it might go further. He feared for a brick through a window. He shuddered at the thought of a lighted newspaper through the letter-box. It had happened elsewhere. He just hoped it wouldn't happen to him. The betrayal and the silent abandonment were bad enough. But what if it got worse?

He was pleased that his home was out of town. 'Allah be praised that they know not where I live,' he thought. Having to face the betrayal himself was an awful thing. He didn't want anyone else affected.

Ahmed wondered if he should close the shop early today. After all, what was the point of burning electricity and heating a place no one wanted to shop in? Maybe he should give in and persuade his uncle to shut the place down. Business might never come back. He would have no way of redeeming himself. Perhaps it would be better if he just walked away. The suspicion was too much to fight against. He had been badly betrayed. He had been defeated. Maybe he just had to accept that.

He slipped inside from the damp doorway and looked around the shop. There were some shelves that needed restocking. The floor beside the freezer needed cleaning of muddy footprints left by the shop's one and only customer. The glass door of the chill-cabinet had fingermarks on it that needed wiping away. There were some stock-sheets that needed completing. There were yesterday's newspapers that needed bundling and tying for collection. There were sell-by-date items that needed repricing. There were a host of things to do.

Ahmed Kahn still felt as miserable as the slate-grey sky he'd left outside. But as he filled his bucket with hot water and began to mop the muddy floor of Kahn's All-Day Store, he figured that, however badly betrayed he had been, he wasn't going to let his standards fall.

Questions

Thirty pieces of silver?
How much is a betrayal worth?
A cheap quote in a tabloid rag?
How is a betrayal to be valued?
'Grassing-up' a mate to get your own back?
What price a betrayal?

A breach of trust?
How much damage does a betrayal do?
A threat to an unsullied integrity?
What destruction will a betrayal cause?
A tarnished reputation?
What can be redeemed after a betrayal?

Moving on, despite being let down?
What hope after a betrayal?
Believing in yourself?
Starting again when the betrayal's past?
Standards that still matter?
A betrayal that cannot win?

Wednesday of Holy Week

Old Testament: Isaiah 50:4-9a
Epistle: Hebrews 12:1-3
Gospel: John 13:21-32

27 Included

Peter had just got back from the cathedral. It had been a magnificent occasion as the celebration of Maundy Thursday Communion always was. The Bishop had been on top form. The washing of people's feet on the altar steps prior to the sharing of the Eucharist – an innovation which the Bishop had introduced the previous year – was deeply moving. Seeing the Bishop, with his robes tucked up under him, gently washing the feet of old and young alike, was one of the most meaningful things Peter had ever seen.

The choir filled the great cathedral with magnificent music, and the singing of the congregation was equally glorious. But amidst all of this, Peter's involvement in the celebration of the Communion was undoubtedly the high point. For, as a young priest, to stand with your Bishop and other senior priests and do the Lord's bidding and facilitate the sharing of the Sacrament, and to do so on the night of Maundy Thursday, *and* in the cathedral, *and* for all these people … Well, it just didn't get any better.

He was on a high all the way home. This Maundy Thursday Communion in this Holy Week had been the best ever.

Peter had just got back from the cathedral when the phone rang. 'Bother,' he whispered, irritated that he wasn't going to have the chance to sit down and bask in the afterglow of the cathedral celebration.

'Hello, St Bartholomew's. Father Peter speaking. Can I help you?' A frail, distressed voice replied.

'Father, I'm so glad you're there. It's John. He's got worse. I think he's going. Can you come round? He's still conscious and he'd like to see you. He'd have been in the cathedral tonight if he'd been well enough, it being Maundy Thursday and all. But that wasn't to be. So can you bring us the Eucharist, today being today? John would like that.'

Peter didn't have to say much. He knew Gillian Goodfellow's

voice well, and he was well familiar with her husband John's failing condition. Gillian's care and attention as a devoted wife of a dying husband was exemplary, and Peter did all he could to support her in trying times. So within minutes, he was at John Goodfellow's bedside, offering care and support to one of his favourite people. John was being comforted by Gillian, and Peter was also introduced to John's sister, Edith, who'd come to stay to provide another dimension of practical support.

Eventually, when it was appropriate, it came time to share another – and very different – Maundy Thursday Eucharist. This humble bed-room was no cathedral, and yet Peter was aware of a holiness which was all-pervading; there was no Bishop washing people's feet, and yet Peter was aware of a tenderness as Gillian held the bony hand of her frail old husband; there was no magnificent choir, and yet Peter was sure he could hear the sound of angel voices; there was no great con-gregation, and yet as Peter looked at Gillian and John and his sister, that was all the congregation that would ever be needed.

When the bread and wine were to be shared, Peter served Gillian and then placed a crumb of the Eucharistic wafer in the corner of John's mouth and dampened the old man's lips with the wine from the Communion chalice. Having done so, he turned to serve John's sister, only to find that she had gone. Undeterred, Peter brought the Eucharist to a conclusion, gave John a blessing, left an old man to absorb the healing moments of another Maundy Thursday Com-munion, and retired to the front room with Gillian, '… for a small refreshment before you go home, Father Peter.'

Taking a seat by a roaring fire, Peter was reunited with John's sister who was bustling around with crystal sherry glasses and a plate of shortbread. Once Peter and Gillian had been served with their 'small refreshment' and Edith had reappeared from the kitchen with a glass of orange juice, Peter remarked to Edith that he was sorry she'd not been able to stay for the Communion. There was an embarrassed silence. Edith's cheeks reddened. It was Gillian who spoke first.

'It's no' for the wantin' or the meanin',' she offered quietly. 'It's just that she can't. For she's no' able to take anything wi' alcohol for this many a long year, for the battle wi' the drink.'

'And I wasn't sure about the Communion wine,' Edith added, quietly, 'so I thought it best not to risk it.'

To this day Peter doesn't know why he did what he did next. He hoped Gillian wouldn't tell the Bishop. Indeed, he's still not sure what came over him. But he reached down into his case, took out his prayer book and placed it on the small coffee-table in front of him. Then he gently leaned over to where Edith was, took the glass of orange juice out of her hands and placed it on the table beside the prayer book. And taking a finger of shortbread, he laid it carefully beside the glass. Within moments, prayers were said, a Bible reading was offered, and crumbs of shortbread and sips of orange juice were shared by another congregation around another holy table. Peter, Edith and Gillian sat in silence for a while, allowing the depth of the atmosphere in the room to embrace them all. Nothing much more needed to be said.

After hugs of thanks, words of reassurance and promises of future contact had been exchanged, Peter took his leave and headed home, giving thanks for each of the three Communions he'd shared on that Maundy Thursday – where *everyone* had been included.

He was on a high all the way home from his cathedral. This Maundy Thursday Communion in this Holy Week had been the best ever.

Included

To be welcomed, without restriction or hesitation,
is the embrace of God.

To be loved, without condition or definition,
is the blessing of God.

To be called, without explanation or notification,
is the voice of God.

To be affirmed, without mediation or accreditation,
is the assurance of God.

To be applauded, without limitation or specification,
is the praise of God.

To be included, without rejection or clarification,
is the very being of God.

Maundy Thursday

Old Testament: Exodus 12:1-14
Epistle: 1 Corinthians 11:23-26
Gospel: John 13:1-17, 31*b*-35

28 Denial

Denial was Eddie's reaction to the news of the death. The shock of it was too much to bear. Any sensible person would have disappeared from sight, to lick their wounds, to cry in private, to stay safe with friends, or simply to try to take it all in. But Eddie wasn't any sensible person, and the hellishness of the death had a devastating effect.

Eddie's sister, Paula, had died. It had been a lonely death. No one expected it to happen so quickly, though the knowledge of her cancer had been communicated appropriately to all the people that mattered. Even admission to the hospice didn't seem to rouse people from their apathetic slumbers. Denial seemed to run in the family and there were few visitors to Paula's bedside in her last days. Maybe they didn't care, or maybe they just couldn't cope. But, whatever the reason, death, when it took Paula, was a devastating reality that had now to be faced.

A few of the family rallied round at the end. Paula had never married, so there were no children. There were a couple of cousins with her when she died and a few neighbours came when they heard she'd gone. 'Not many people for a long life,' one of the hospice staff remarked.

Eddie was his sister's twin, but Eddie hadn't been around much in recent times, and sadly the family couldn't get in touch with him on the morning of the death to tell him what had happened. The hospice staff discovered later that he had been on 'a bender' the night before and was unrousable that morning, sleeping off his over-indulgence – a not-uncommon occurrence, apparently. So when Eddie appeared to visit his twin sister early in the afternoon, expecting to be able to see her and talk with her, the cousins, neighbours and hospice staff were faced with a man who would have to be told, there and then, that his sister had died.

When Eddie heard the news he went mental. 'I don't believe you,' was his immediate response. 'You're all bloody liars,' he shouted. 'She was OK yesterday. No one said she was going to die. It's a lie. She can't be dead.' Eddie was ferociously angry, lashing out, swearing at the doctors, scaring even the most experienced of the nurses, and not doing much for the peace of mind of his cousins either! Eddie was not to be convinced.

Eventually his younger brother arrived and everyone tried to help Eddie grasp the reality of what was happening. It became clear that he would not and could not accept the reality of the death – unless he had the chance to see his sister. By this time she was in the hospice mortuary, and yet, if reality could only be grasped in this way, then seeing his sister in the mortuary had to be the way forward.

Two of the hospice staff had the task of taking Eddie and his brother to the family room adjacent to the mortuary where their sister had been laid out. It took some time to get this organised, and in the meantime it took all the support of the staff, family and friends to keep Eddie calm.

In time, a small band of mourners made their way to the mortuary viewing room. It was a heart-rending scene. Eddie broke down when he saw his sister. He rushed over to the bed on which she lay. He held her. He shook her. He shouted, 'Don't leave me, Paula, don't leave me!' He raged and he swore. The reality of the death was too hellish for him to bear. The two hospice staff confessed to each other later that they had been really scared. Neither of them had witnessed grief like this before. It was like watching a scary movie.

Eddie was with his twin sister for a long time. Sometimes his weeping would subside to a deep sob, and sometimes the sobbing would calm down into silence. Then it would all start again, and the wailing, and the shouting, and the anger, and the tears would fill the room once more. Eddie's brother didn't do much. Occasionally he would put a hand on Eddie's shoulder. But mostly he just stood, watching, letting things happen, sometimes wiping away his own tears, but mostly just standing behind his broken brother in sentinel silence.

In time, Eddie's brother took him home. None of the hospice staff ever found out what happened next to Eddie and the rest of Paula's family and friends. No one ever discovered how they'd coped. They retreated into the privacy of their mourning.

Maybe it took Eddie a long time to believe the reality, even though he'd now seen his dead sister. Maybe he was hysterical at the funeral service. Almost certainly his brother and the rest of the mourners would have to struggle with Eddie's grief as well as their own. And probably there would be a few more 'benders' to contend with. And, who knows, maybe Eddie still doesn't want to believe his twin sister has gone.

Not to believe

Not to believe that death is real –
it is the worst of things;
not to accept the awful truth,
the hellish pain it brings;
not to attend the bell that tolls,
the mourning-chime that rings –
for this is who I am.

Not to absorb the news of death,
pretending it's a lie;
never to trust the messenger –
my loved one cannot die;
not to respond to careful words
with frown or gentle sigh –
for this is where I stand.

Not to betray that I have heard
the truth your words reveal;
not to show signs of gratitude

for love's attempt to heal;
not to accept the awfulness
of what I now must feel –
for this is what I know.

Yes, and until the truth takes hold,
I'll wait and be aware;
and when the gates of hell burst wide,
you'll ever find me there;
whatever storms of grief will rage,
your brokenness I'll bear –
for this is who I am.

And when your curses rend the skies,
with faithfulness I'll wait;
and when you rail against the truth,
I'll not respond with hate;
when I'm too scared by who you are,
your pain I'll not negate –
for this is where I stand.

And when the awfulness takes hold,
I'll hold what you've become;
when tears are ever flowing, now
you'll know that we are one;
when awesome death has done its worst,
love will not be outdone –
for this is who I Am.

Good Friday

Old Testament: Isaiah 52:13-53:12
Epistle: Hebrews 4:14-16; 5:7-9
Gospel: John 18:1-19:42

29 A better view

James hated being stuck in traffic. But here he was again, stuck in the long line of stationary traffic that was the bane of every driver's life – especially in the High Street. The High Street! The infernal High Street! A car park most of the time rather than a moving thorough-fare through the centre of the town ... Everyone knew that you should avoid the High Street at all costs, even if it meant taking an extensive detour through the suburbs. But sometimes you just couldn't, and negotiating the High Street was simply inevitable – and a total pain!

So this was one of those inevitable and painful times for James. He wasn't in a rush. He didn't have an appointment to get to. He wasn't keeping anyone waiting. It's just that he *hated* being stuck in traffic. It was such an *unbelievable* waste of time.

Today it was driving behind a bus that was the problem. The High Street was narrow as well as permanently busy. So being stuck behind a bus was the worst thing of all. There were no designated parts of the High Street that would allow a bus to pull in and let the queue of traffic behind it pass with ease. So when the bus in front of James stopped, everything else had to stop too. And if you were right behind the bus, as James was now, right up close, you couldn't see round the bus to find out if there was a break in the traffic coming the other way that would allow you to pull out and zoom off (tem-porarily, at least) on the rest of your journey.

So when the bus stopped, James stopped. And when the bus moved off slowly, James crawled behind it. And when the bus stopped again, James – close up behind it once more – had no chance to pull round it or even to see what was up ahead. So he had to stop too. It was one of *those* journeys up the infernal High Street.

That's the way it had been since Katy had died too. Six months it was since he'd lost the love of his life, his beloved wife of forty-eight wonderful years. It was *so* slow adjusting to his loss, and if it was stop-start at all, the stopping was more common than the starting, and the starting never seemed to get him very far or very fast.

People said it would be like this. 'It takes time' had been people's mantra. 'But how long, how much time?' was James's silent response. And so, stopped for the umpteenth time behind the bus, James felt as hopeless as he did on his journey of bereavement. And close up behind the bus was like still being so close to Katy's death. Was it always going to be this slow? Was he never going to see the way ahead?

Stopped behind the bus once more, James mused on a vacation he and Katy had shared with friends in Salt Lake City in the USA, where the streets at the heart of a modern city were twice as wide as they needed to be – cars parked on both sides, and *still* room for cars, trucks and vans to pass each other in two wide lanes each way. 'No need to be stuck behind a bus on *these* roads,' he'd remarked to his friend, recalling the nightmare of negotiating the High Street back home.

'The city streets were built this wide by the Mormons when they settled here,' James had been told, 'wide enough so that a horse and cart could do a complete u-turn without blocking the road.'

'If you tried to turn a dog-cart in our High Street,' James had commented, 'you would cause a traffic-jam that would take a week and a half to disentangle.'

'Why is our High Street not like the streets in Salt Lake City?' James asked himself as he watched the bus in front disgorge another bunch of travellers. 'Why is bereavement not like wide streets with plenty of space to travel, and turn around if you want to, or see the way ahead?'

In time – an inordinate length of time – James got to his destination, a small lane off the end of the High Street where he could find his favourite book shop. *Larry's Library* had often been James's salvation, even on the worst of days, when loss or traffic – or both – were hard to bear. Today was no different. Browsing the packed shelves, absorbing the familiar musty smell, and buying his usual out-of-print books did their job. His spirits lifted. Even the return journey down the High Street could be faced with a renewed energy.

It was just as slow. James was stuck behind a bus again, so it was stop-start, stop-start, stop-start as the traffic inched itself through the High Street bottleneck. But this time James was half-a-dozen cars behind the bus, not hard on its tail. And at one stage, from his vantage point further back, he could actually see that the road ahead was absolutely clear. 'Why's nobody moving?' he muttered to himself. 'Why's that guy behind the bus not pulling out and getting on? The road's clear. Can't he see that?'

But of course the guy behind the bus couldn't see the clear road that James could see – because he was too close behind the bus, just as James had been an hour or so earlier. But now that he wasn't so close himself, James could see better. Not being so close any more, he could see there was a way ahead.

James smiled to himself. 'Looks like bereavement's going to be like this?' he said out loud. 'Maybe it's only when you're not too close that you can see the road is clear ahead ...' James smiled again as the traffic moved off once more, and he thought of Katy and his slow journey of loss.

Stuck

I hate being stuck,
waiting,
in a holding-bay,
in the ante-room,
before participating in the main event.

I hate not being in control,
hanging about,
in limbo,

in the waiting-zone,
before getting on with the business in hand.

I hate not knowing,
being in the dark,
uncertain,
not having things clear,
before making decisions to go on.

Maybe I need to understand 'being stuck',
and learn to wait,
in a holding pattern,
for a few minutes longer,
before I can go on my way.

Maybe I need to let go of being in control,
and enter into
a limbo time
with better grace,
before getting frustrated about what's coming next.

Maybe I should understand that I'll not always know
when a light will come,
when I can be sure
that everything is crystal clear,
and know what tomorrow will bring.

Holy Saturday

Old Testament: Lamentations 3:1-9, 19-24
Epistle: 1 Peter 4:1-8
Gospel: John 19:38-42

30 Time for some fun again

Norman and Connie were old. There was no getting away from it. At eighty-nine and eighty-seven, Norman reckoned that they weren't far from being in their coffins far less being in their dotage – and he would make such quips to anyone who was prepared to listen. That's what had kept Norman and Connie going for so long, it seemed – an unquenchable sense of fun.

For fifty-seven years of married life Norman and Connie had enjoyed fun together. Norman was indefatigable with his wise-cracks. Connie was a tonic with her infectious laugh. As the years passed and the family expanded through the generations, children, grandchildren and great-grandchildren had shared many fun times with 'the oldies' and marvelled at their spirit and love of life.

But the last couple of years had been different. Life in old age had become very serious. 'Old age doesn't come by itself,' Norman was fond of saying – without a smile – as he struggled with the crippling pain of arthritis and the chronic effects of his bronchitis. And Connie had lost her sparkle too and had almost forgotten how to laugh. The loss of mobility since her stroke and her increasing – and embarrassing – incontinence were harder and harder to bear.

So life for Norman and Connie had got to the stage where it wasn't much fun any more. It had become very serious indeed, as days revolved round when pills were due to be taken, and when the carers were expected, and wondering what was worth making for tea, and there being nothing good on the telly. The family were great, of course, and the carers were good too. But life was a grind of serious things, and there was little room for fun any more.

The doctor said they weren't depressed. The family weren't so sure. Norman and Connie didn't much care. It was simply a struggle getting through another day. 'Old age doesn't come by itself,' Norman would mutter again, as an indication that he and Connie should just resign themselves to their lot. It was like living with death …

Connie wasn't sure they could survive like this. 'We don't laugh any more,' she remarked one fun-free teatime.

'Nothing to laugh about,' replied Norman grumpily, and the two of them lapsed into silence once again.

'You don't cuddle me any more,' Connie said after a time.

'Too sore,' Norman responded, and the silence returned.

'You don't even smile at me any more,' Connie remarked.

'Neither do you,' Norman retorted.

'Nothing to smile about,' Connie snapped back, 'not looking at your miserable face anyway.'

'And is your face any less miserable, you old bag?' Norman rejoined.

Connie was furious. Flushed in the face and raising her voice as much as she was able, she snapped back, 'Old bag, is it? You didn't think that when you and I had yon fling in the woods at the back of the village when we were first married, eh, auld yin …'

Norman was about to shout in response. But he didn't. He stopped himself, turned slowly towards Connie, and looked at her for a long while. And then he smiled for the first time in ages. 'Aye, lassie, but you were a bonny young thing.'

'An' you wernae bad lookin' yersel',' was Connie's reply. And two old lovers smiled as they both recalled, in their own way, 'yon fling' in the woods fifty-odd years before.

Silence resumed and embraced them both for a time. It was Connie who broke the quietness.

'I've been thinking,' she said softly. 'You and I need to have some fun in the middle o' a' this. Why no' dae it this way. Once an hour, on the hour, one of us, or both of us if we remember, should do something silly, just for a laugh, eh, Norman. What d'ye think?' There was a long pause. Norman smiled.

'It's a deal, lassie ... time for some fun again ... if either one of us remembers.'

That's why Connie was woken up out of a doze when the six o' clock news was just starting and was surprised to find Norman giving her a wee peck on the cheek. 'Good God, man, it must have taken you an eternity to get from there to here wi' a' your aches and pains. But it was worth it, you daft bugger.'

And that's why, an hour later, with Norman now dozing in his chair, Connie tapped him on the knee with her walking stick and announced, 'I just wanted to check that you wernae dead yet.'

And that's why, just as 'Coronation Street' was finishing, a little paper aeroplane made from a sheet of writing paper landed in Connie's lap, and she could make out a love-heart in red pen on either wing.

And that's why, when Connie came back from the toilet before bed time, she had a plastic rose from the vase in the hall behind her ear.

'A rose for a rose,' Norman chuckled.

'Bloomin' gorgeous, eh?' Connie replied, and an old, engaging, infectious laugh came back and filled the room once more – as the clock on the mantelpiece struck nine.

Norman and Connie were old. There was no getting away from it. At eighty-nine and eighty-seven, Norman reckoned that they weren't far from being in their coffins far less being in their dotage. But old age and coffins weren't going to win any more – now that it was time for fun again.

Resurrection

To rise from despair
when despair has had its victory,
is a thing of wonder and of joy.

To rise from the gates of hell,
when death has lost its sting,
is a resurrection beyond imagining.

To rise from the chains of fear,
when freedom is the gift we hold,
is the new beginning we dared not expect.

To rise from hopelessness,
when 'all things new' are being revealed,
is our promise now fulfilled.

To rise from a darkened tomb,
when we believed our Light had gone,
is our glory, conquering all.

Easter Day

Old Testament: Psalm 118:1-2
Epistle: Colossians 3:1-4
Gospel: John 20:1-18

31 Saint George

'GEORGE SLAYS THE DRAGONS' the billboard outside the newsagent's boldly proclaimed, prefacing the headline in that day's local paper, 'Dragons no match for George's lance.' It had been a long time coming, but the story was clearly worth broadcasting. There was no doubt about it; Danny George was the hero of the hour.

The 'Dragons' in question were the darts team from The Dew Drop, the pub at the end of Main Street. 'The Drew Drop Dragons' had reigned supreme in the county's darts league for a decade or more. They'd been odds-on for lifting the trophy once again. But they hadn't. And that had been down to Danny George.

Danny was an unlikely hero. He was a regular at the Dog and Duck, a 'working-men's' establishment that had seen better days. The 'working' in the label was definitely a misnomer, as most of the regulars in The Dog and Duck were out of work, the more so since the brewery, the town's main employer and recent victim of the recession, had been mothballed. The 'men' part, however, was more than accurate, as no self-respecting member of the female sex would have been seen dead in such a place. Danny was a regular. But Danny had once been a stranger too.

Danny George's real name was Dobrilo Juraj. A refugee from Serbia, Danny and his family had fled from the Kosovan conflict in the late 1990s, and after working their way through Europe, had ended up in the town. It was hard being a refugee. Accommodation was seldom the best. Money was never in plentiful supply. Schooling was tough for the children. And work was well-nigh impossible to find. Oh, there were jobs that could be had – cash in hand; no records kept; no insurance; no questions asked; the risk of being found out. But Danny had his pride. And it was too risky anyway, as imprisonment would have threatened the fragile stability he and his family had found.

It wasn't a good life. But it was a better life than he would have had in Serbia. He might have been dead – as many of his friends and family were. It wasn't a good life in the town. But it was a life.

Danny had changed his name to make things as easy for his family as possible. It wasn't that he was ashamed of his heritage, but he had already experienced discrimination. So Juraj was adjusted to the anglicized form 'George', and 'Danny' replaced Dobrilo. It was easier that way.

Danny had been going to The Dog and Duck regularly for months before anyone had even looked his way. He wasn't a big drinker and would seldom have more than two half-pints. But the big TV in the pub was an attraction, and Danny loved the European football matches. No one bothered him. No contact meant no discrimination. That suited him just fine. And on some evenings he enjoyed watching the regulars playing darts. Some of them were good. Some tried hard but were no great shakes. Some played for money or beer. Some just enjoyed a friendly game. And one big guy was a regular hustler, challenging all-comers, usually for a moderate stake, and usually with the certainty of a victory. But the big hustler had run out of people to hustle. The regulars obviously knew him too well, and no casual callers would find their way into The Dog and Duck …

Until, that is, the two unsuspecting students arrived one night. In they came, had a few pints, and quickly became the latest victims of the big guy's hustling. He took them on one at a time. They lost the first game. Money changed hands. They went double-or-quits. They lost the second one. They took him on together. They lost again. More money was passed over. They were out of their depth. And now, being taunted and cajoled into another game that would inevitably compound their losses, they were finding it hard to back out with good grace. Things were turning ugly … till Danny offered to help.

'I play too,' he interjected. The pub fell silent. 'You want me play? I play beside young men,' Danny suggested. The big man grinned from ear to ear.

'Another victim, lads,' he suggested to the assembled company. There was much laughter. Danny stepped over to the two students.

'He's made mincemeat of us,' they whispered to their new colleague. 'You're a gonner, so you are …' Danny smiled.

'You give me arrows. You just hit board. I do rest.' A wager was laid. Danny and the students pooled their limited funds to make up their stake. 'Money for old rope,' one of the regulars suggested, as several side-bets were laid among the viewing crowd.

Danny scored one hundred and eighty with his first three darts, one hundred and forty at his second turn, and went out on a hundred and twenty-one, ending with a double-top – a rare nine-dart finish. That silenced the onlookers and put a frown on the big hustler's face. Danny and the students won the first leg three-nil, the second three-two and the third three-one, taking the best-of-five match by three to nothing. The next two games got the students their money back, with a few pounds to spare. And that was enough. Danny wasn't greedy. A point had been made. Everyone seemed satisfied.

When the students had gone and the evening's excitement was over, the big darts hustler brought a pint over to Danny's table.

'You're a dark horse, eh? Seen you in here a few times … but never seen you at the 'ockey. You're good. Where did you learn to play like that?'

'Back home,' replied Danny, trying hard to soften the thickness of his accent, 'back home in own country, I play. Not many people play. But I play, and I play good. I win champion. I best player in country. I go Holland once and I win international game. But I no play since I come here. I not know where I can play.'

'Well now! There's a thing. So you're an international champion, eh? Well pal, you've just found a place to play.' And, turning to the regulars at the bar, the big guy announced, 'Hey, lads, we've just found a new member for our darts team.'

It's a simple story from there. Danny became the star member of the Dog and Duck darts team. They shot up the County League. The play-off against 'The Dragons', the reigning champions, was a triumph. Danny George was the hero of the hour.

'GEORGE SLAYS THE DRAGONS' the billboard outside the newsagent's boldly proclaimed. But the truth was even more important – that one outsider had found a home; one refugee family came to be accepted in a strange town; one darts team had found a hero; one run-down pub had found a saviour. No one had called Danny George a saint, but, if he was to slay any more Dragons, who's to know?

Saints

Saint Peter, Saint Matthew, Saint Andrew, Saint George,
Saint Patrick, Saint David, Saint John,
Saint Thomas Aquinas, Saint Martin of Tours,
Saint … what's-his-name … bother, it's gone!

Saint Margaret, Saint Mary, Saint Bridget, Saint Anne,
Saint Rhoda and sweet Bernadette,
Saint Agnes, Saint Frances, Saint Sarah, Saint Joan,
Saint … thingummy … Oh, I forget.

But what about Danny who's everyone's mate,
And Evelyn who washes the stair,
And Trevor who cares for the folk the Home,
And Michael, and Barbara, and Claire

Who go out collecting for Oxfam each year,
And ask for no praise or renown,
And Tracy who's fostered a whole host of kids,
And Bob, the street-sweeper in town,

And all of the people whose names are not known,
The quiet ones, the gentle, the shy,
Well out of the limelight, not seen in stained-glass,
The ones who will quietly slip by

Unnoticed, unheralded, out of the gaze
Of publicity, seeking no praise,
Who live lives of sacrifice, service and love,
And have done for all of their days?

Look out for the heroes that nobody knows,
And saints all around us you'll see …
And maybe one day you'll be noticed as well –
Saint so-and-so … Goodness! That's me!

St George's Day

Old Testament: Psalm 125:1-5
Epistle: Acts 12:1-11
Gospel: John 15:17-16:2

32 The twisted face

Alison was fascinated by the twisted face. In fact, if she was honest, ever since she had first seen it, she was just a little bit scared of the tormented image that stared down at her from high up on the abbey wall. But it had been *the* most fascinating thing that had been pointed out to her and her family along with a crowd of other tourists on their guided tour of the abbey church.

This wasn't Alison's first time visiting the island of Iona and having a tour of the restored abbey and its Benedictine living quarters. Alison's family had often visited Iona, and the abbey, its buildings and grounds were familiar surroundings for her. But this was the first time that the tour of the abbey actually mattered for her. Till then it had been much more fun running up and down Tor Ab, the 'hill of the abbot', outside the abbey's west door, exploring the pillared cloisters, or finding which door led to what part of the abbey complex and allowing a small child to hide from her parents into the bargain.

But this year it was different. Feeling more grown up, Alison wanted to be with the 'big people' and go on a proper tour with a proper guide who had a proper badge and carried a proper pointy-stick. She wanted to take photos with a proper digital camera – a present for a recent birthday – and feel she was a proper tourist. That's what big people do.

Her parents weren't too keen. What was new for them to learn when they knew the place inside out already? But for the sake of an excited mini-grown-up – and why would you refuse any child who actually wanted to learn something? – they signed up as a family for the early afternoon tour.

Alison loved it. She smiled when she heard the story of the monkey and the cat on either side of the window to the south of the communion table, almost too small to see, but representing the two sides of the monastic life – the monkey standing for activity and busyness, and the cat for contemplation and rest. (*Good idea for a project in school after the summer*, she thought.) She was amazed at the description of the huge communion table, and how it had been made from the green-flecked marble mined from a quarry at the south end of the island of Iona itself. (*I must visit the marble quarry one day*, she decided.) She was transfixed by the carvings on the stone pillars showing Bible stories for the people in olden times who couldn't read. She loved the story of St Columba, and wondered if the picture of him in the little stained-glass window high in the north wall was what he actually looked like. She was intrigued by the 'quiet space' in the south aisle, with its flickering candles and requests for prayer on scraps of paper pinned to an old wooden cross. And she was fascinated by the twisted face.

The guide showed the tour-party where it was using his pointy-stick or otherwise no one would have known it was there. Indeed, Alison had been in the abbey church *hundreds* of times and never noticed the twisted face. But there it was, right enough, half way up the archway that led from the crossing to the abbey's nave, a small, twisted, scary face carved in the stone – and it was looking right down at her!

The guide was explaining what the twisted face was about, as Alison and the other visitors turned their heads upwards to have a good look. 'Some people say it was put there to face the pulpit so that the preacher would know how people would feel if he said the wrong thing,' he intoned, 'for they would all look at him with a twisted face like that.' The tourists laughed, 'And,' the guide continued, 'others say it's a reminder to the preacher that if the true message isn't given, people will go to Hell and be tormented – so that they'll look like that!' Sniggers and knowing looks all round ... 'And I've heard it said that some people believe it's an image of an old monk getting out of bed to say his prayers on a cold winter morning.' There were smiles and acknowledging nods. Photographs were taken.

The guide moved along, taking the tour-party with him.

But Alison lingered at the twisted face – scarily fascinated. And as she gazed upwards, she wondered what the twisted face was *really* saying. She decided it was nothing to do with old monks having a bad day, or a congregation not liking a preacher, or scaring people with stories about Hell (whatever that was …) It would be *much* more interesting if it had been put there deliberately to say something – different. *But what might that be?* she wondered.

So every opportunity Alison took to spend time listening to the twisted face and to hear what it was saying – and she sneaked into the abbey church many times during that holiday – the twisted face said something new. One day the twisted face looked like the faces of the starving children she'd seen on TV after a famine in Africa, and was crying, 'I need your help.' Another day it looked like her friend Kirsty after she'd been bullied by the big girls, and was very frightened. Once it looked like her teacher when she was *very* angry when Johnny Kennedy was cheeky in class. And it had even looked like the way Alison herself felt inside when she *hated* her cousin for scribbling in her homework book so that Alison got a row for something that wasn't her fault. Or maybe it was showing someone who just didn't understand things at all …

Alison decided the twisted face really, really mattered. And she wondered if the twisted face could ever get untwisted to show her that, sometimes, even a twisted face could smile.

I believe

Hi, Josh, thanks for the text. I hope you don't mind the e-mail. It would be too long to text you back. So you've heard then. Well, it wasn't my fault, so there's no use in giving me a hard time. Listen! I wasn't there, right? I wasn't there. I was busy, so I missed it. All the other guys said it was great. They were buzzing when I got back. Jake was as high as a kite. And Matt was flying, almost as bad as he was at his birthday bash. But it couldn't have been *that* good, I said. They said it was true, it was the best. But it was just too over-the-top for me. So I told them to get real. And, blow me, that was just the start of it. Dog's abuse, I got. All because I didn't believe it. But I WASN'T THERE, right? And you know what the guys are like, especially Andy with his messing about. I thought it was a wind-up, big time. So I told them to take a hike. Well, you could have knocked me down with a feather when I found out it wasn't a joke after all. I was there the next time. And, wow! They were right. It was unbelievable! Amazing! Indescribable! It wasn't a wind-up at all. I wish I hadn't doubted them now. But, I wasn't there the first time. Was I? But am I glad I didn't miss it altogether. They've just about scraped me off the ceiling. Anyway, I'm off back to the guys. Keep in touch. Cheers. Tommy.

★★★

Hi T. thx 4 ur msg. omg. i bliev u. w@ a do. w@ a buz. must hv been gr8. bet it 2k frown off ur twstd face. Kp smilg. LOL :) J

First after Easter

Old Testament: Psalm 16
Epistle: Acts 2: 14a, 22-23 & 1 Peter 1:3-9
Gospel: John 20:19-31

33 The crossroads

Chris sat down at the crossroads. He slipped off his rucksack and laid it on the ground at his feet, took his ease for a moment on what remained of a low, stone-built wall on the edge of a field, and pondered his options.

In front of him the road split in two, each of the roads appearing to be just as much a 'main' thoroughfare as the other, with both disappearing out of sight after a few metres behind high beech and thorn hedges. To his right a smaller lane stretched out, over a ridge in the undulating ground. It was no more than a farm track, with a line of green turf running up the centre. To his left ran a more rutted path, too rough even to be labelled a lane, far less a road, which disappeared through a broken-down gate into a field and was quickly lost in high grass.

There was no signpost at the crossroads to offer the confused Chris the direction he needed. His conclusion was – he was lost! And he had no one to blame but himself. He thought he knew the way. 'Down past the church, half a mile to the crossroads, and it's about a mile or so to Oakfield from there. You can't go wrong,' he'd been told. But his informant had failed to point out that the crossroads had no signpost. So now Chris was lost.

He was ruminating on his choices when a man came along with his dog. He was clearly a farmer-type, his faithful border collie joined by invisible elastic to his right calf. He was carrying a long stick and he was sucking on a big, unlit pipe.

'Mornin', he offered, raising his battered hat a millimetre off his forehead in greeting.

'Good morning,' Chris responded.

'Fine day,' the farmer continued.

'Yes, indeed,' was the reply.

'Lost, are you?' the farmer enquired. Chris smiled.

'Well, not lost exactly,' he said, forlornly. 'I just don't know where to go next.'

'So, where are you wantin' to go next if you're not exactly lost?' the enquiry continued.

'I'm heading to Oakfield,' answered Chris.

The farmer paused, deep in thought. Then after a while he announced, 'Well, now, if it is to Oakfield you are going, it's that-a-way.' And with that he raised his stick and stretched it in a wide arc that embraced all the roads from the crossroads onwards. Chris struggled to conceal his irritation.

'Yes, I know it's out there *somewhere*, but which road do I take?'

The farmer smiled, leaned on his stick and was silent again, as if pondering his next contribution. Then, using his pipe as a pointer, he said, 'Well now, Oakfield's down there,' and he swung his pointer across the same arc his stick had traced a few moments before. But this time he stopped with his arm pointing 90° to the right. 'You can go that way, past Ben Crawford's farm, follow the track at the side of the wood, pass along the edge of the lower meadow, and there's Oakfield. Just follow the track, and there you are.' A relieved Chris rose to his feet.

'Thank you,' he said with obvious gratitude. But the farmer wasn't finished.

'Or,' he continued, without acknowledging Chris's attempt to move on, 'you could go that way,' and swung round to point his pipe down the right fork in the road. 'Go round the corner, over the wooden bridge and go into Oakfield past the village school. It's shorter but not nearly so pretty.' Chris picked up his rucksack, ready to make the choice between short and pretty and be on his way. But the farmer still wasn't done.

'Or,' he went on, now indicating the left fork, 'you could go that way, swing round past the green hay-silos, work your way to the next crossroads, go right, and you'll come to Oakfield through the cemetery at the east edge of the village.' Chris sat down again, reckoning the farmer's instructions may not yet be complete. He was right.

'Or,' the instructor intoned, 'if you want a bit of a hike,' – and now his pipe was indicating the track to the left – 'you could start through yonder field. Go over the style at the bottom end, through the pine-wood – and there's no track there, mind – go across the ford in the stream – provided it's passable – follow the path up to the ruined mill – and it'll be muddy this weather – and Bob's your uncle.' Silence again, for at last the farmer was done.

'So let me get this right,' said Chris, scratching his head. 'No matter what road I take, I'll get to where I need to go.'

The farmer smiled, sucking once more on his empty pipe and resuming the use of his stick as a leaning post. 'Aye, laddie, you'll get there right enough, no matter which way you go. It's more a matter of what kind of journey you want and what you want to see on the way. Easy or hard, pretty or short, it's up to you. But you'll get there in the end.'

'Thanks,' Chris offered, somewhat sceptically as he rose to his feet and swung his rucksack onto his shoulder.

'Enjoy your journey,' the farmer said, and turning on his heel, with his faithful dog nudging his calf, he set off the way he had come.

'You not going on to Oakfield, then?' Chris enquired.

'No need,' the farmer replied. 'I just wanted to check at the cross-roads whether they'd put up a new signpost yet.'

Emmaus

I can't remember for the life of me
why we were going to the town.
There was me and Brenda –
I remember that much –
but why we were on that road,
I haven't got a clue.

I can remember we were in deep conversation –
well, it's always the same
when me and Brenda are together –
catching up on the news,
swapping stories,
putting the world to rights.
It was ever thus …

And then we met this guy.
I can't remember whether we caught up with him
or he fell in with us.
No matter;
he just appeared.
And pretty soon we were into this heavy discussion –
about the meaning of life, and stuff like that.

You know,
sometimes that's how a conversation goes –
you're on trivial stuff,
you know, just on the surface of things,
and then, bang!
and you're into some deep areas,
and you've no idea how you got there …

Well, it was like that.
I remember thinking,
how has this guy got me to talk about things
I've never shared with anyone before,
not even with Brenda?
And why am I talking about meaning and purpose,
and hope and fulfilment for my life
when I'd never given much thought
to that kind of stuff before?

And then he was gone.
I don't remember whether he shot on more quickly,
or fell behind,
or went off down a side road.
But me and Brenda just stopped,
and looked at each other,
in silence,
for ages and ages ...

And then,
just like that,
we carried on walking together
and got straight into a right, good-going discussion
about the meaning of life.

Second after Easter

Old Testament: Psalm 116:1-4, 12-29
Epistle: Acts 2:14a, 36-41 & 1 Peter 1:17-23
Gospel: Luke 24:13-35

34 Counting to a hundred

Elvis had lost his job. Martin Miller didn't know when or why, but when he heard that Elvis and employment had parted company, he was very worried indeed.

Martin hadn't seen Elvis in a while. Elvis had promised to keep in touch when he moved away, but Elvis wasn't a writer, and in the days before mobile phones, Skype, Twitter and the like, communication with him was scant to say the least. News filtered through from time to time. Occasionally Martin would come across Elvis's mother in the shopping centre, enquire after the young man's welfare, get a brief update on current circumstances, and be satisfied with the news. That had to be enough.

Elvis had moved away from the area to keep out of trouble. An understanding Sheriff – hearing that Elvis had a chance to go to stay with his grandparents and get a job, well distant from peer-group pressure and trouble with the police – had given him a suspended sentence. Martin had done his bit to help. Elvis had a new start. That was enough for a concerned Martin Miller.

Martin had a soft spot for Andrew Wallace Burns Lenin Presley – hence the 'Elvis' tag – ever since he'd known Elvis in the latter stages of his school career. He'd visited Elvis when he was on remand and he'd spoken with the Sheriff when Elvis was up in court. He'd always believed that Elvis could make it, that there was enough potential for this likeable rogue to do something good with his life. He would have preferred for Elvis to have stuck around locally – and so would Elvis's mother and his mates. But if the only way for Elvis to keep on the straight-and-narrow was for him to go somewhere else, where caring grandparents and a job in the local garage were waiting, then so be it. Elvis would come through. Martin always believed that.

So when he heard from a distraught Mrs Presley that Elvis had lost his job, Martin Miller was mighty concerned. Information was sketchy. 'I got a phone call frae ma maw last night,' explained his anxious informant. 'Ma boy's been given the heave-ho from the garage. Something about money goin' missin'. An' worse still, he's done a runner. Ma maw disnae ken where he is.'

It was as much as a distressed woman could communicate. Martin didn't know what to say. Elvis's mother didn't hang around for an extended conversation. So Martin was left alone to absorb the worrying news and ponder his options. He decided there and then that he had to go and find out for himself what was going on.

That's why, two days later, having taken a day's leave-of-absence from the school, Martin was knocking on the door of the Presley grandparents' council house in a small town with which he was quite unfamiliar. He'd let them know he was coming, and there was a welcoming cup of tea waiting for him after his long journey. He was much relieved to hear that Elvis's 'runner' had come to an end and that he'd come back home to his grandparents' house the previous day. But it was the young man's state of mind that was the main topic of conversation and the major cause of concern. Elvis wasn't communicating. All he had said was that he was planning to go 'back tae ma mates' and abandon his new start. 'Whit's the point, eh?' had been his final words. 'Is he with you now?' Martin enquired. 'Naw, son. He's oot. On the wander. You could find him doon by the canal, or at the shops, or wi' a bottle o' cider in the woods. Who knows? He could be onywhere. He's a lost laddie, that wan, that's fur sure …'

There was nothing for it but to go on an Elvis hunt. What was the point in Martin's coming all this way if he didn't try? There was no sign of Elvis down by the canal. It was closing time at the shops, and apart from a few kids hanging about there wasn't much life on the streets. So Martin Miller took the path through the small wood not far from the centre of the town. He found Elvis on a half-rotting bench in a clearing. He'd hardly touched the cider from the bottle at his feet.

In an instant, Martin Miller was back with a forlorn, pathetic young lad, with shorn hair and a battle-tunic two sizes too big, in the visiting room in Shortlane Remand Centre before Elvis had appeared in court. How could you not go to the ends of the earth for this lost soul?

Elvis had his head in his hands. He glanced up at his visitor before returning to his maudlin reverie. 'Ah knew it was you, Mr Miller. Ma gran said ye were comin'. But ah wisnae sure. Ah've let ye doon, Mr Miller. Ah've let a'body doon. Why wid ye come a' this way fur the likes o' me, eh? Ah'm no worth it. Ye've got ithers who're worth the bother. But no' me. No' the likes o' me. Awa' hame, Mr Miller. Ah'm no' worth botherin' aboot. Ah'm no' worth a hang.'

By now Elvis was sobbing into his hands. Martin offered him a handkerchief. He put an arm round the lad's shoulders. He knew he wasn't supposed to in these 'PC' times. But what did that mean now? He put an arm round the shoulder of a lost soul. He didn't know what to say. So he said nothing. He hoped he was doing enough.

The two men sat in silence for an age. Elvis made good use of Martin's handkerchief. Martin had surreptitiously to wipe his own tears on the arm of his jacket. After a time, Elvis lifted his head, looked at Martin Miller with bloodshot eyes, and whispered, 'Thanks for comin', Mr Miller.'

The following day, Martin's colleagues were desperate to find where he'd been on his mysterious day off. 'Fancy woman, eh?' one had suggested in the staffroom at the lunch break. 'Sleeping off a hangover,' offered someone else. 'Family stuff?' was another idea. Martin didn't enlighten them. He didn't think there was any point in going into all the details. All he would tell them ('very enigmatically,' someone said) was that he'd spent the day counting to a hundred, but no one really bothered trying to figure out what he meant …

One, two ...

One, two, three ...
All safe.
Good!
No bother there, then.

Fourteen, fifteen, sixteen ...
And one more over there ...
Excellent!
It's looking good.

Thirty-seven, thirty-eight, thirty-nine ...
Like ducks in a row –
except they're fleecy ones.
I hope I don't fall asleep.

Sixty-nine, seventy, seventy-one ...
Getting there!
Not too bad.
No problems thus far ...

Ninety-two, ninety-three ...
Nearly done!
Ninety-four, ninety-five ...
Yes, OK.

Ninety-six, ninety-seven ...
Close ...
Ninety-eight ...
Yes ...

Ninety-nine ...
Ninety-nine ...
Good!

And that makes one hun …
Oh, fff … for goodness' sake!
Where's the last one?
It was all going *so* well.
Ninety-nine, safe and sound …
So where are you, you little toe-rag.

Come on!
Where've you gone, eh?

Ninety-nine …
Safe and sound!
Ninety-nine … ONE HUNDRED …
Here I come, ready or not …

Third after Easter

Old Testament: Psalm 23
Epistle: Acts 2:42-47 & 1 Peter 2:19-25
Gospel: John 10:1-10

35 The whisper

Connie always looked on her uncle as her great hero. Even though William Henry Rankin was actually her father's uncle, and therefore, technically, Connie's great-uncle, he had always been her uncle William, and had always been her hero.

Uncle William was an old man, and he had been old all the time Connie had known him. By the time she was mature enough to get to know and admire Uncle William, he had been retired for many years. But it was the quiet wisdom of the great man that had had such an effect on Connie, and she liked nothing better than spending time in his company and absorbing some of his depth and experience.

William Henry Rankin had been a great preacher in his day and, in his latter working years, in great demand as an orator, a guest speaker, a rousing evangelist and a stirring preacher up and down the land. Diligent and committed to his own parish, his fame had also spread far and wide. The name of the Reverend William Henry Rankin had become synonymous with preaching of the highest order.

He'd never lost the common touch, though, and as well as his preaching he'd also been a popular and much utilised after-dinner speaker. For his ready sense of humour, ability with language, captivating delivery and, of course, his endless supply of jokes and funny stories appropriate for every conceivable occasion made William Henry Rankin the first name on the lists of organisers of award dinners and Burns' Suppers, national rallies and anniversary celebrations, school reunions and presentation ceremonies.

Yes indeed, as a preacher and public speaker, the Reverend William Henry Rankin was almost unsurpassed.

All of this was another world to Connie. And though she'd been regaled with countless stories of Uncle William's renown, she'd never seen him in action, for his preaching and speaking days were well in the past and old age had taken its toll on the great man. So to Connie he was simply Uncle William, a teller of stories, a sharer of jokes, and a hero to a young woman.

'Did you hear of the minister who went to visit a sick man in hospital one day and found him very frail and weak, lying in his hospital bed, fixed up to machines and drips, and wearing an oxygen mask to help his breathing?' her uncle William would begin, and Connie knew she was in for another treat. 'Well, there he was, standing at the bedside, wondering what he could do to comfort the sick chap. And then the frail man in the bed slowly raised his hand and beckoned the minister to come closer. The minister leaned over to hear what was to be said. The patient beckoned him to come even closer. Was this an end-of-life revelation, a question of meaning, or a death-bed confession that only his minister could help with? The man signalled the expectant clergyman to some so near they were almost touching, cheek to cheek. The minister put his ear close to the sick man's lips. "What is it, my friend?" And the patient looked at his minister with a contorted face, and in a frail, hoarse, agonised voice, whispered, "I can't breathe … 'cause you're standing on my oxygen tube!"' And Uncle William would laugh uproariously, and Connie would once again be thankful for the greatness of her hero.

All of this and much, much more made the tragedy of Uncle William's throat cancer all the more devastating. For it robbed William Henry Rankin of his greatest gift, the most important tool of his trade – his fine, rich, resonating voice. From pulpit to family meal-table, from a speech from a podium to a story for his great-niece, from top table to intimate gatherings, the voice of William Henry Rankin had been his life.

So when Connie went to see her uncle William in hospital after yet another operation, she just didn't know what she was expected to say. He smiled when she came to his bedside. She took him by the hand. He beckoned her to come close. She leant over to hear what he had to say. He summoned her even closer – *Obviously because he can't speak much*, Connie figured – until she had her ear next to his lips. 'Don't try too hard, Uncle William, but what is it you want to say?' William Henry Rankin screwed his eyes tight, squeezed Connie's hand, and whispered in a hoarse, frail but distinctive voice, 'You're standing on my oxygen tube …' and, opening his eyes wide, broke into a typical, beaming, Uncle William-type grin.

'But,' Connie protested, 'you don't have an oxy …' and then she got the point, and grinned widely too.

Uncle William kissed her gently on the cheek, and whispered, 'I love you, Connie.'

And catching the mood of the moment she kissed the old man on his cheek too and whispered, 'And I love you too, Uncle William.'

It was to be the last time Connie was to talk with her hero. Now she wonders what it would have been like to hear William Henry Rankin preach a stirring sermon, or to clap with appreciation at the end of an excellent after-dinner speech. And then she knows that a whisper of love is worth a thousand sermons and a million words, and she gives thanks again for the greatest hero she's ever known.

Whispers

When death was close, the whisper came –
'I have a place for you.'
So clear, the sound of my own name,
'There's always room for you.'
As sure as love's eternal flame,
The whisper's word was true.

When I was lost, the whisper was –
'I am the way for you.'
So clear, the voice of comfort's cause,

'Come, here's my path for you.'
And stepping out, with ne'er a pause,
The whisper's word was true.

When I had failed, the whisper said –
'I am the truth for you.'
So clear, insisting guilt be shed,
'I have forgiven you.'
Redemptive oil anoints my head;
The whisper's word was new.

When all is done the whisper sounds –
'I am the life for you.'
So clear – I grasp this truth profound –
'Life's fullness is for you.'
In promised hope, true Love abounds,
The whisper's Way,
The whisper's Truth,
The whisper's Life anew!

Fourth after Easter

Old Testament: Psalm 31:1-5, 15-16
Epistle: Acts 7:55-60 & 1 Peter 2:2-10
Gospel: John 14:1-14

36 A good man

Peter had watched eight half-hour episodes of comedy shows from the box-set of DVDs of Comedy Classics he'd got as a Christmas present from his son a few years ago – and it still wasn't lunchtime. That had been the way of things recently – at least it was better than morning TV, he reckoned – and Peter almost had every episode of 'On the Buses' and 'Hancock's Half-Hour' off by heart. That had been the way of things – that and the drink, as Peter looked down at the half-empty bottle of Scotch and the grubby tumbler on the table in front of him.

What was he to do next? Change the DVD? Pour another drink? Fix some lunch? He dismissed the third option quickly enough. He didn't eat many lunches these days. He decided a drink was the priority, and he was just leaning forward to do the necessary with the bottle and glass when the doorbell rang. 'Damn!' Peter muttered. He uncorked the bottle. The doorbell went again. 'Damn and blast!' cursed Peter. He paused, reckoning that if he ignored the unwanted interruption the caller might just go away. No such luck. The caller was persistent. Peter replaced the bottle and glass on the table and went to the front door to give the uninvited visitor short shrift! He was going to be rude. But he couldn't be when he saw Maggie standing there.

No one could be rude to Maggie, not even a belligerent drunk. For Maggie's disarming smile always got people on her side. Well, it's what a good church deaconess should be like, she always said. So there they stood in the doorway, Peter staring at Maggie, not saying a word but willing her to go away, and Maggie staring at Peter, and being very uneasy about what she saw.

Clearly, Peter had not been looking after himself. He was unshaven. The collar of his blue shirt was extremely grubby. He had stains on his trousers. His carpet slippers were torn. His hair was all over the place. And his hands had a distinct tremor.

'Oh Peter,' blurted Maggie once she'd got her voice back. 'Oh Peter McLafferty. Look at the state of you. What's happenin' to you man?' 'Och lassie,' the forlorn figure replied, 'ah'm no masel' since Jeanie left. It's awfey hard, ye ken. Ah cannae get oot of the bit.' Maggie smiled. 'That's what I'd heard,' she replied, and after a pause enquired, 'Are you not going to invite me in?'

Peter was embarrassed and, his face reddening, he stumbled, 'Och, no' the noo – the hoose isnae tidy – washin' up lyin', ken?' along with more mumbled excuses. Maggie smiled again. 'OK, that's fine,' she responded. 'But I'll be back. Let's make it … this Friday afternoon … half past three. OK?' Peter nodded reluctantly. Maggie turned to leave. 'Now, don't forget. Friday. 3.30. OK?' She looked over her shoulder to make sure Peter understood. But she was looking at a closed door.

Maggie was sure Peter would forget the arrangement. So, before she finished work for the day, she wrote Peter a letter on the church's headed notepaper – handwritten – 'more personal' she always reckoned. She reminded Peter of the appointment on Friday at half past three. She said she was sorry for what had happened but that she'd do all she could to help. She wrote that Peter was a good man and deserved better than 'letting things go'. She suggested there might be some bits and pieces he needed help with, and to remember he could be in touch if there was anything she could do. The letter was put in the post on the way home from work.

But it was with apprehension that Maggie stood on Peter McLafferty's doorstep the following Friday on the stroke of half past three. She rang the doorbell, not at all sure what she would find or whether she could handle things if they were bad. The door opened promptly and Maggie was surprised with what faced her. For there was Peter, clean-shaven and wearing a white shirt and neatly-knotted tie. He sported polished black shoes. His hair was carefully combed. And he was smiling.

He held out his hand without a tremor and, shaking Maggie's hand firmly, he announced, 'Come away in, lassie. I've been expectin' ye. Right on time. Weel done. Come on through. Ah'm in the kitchen, wi' the makin's o' a brew o' tea. Come in bye, and ye can help.' And with that the bold Peter ushered the speechless deaconess through his living room and into the little kitchen beyond.

As Peter busied himself with the teapot and hot water, Maggie looked around. The kitchen was clean and tidy. *'Well done, Peter,'* she thought. And her eye fell on … her letter. There it was, fixed to the door of the fridge-freezer with a fridge-magnet for all to see. And, as she studied it, she couldn't help noticing that Peter had underlined – in red, no less – the words 'Friday at half past three'. *'Sensible man,'* Maggie thought.

But there was more. For, lower down the letter, Peter had also underlined in red Maggie's words 'You're a good man'. Maggie stared, forgetting she'd even included that in her missive, but pleased she had, and even more pleased that Peter had singled it out for underlining.

Peter saw Maggie staring at the letter. 'Puzzled, lassie?' he asked, laying the teapot on the stove. 'No,' Maggie replied, 'not by that bit,' pointing to 'Friday at half-past-three'. 'I was concerned you wouldn't remember. That's why I wrote. And that's why you've underlined it and stuck the letter up there.' She paused. 'But why that bit down there?' she asked, quietly. 'Why have you underlined that?'

Peter smiled. 'You're a good man,' he said, almost to himself, as if reading the words again from the letter. 'You're a good man … I needed to underline that bit, lassie. For it jumped oot at me frae the paper. For, ye see, naebody's ever said that tae me in the hale o' ma life.' And, as he turned back to the stove to pour the tea, Maggie saw a tear in his eye. For *she* knew that Peter McLafferty was seventy two years old.

Good?

What is 'good'?
    'Good' is good.
I know *that* … But what does being 'good' mean?
    'Good'?
Yes, 'Good'.
    'Good' means you're good.
Doing it right, you mean.
    Well, that too.
    But 'being good' isn't the same as 'doing good'.
Now, you're confusing me.
    Well, if 'good' was doing it right all the time,
    then none of us would be 'good', would we?
No, I suppose …
    So 'good' means who we are and what we are,
    not doing things right and being perfect all the time.
Am I good?
    Yes. You were made good.
Am I good all the time?
    Yes, you are.
Even when I'm not good at things?
    Yes, even then.
Good!
    OK?
Yes, thanks.
    Good man!

Fifth after Easter

Old Testament: Psalm 66:8-20
Epistle: Acts 17:22-31 & 1 Peter 3:13-22
Gospel: John 14:15-21

37 Conversations

Paul wasn't really worried about his aunt Reta. Well, in actual fact, he was as worried about her as everyone was, as anyone would be who had concerns for an elderly lady who'd been left alone after the death of her husband. After all, fifty-two years is a long time to be together, and being on her own must be hard. But Paul wasn't *really* worried. For, truth be known, his aunt Reta had done pretty well in those early months of her loss.

Uncle Terry had been ill for a long while and the end of his life had been difficult for Aunt Reta to cope with. She was suffering too, clearly weighed down by the burden of being a carer for a frail old man. So when Uncle Terry had died it was, pure and simple, a relief all round and a chance for Reta to look after herself again. And so she had. She'd done well. Everyone was pleased for her. So Paul wasn't really worried about his aunt Reta. Not *really* worried, anyway … But he was concerned enough to make sure he visited her regularly just to be certain.

Aunt Reta wasn't his real aunt. She was his father's aunt by marriage, and that made her … Oh, he could never figure it out. It was something like a great-aunt, but that made her sound like someone out of a Jane Austen novel, and that would never do. So it was what it had always been – to Paul she was Aunt Reta.

He wasn't the only one in his family who cared either. But he was the one who lived the closest, and given that his college was only a forty-five minute bus ride away, Paul visited his aunt Reta as often as he was able and dutifully reported progress to his family. As time went on, he wasn't *really* worried about Aunt Reta, but he made sure that, every second or third time he came through to see her, he touched base (on the quiet) with one of her neighbours, just to make sure everything was OK – some additional reassurance he could further report to his family.

It was on a Friday afternoon that he met Mrs McCracken taking out her bin to her front gate. 'Afternoon, Mrs McCracken. Nice day,' he greeted his aunt's neighbour, whom he knew well. 'Can I help you with that?'

'Oh, thanks son, but no. Ah'm fine.' She rested her bin halfway down her path and beckoned Paul to come closer. 'C'm'ere, son. Ah need a wee word.' Doing as he was bid, Paul approached Mrs McCracken till only her bin was between them. 'Naw, c'm'ere, roon this side, up close, fur there's somethin' ye need tae know.' Intrigued, Paul was now up close and personal with Mrs McCracken. She was clearly satisfied with their intimacy, and, putting her lips as close as possible to Paul's ear, she whispered, 'Ah'm worried aboot your auntie Reta, son.'

Recoiling somewhat – more affected by the unexpected concern than he was by the unexpected closeness – Paul replied, 'Why? What's wrong? Is she not well?'

'Ah think she's goin' mad, son, doolally, kind of thing.' Paul recoiled further, horrified by this revelation.

'Mad? Aunt Reta? Whatever do you mean?'

'Well, son, it's the conversations. I can hear her – clear as day – through the wall – conversations – wi' hersel' – not a soul else in the hoose – talkin' tae hersel' – wan-sided conversations … Doolally, ah call it. Ah wis just saying to Connie Roberts this mornin' …'

But Paul wasn't for hanging about for any further explanations, and with a somewhat curt 'Bye' and 'Thank you' to the bearer of concerns about his aunt's state of mind, Paul made a beeline for his aunt's front door.

Paul's aunt Reta was fine. She was as fine as she always was. She was no different from the last time Paul had visited. So he had no idea how he was going to get round to the subject of the reported 'conversations' which Mrs McCracken had picked up through the wall. He needn't have worried. Aunt Reta brought the subject up herself.

'Ah see ye were collared by that nosey besom next door, afore ye came in. An' ah'll bet I ken whit she wanted tae bend yer ear aboot, eh?' Paul could offer nothing more than an embarrassed grin by way of response. That was apparently enough. 'Ah thought so. She's bin tellin' ye that ah'm talking, eh? Wi' naebody else here, eh? Conversations, eh? An' ah'll wager she thinks ah'm aff ma heid, eh?'

Paul nodded, but thankfully found his tongue again. 'But *do* you, Aunt Reta? Is she right? Do you talk to yourself?' Aunt Reta put both hands on her hips and looked as indignant as Paul could ever remember.

'Masel'? Talkin' tae masel'? Is that whit she's sayin'? The auld goat. Ah've niver talked tae masel' in ma life, son. Noo, that would *really* be doolally, eh?'

'But if you're *talking*, Aunt Reta, who on earth are you talking to if there's no one here?'

'Ach, son, d'ye no see? Ah'm talkin' tae yer uncle Terry, eh? Ah'm talkin' tae ma man …'

'But he's not here, Aunt Reta,' blurted Paul, now responding with increasing incredulity. He took a deep breath and stated the obvious.

'He's dead, Aunt Reta, my uncle Terry is dead.'

Aunt Reta was silent for a moment, trying to work out how the conversation had taken such a turn. And then, as if it all had suddenly fallen into place, she grinned widely and announced, 'Ach, son, ah ken that fine. Ah ken he's dead, an' ah still miss him sair.'

'But how can you talk to him if he's gone?' Paul asked. His aunt Reta grinned even more widely, as if realising that her great-nephew had an *awful* lot to learn.

'Weel, son, me an' yer uncle Terry were together for fifty-two years. So am ah goin' tae stop talkin' to him when he's no' here? He's as real in this hoose as he's aye been. So ah tell him things, and ah ask his advice, an' ah let him ken how ah'm gettin' on, and that you've been tae visit an' a'. Conversations, son. Wi' ma man, like it's aye been.'

Paul was now wide-eyed. 'An' ah'll tell you somethin', young man, ah'll dae it for as lang as ah need tae dae it. For he'll aye be wi' me. An' there's aye a bonus – there's nae arguments onymair, an' ah aye get the last word ...'

Paul was on the phone to his dad later that evening to report diligence on that day's visit to Aunt Reta. 'How is she doing?' his dad enquired as usual.

'Just fine,' Paul replied.

'*Really* fine?' continued the enquiry.

'Really, really fine,' Paul responded, mirroring his aunt Reta's wide grin, and thanking her silently for her object lesson on loss, 'absolutely, really, really fine ...'

Gone?

Gone, but not forgotten.
Gone, but yet, still known
in memory's words,
and cherished pictures,
which time and separation
will not erase
from what I am
and what I will become.

Gone, but still remembered.
Gone, but present still,
in what you've left
of life and love,
of words and truth,
and changes wrought in me
by what you are
and always will remain.

Gone, beyond the blue.
Gone, but yet still seen;
never obscured by clouds of grey
or sparkling light,
but here, with me,
in all the fullness I recall,
in all the living vibrancy
of what I've known and loved.

Gone, yes you have gone;
gone, and I must let you go.
but going does not end
how close we are and will remain.
In form you go;
in me you'll always stay;
for we are one communion
in love's eternal span.

Ascension

Old Testament: Psalm 47 *or* 93
Epistle: Acts 1:1-11 & Ephesians 1:15-23
Gospel: Luke 24:44-53

38 A place of holiness

Julie liked her visits to Bert Montgomery's house. Among the distressing and difficult chores of being a District Nurse in a busy, inner-city medical practice, visits to Bert's were always a pleasure.

Julie had got to know Bert after his stroke, when he and Edith, his wife, had needed a fair bit of reassurance and support. Then she'd been with him through the loss of his wife, and since then she'd always tried to find a way of popping in to see him even when there was no medical reason for a visit. In recent times, she was back to being a regular visitor once more, as Bert needed the dressings on an ulcerous leg changed pretty well every day.

The visits were as beneficial to Julie as they ever were to Bert. His cheery smile, gentle teasing, amiable flirting (*'If only he was forty years younger,'* Julie sometimes allowed herself to think …) and irrepressible sense of humour were a tonic to a hard-pressed District Nurse. But best of all were the stories …

Bert Montgomery was a veritable fund of stories – from childhood; from his time in the pit; from his travels; from his reading – all told with colour, enthusiasm and clarity. There was always a story, and Julie loved them all.

But *best* of all were his stories about the war. Bert had been in North Africa with the army during the Second World War – 'They'll tell you that it was Monty that won the war, lassie. But it was *this* Montgomery that did most of the work.'

An oft-repeated tale – and Julie never figured out whether it was true or not – was the one when Field Marshal Montgomery decides to offer the soldiers a special treat at Christmas time, and provides them all with a portion of caviar. It's not well received. Aware of the murmurings in the ranks, Monty calls over an RSM and enquires as to the disquiet among the troops, and why they are so ungrateful for such an expensive delicacy. 'The men are grateful enough, sir,' the RSM reports. 'Why the grumbling, then?' Monty asks. 'Well, sir, they're complaining that the bloody bramble jam tastes of fish.'

But the story that meant most to Julie, and one that she *knew* must be true because of the hushed tones Bert used when he was telling it and the tear that was always in his eye when he'd finished it, was the one about the strange experience in the desert.

'It was a slack day,' the story ran. 'Me and the lads had spent the morning repairing a truck, and in the heat of the day sheltering underneath it to get some respite from the sun. After a brew of tea, when things started to get cooler, I went for a wander and a smoke, keeping sight of the camp, but exploring a bit further away. We knew there was no danger, and ... well ... I was bored. So I went on a wee recce. I'd not got two hundred yards from the boys when I stopped. I don't know why I stopped. There was nothing to see, just the usual scrub and sand and rocks. But something made me stop. I had this strange feeling. I can't describe it. It made me all tingly, kind of like I was in the presence of something weird. Not scary or anything like that, just good ... right ... holy ... that kind of thing. It was amazing. I sat down for a bit, and it never left me all the time I was there.

Then after a while I went back to tell the lads. And I got halfway back, and the feeling disappeared. So I retraced my steps, and when I got back to the place where I'd been sitting down, there it was again, this amazing feeling. I marked the spot with a bundle of stones. Then I took the lads over. None of them knew what I was talking about. They said it was the heat, or that I was imagining things. But I knew what I'd felt.

I made sure I got the coordinates of where we were and marked the location on the map in the truck. I never thought much more about it after that. There was too much to do, other things to think about – like bramble jam that tasted of fish, and the like.

But, d'you know, it's a funny thing. When I had some leave in Cairo later on, I went to a library and dug out some old maps of where we'd been, you know, old, old maps, from centuries ago. And d'you know what I found out? Right at the spot where we'd been camped, right there where I'd had this weird feeling, had been the site of an ancient Christian settlement, centuries before. It was called "Mkan Llqdash", which roughly translated means "A dwelling place of holiness". I'd been standing in a holy place, and that's what I'd been feeling – all these centuries later.'

Julie would marvel at Bert Montgomery's story of 'a dwelling place of holiness'. Who was she a sceptical agnostic – to argue against the idea that the prayer and worship of an ancient Christian settlement could stick around, long, long after the walls and stockades had been obliterated by the desert, so that its holiness could still affect a hard-nosed soldier in the North African desert in the heat and the sand and the horror of war?

Julie liked her visits to Bert Montgomery's house, especially his stories about the war, and particularly the one about the 'dwelling place of holiness'. Because, after all, if Bert had really found the holiness there, he must have brought a fair bit of it back with him from the North African desert, for there was enough of it around to give Julie a wee tingle every time she visited his home.

Holy, holy, holy

Holy places, holy people, holy signs are seen;
Holy feelings, holy auras, offerings serene;
Holy moments, holy tingles, holy blessings found;
Holy, holy, holiness abounds.

Holy places offering some comfort in distress;
Holy people giving hope when life's a wilderness;
Holy signs appearing which can smooth a furrowed brow;
Holy, holy, holiness is now.

Holy feelings way beyond the scrutiny of thought;
Holy auras bringing peace when battles are being fought;
Holy moments happening, even when they're not so clear;
Holy, holy, holiness is here.

Holy tingles, felt and known, though seldom understood;
Holy blessings, making sense when things are far from good;
Holy for the moment, when quite nothing else will do;
Holy, holy, holiness,
Blessèd times of holiness,
Precious gifts of holiness for you.

Sixth after Easter

Old Testament: Isaiah 2:1–5
Epistle: Romans 13:11–14
Gospel: Matthew 24:36–44

39 What kind of spirit?

'What's God like?' Nathan asked at random one morning when he was tucking into his cereal. Nathan was on holiday at his nan's and he was always down first for breakfast-time leaving his big sister and his mum and dad trailing behind. He liked to be up early at Nan's so that he could get his nan to himself – without interruptions from grown-ups and a talkative sister. 'Eh, Nan,' Nathan continued, 'what's God like?'

Nathan's nan was well used to such questions from a small, inquisitive boy. They always seemed to come at breakfast time when they were alone together, as she busied herself making porridge for the others and Nathan enjoyed his Rice Crispies. Yesterday his questions were about spaceships. The day before he had wondered why Mrs Rennilson next door walked with a limp. And the day before that he had been enquiring about … No, she just couldn't remember. All she could recall was that there were lots of questions. Today it was God's turn.

If she was honest, 'What's God like?' took her somewhat by surprise. But always having up her sleeve her well-practised technique of answering a question with another question because it gave her time to think, she carried on stirring her porridge with due diligence and replied, 'And what's put that in your mind today, young man?'

Nathan never looked up from his cereal bowl but was clearly ready with his response. 'Well, Nan,' he began. 'Mr McCauley, the minister who comes to our school, says God is a spirit and is all around us, all of the time. So I wondered, what's God like if you can't see him but he's always there? How do you know what's he's like, eh? Have you met God, Nan?' There was much porridge stirring and a long pause. Then Nathan's nan turned round.

'Yes, Nathan, I have,' she replied softly. And before Nathan had time to enquire further as to the kind of God his nan had *actually* met, his nan sat down beside him at the table and returned to her well-used ploy. 'But let me ask you a question first.'

'Ok, Nan,' chirped Nathan through a mouthful of cereal.

'Well, young man, here's my question for you.' Nathan was all ears. 'Do you ever take a bath?'

Nathan stopped his spoon halfway between his plate and his mouth. He was suspicious of questioning of a personal nature. Had his mum been talking? 'Of course I do, Nan,' he protested, 'though my mum says I don't wash myself properly and only mess about in the bath, and then she comes and scrubs behind my ears because she says she could grow potatoes there, and she makes sure *everywhere* else is clean as well. So I *do* have a bath, honest I do … I know I get a bit smelly at times – or so my mum says – but it's only because I run about a lot and play football and stuff. But I do have a bath, Nan, honest I do, *honest* …'

'*Methinks he doth protest too much,*' Nan thought, choosing not to pursue this line of enquiry. 'So, when you're in the bath,' she continued, 'do you use soap?'

Now Nathan was *convinced* his mum had been blabbing about his bath-time exploits. His face reddening and his voice louder he insisted, 'Yes I *do*. I always do. I use soap all the time, even though my mum says the soap isn't wearing down quickly enough so I can't be using it as much as I need to. And anyway …' His nan interrupted what was likely to be another lengthy protest.

'Well,' she continued, 'if you use soap, does it sometimes slip out of your fingers and disappear into the water and when you try to find it, it isn't where you thought it should be?'

Now she had her grandson's full attention. 'How did you know that?' Nathan asked.

'Because I have baths too, and that's what happens to me. Does it happen to you too?'

'Yes, Nan,' Nathan replied, now wide-eyed. 'I've got hold of the soap and I'm just about to wash my knees and then, woops! it's gone.

And then I can't find it any more, and I look and look – and that's when my mum thinks I'm playing, and I know I'm not. I'm just looking for the soap …' Nan smiled as Nathan rushed on excitedly. 'And I look and look, and then, when I think it's gone for good, woops! again, and there it is, right there, from nowhere, it's back. And I've no idea where it came from. Does that happen to you too, Nan?'

'Exactly!' Nan announced triumphantly, clearly catching Nathan's excitement. 'Exactly! You've got it for a while, and then it's gone. And you try to hold on to it, so you grip too tightly, and it slips from your fingers. And it's gone! And you don't know where it is until it comes back and you've got it again. Exactly!'

She stopped and returned to stirring the porridge. There was silence for a while. Nathan returned to his Rice Crispies and wondered how come they'd got to talking about baths and soap. Then he remembered what his original question had been. 'But Nan,' he blurted, breaking the silence and turning round accusingly, 'what's that got to do with God?'

'Well,' replied Nan, 'it's like this. I don't know what God is like. But I know when he's there. I don't know how I know. I just do. And I've got him for a while, and I know it's OK. And then he slips out of my fingers, and he's gone …'

'Like the soap, Nan …' Nathan interjected.

'Exactly! Just like the soap. And I get really worried, and I wonder where he's gone. And I look and look, and I start to panic, thinking I'll never find him again. And then, woops! out of nowhere, God comes back, and I just know he's there again. I just *know*! And then, he's gone …'

'Just like the soap in the bath,' shouted Nathan excitedly, 'but he's always there, and it's just that you can't find him for a while, but he never really goes away, eh Nan?'

'Exactly!' responded Nan, and the two questioners fell silent once again. Nathan finished his cereal as his nan concentrated on the porridge, until Nathan was ready for another bout of questions. 'Nan,' he began, 'what if ...?' but his question was interrupted by his sister, mum and dad coming down for breakfast.

'What was that, Nathan?' Nan enquired.

'Oh, nothing much, Nan. It can wait ...'

Do I?

This God business ...
Do I need to know what God is like?
No ...
Will I need to figure it all out?
No ...
Do I need to understand things?
No ...
Do I need ...?
Yes ...
Will I find ...?
Yes ...
Do I ...?
Yes, indeed you do ...

Pentecost

Old Testament: Psalm 104:24-34, 35b
Epistle: Acts 2:1-21 & 1 Corinthians 12:3b-13
Gospel: John 20:19-23 or John 7:37-39

40 How does the fire work, Daddy?

'How does the fire work, Daddy?' Chloe asked one day. Graham was too tired to answer. There had already been too many questions, too much enquiring for a daddy's weary, end-of-a-long-day mind to cope with.

'Not now, darling,' he answered, 'not just now. Perhaps Mummy might know.' Graham had vowed he'd never say that, but you have to sometimes – don't you? Isn't it written somewhere in the job-description of being a dad? And with a shrug and a resigned smile, off went an enquiring Chloe, having to learn to live with her unan-swered query.

Graham closed his eyes, relaxing into the soporific heat emanating from the two-barred electric fire – with its hypnotic artificial coal effect – that filled the grate. It really was too warm. He didn't actually need the second bar. But the embrace of the warmth was *so* welcome at the end of a long day and after a big meal. He drifted into that pleasant, sleepy state that was a more than welcome antidote to a hard day at the office. And as he did so he pondered …

'How does the fire work?' The question had stuck, planted in his mind by a little sower of seeds. Graham didn't know the answer, and tried to drag his own childhood learning to the front of his mind – along with any helpful adult learning that would do the job too. But he couldn't work it out. And, indeed, unless pestered further by she-who-always-asks-questions, he decided he didn't really need to know.

All he knew was what he knew – such a wonderful invention as a two-bar electric fire was working wonders on his weary body and tired mind.

Didn't the bars glow and the coal-effect shine when he flicked a switch? Wonderful thing, electricity! All he knew was what he knew …

And when the bars glowed, wasn't he surrounded by the warmth they created? Wonderful thing, heat! All he knew was what he knew …

And when he saw the light and felt the heat, didn't that prove the fire was working? Wonderful thing a two-bar electric fire. All he knew was what he knew …

Did he really need to understand how it all happened? Graham decided he didn't … All he knew was what he knew … That would have to be enough for now.

'How does the fire work?' Graham pondered the question as he gently let himself go into sleep. The light, the unseen warmth, the hidden power making it happen. Light, warmth, power … power, warmth, light … power, light, warmth … not one without the other … each a part of the whole … All he knew was what he knew … That would have to be enough for now, as a tired daddy slept peacefully by the fire.

'How does the Trinity work?' the preacher asked at the start of her sermon in church the following Sunday. 'A good question,' Graham thought. But he never heard much of the sermon, for the church was too warm, and he was struggling not to let himself drift off to sleep … But for some reason or another, he kept thinking about power, light, warmth … light, warmth, power … power, warmth, light … power, light, warmth … not one without the other … each a part of the whole … three in one, and one in three …

Graham was wide awake by the time the offering was taken. But he'd made a decision. God the Trinity? No, I'll leave that to the vicar. But 'How does the fire work?' Well, if Chloe came out with *that* one again, he would just tell her not to worry, and just to enjoy the fact that it works. After all, he only knew what he knew, didn't he?

Three

I visited a castle once,
and, not surprisingly,
it had a grand entrance,
with a long driveway up to it,
and steps,
and an archway,
and huge, iron-studded oak doors.
Well,
that's what you would expect from a castle.

And then the tour-guide took us round the back,
to another door,
where the tradesmen came and went,
and the servants went in and out,
unseen, unknown.
Not for them the grand entrance.
They had their own door.
Well,
how else were they going to get in and out of the castle?

But at the end of the tour,
we found another door,
a secret door, we were told,
where special visitors got in,
and personal liaisons were arranged,
and, in later years,
which people used as an escape when they were in danger,
and, in recent times,
where the children played 'hide-and-seek'
because they had their own door.
Well, it was their castle too, wasn't it?

I liked that.
Here was a great castle,
with three doors –
and probably more, for all I knew –
where people could come and go,
depending on who they were,
and what they needed,
and what else was going on.
I liked that.
What a great place …
Well,
even a castle's all the better for having three doors,
don't you think?

Trinity

Old Testament: Genesis 1:1-2:4a
Epistle: 2 Corinthians 13:11-13
Gospel: Matthew 28:16-20

41 Tested

It was the most challenging test Mandy had ever had to face. She's still not sure she passed. She'd had sleepless nights thinking about it since. And she is very sure she never wants to have to face it again.

It all began quietly enough with a gentle walk through the parish on a balmy summer's day. Mandy loved her parish, a quiet, unspoiled village set in rolling hills, its jumble of old houses and cottages clustered tightly around the village green with its pub and its shop and, of course, Mandy's church. There were the two new housing developments on the outskirts of the village too. Well, you can't stand in the way of progress, can you? And she had to admit it was the influx of newcomers which had given the village much-needed new life – and kept the school, the post office and the church functioning as before. Not to put too fine a point on it, the expansion of the village had kept Mandy in a job, for no rural vicar could survive on the remnants of what the village church had been.

Mandy loved her gentle walks through the old part of the village – a cheery word here, a deeper conversation there, checking on the welfare of the postmistress's son, hearing about the arrangements for the School Fayre, learning about the birth of someone's grandchild in the nearby town, hearing how the local bobby's daughter was getting on in college. Today's stroll through the village was that kind of walk. Until, that is, she bumped into Mrs Peterson. Mrs Peterson had a story to tell, and it was a story that was to be the beginning of Mandy's challenging test and recurrent sleepless nights.

Mandy knew Mrs Peterson very well and was more than familiar with her circumstances. Mrs Peterson had nursed her husband through several debilitating years of motor neurone disease. There were times when the disease was stable and, with good support and the commitment of a loving and devoted wife, Mr Peterson was able to stay at home. The occasional crisis necessitated a spell in the hospital in the town and, to be honest, that was the only respite Mrs Peterson ever got. She'd been offered a break, of course, when respite care for her husband in a specialist care-facility would allow her to get away for a holiday. But she never took up the offer. 'How can I be away enjoying myself,' she'd once confessed to Mandy, 'when I've put my husband in a home?'

Recent months had seen a steep decline in Mr Peterson's condition. He was now almost completely helpless and, having lost his swallowing reflex, was now being fed through a tube. It was hard to watch, and Mandy's visits to the Peterson home were among the hardest things she'd ever had to do as a vicar. She never knew what to say, or whether her support for either of the Petersons in their trying circumstances was ever enough.

The strain was beginning to tell on Mrs Peterson too. She'd lost weight. Her eyes were dark and lifeless. She looked weighed down by an intolerable burden.

Meeting her again on today's walk through the village, Mandy got her typical update and offered her usual sympathy. It was common enough, and both parties were familiar with their roles, Mrs Peterson pouring out her soul, and Mandy listening with focus and sensitivity. But today, something was different, for, as they were about to part, Mrs Peterson gripped Mandy by the arm and whispered, 'Mandy, I've had enough. It's too much, more than I bear any more. When I look into my man's pleading eyes, I know he wants it to be over too. Last night I asked him outright, "D'you want it to be finished?" He started to cry and blinked his eyes hard. That's what he does when he wants to make his views clear. He knows there's no quality any more. He sees what it's doing to me. So, I've decided it's time. Don't be surprised if you hear … '

By now, Mrs Peterson was in tears, and fishing in her handbag for a tissue she looked straight at Mandy and said, 'I believe that's what God wants too, and if he doesn't then he damn well should.'

Mandy's words of consolation to a distraught Mrs Peterson felt less than adequate. And as she returned to the vicarage after their encounter, she wondered what she should have said – Persuaded Mrs Peterson she was taking the wrong approach? Given a different interpretation of what God might be wanting for Mrs Peterson and her husband? Talked about the sanctity of life? Quoted scripture? Agreed with her distraught parishioner? Empathised to the extent of understanding why Mrs Peterson would think like this? And anyway, what would *she* do herself if it was her husband, or mother, or sister?

Mandy never slept that night. When the phone rang first thing in the morning, it was the Petersons' eldest daughter informing her that her dad was dead. He had been found by Mrs Peterson first thing in the morning. It was a blessed release. Mrs Peterson was remarkably calm and at ease with herself. Could the vicar come round?

Mandy's blood ran cold. Her mind was in turmoil. She didn't know what to think, or what she would find, or what she should say when she went round to the Peterson's home.

She arrived to find Mrs Peterson as calm and dignified as her daughter had described. The doctor had just left, having certified the death as the natural processes of the end stages of MND. The family were waiting for the funeral director's people to come to take the body away to their rest rooms. Mrs Peterson asked Mandy if she could have a quiet word with her in the kitchen. And in the privacy of an intimate conversation she began, 'You remember what I was saying to you when we met in the village yesterday? Well …' She was interrupted by the ringing of the doorbell. 'That's the funeral director, mum,' a voice came from the hallway. The intimate conversation was never continued – ever …

That was Mandy's challenging test, and she's still not sure she passed …

Tested

Tested beyond my endurance;
Tested to do what is right;

Tested right up to the limit;
Tested to take up the fight;

Tested to challenge what's evil;
Tested my debts to repay;
Tested, when testing's beyond me;
Tested, at once to obey;

Tested to face a new challenge;
Tested to answer the call;
Tested to go where I'm bidden;
Tested to give up my all;

Tested like no one before me;
Tested, decisions to make;
Tested with burdens too heavy;
Tested – my spirit to break?

Tested, and tested, and tested,
And tested, and tested, and then …
Goodness me, would you believe it?
I'm tested and tested again …

Tested, it seems like for ever;
Tested! Do I sound obsessed?
And will I be up for the challenge,
Ready to cope with the test?

Ninth after Easter

Old Testament: Genesis 22:1-14
Epistle: Romans 6:12-23
Gospel: Matthew 10:40-42

42 About the children

Mildred had been in the coffee shop for a long time. She was on her fourth decaf skinny latte, and each of these she had taken an age to finish. Customers had come and gone; the lunchtime rush had swirled round her, the coffee shop returning to its quieter ambience in the early afternoon; tables had been cleared and cleared again; the floor had been mopped several times; the napkin holders and milk-jugs had been appropriately replenished. And still Mildred sat alone at a corner table. And all the time she was thinking about the children.

She was thinking about the children when the waiter wiped her table – a kindly and momentary interruption – and she was thinking about the children after he had gone; she was thinking about the children when two mums with babies in pushchairs had their 'let's-do-lunch' rendezvous, and she was thinking about the children after they'd packed up and left; she was thinking about the children when a business type asked if the other chair at her table was free, and she was thinking about the children after the chair was vacated once more.

It was the children she missed the most after Dan had gone. She missed Dan too. Of course she did, especially when she remembered the times when things were good, not so long ago, really. But after her breakdown, things just hadn't been the same.

He'd tried awfully hard, she had to concede that. Oh, how he had tried … She could remember his visits to her in the hospital when she was doped up on medication, and she could see him come, looking so helpless, but she couldn't reach him and he couldn't reach her. It was as if she was inside a glass box and could see what was happening around her. But she was powerless to interact with what was outside the box. And Dan couldn't reach into the box to help her either.

She could remember how Dan looked so helpless, the pleading in his eyes. She could remember how she winced when he tried to before the coffee shop closed. She had a lot more thinking about the children still to do …

Mildred had been in the coffee shop for a long time. She was on her fifth decaf skinny latte, and this one, like the others, would take an age to finish. But still Mildred sat alone at a corner table. And all the time she was thinking about the children.

And she wondered if she would ever, ever get any respite from this intolerable burden …

Too heavy

I once helped carrying a piano …

I don't know if you've ever tried to lift a piano,
but, if you have, you'll know how heavy it is.

Well, I put my back out.
Not too clever, eh?

But then,
I was lifting it the wrong way,
wasn't I?
And anyway,
me and my mate were too stubborn to ask for help,
and too impatient to wait for it,
even if it had been available.

So we tried to move the piano ourselves.

Bad decision!

So, while I was nursing my bad back,
and not being allowed to lift anything at all,
far less an awkward piano,
I got to thinking –

the obvious, really −
that when there's something heavy to carry,
it's better to get things organised,
and not be too proud to ask for help.

That way,
the piano gets moved properly,
and everyone's happy;
and I don't have a bad back;
and I can try to help carry someone else's piano,
some other time,
when they need my help with the lifting.

Tenth after Easter

Old Testament: Genesis 24:34–38, 42–49, 58–67
Epistle: Romans 7:15–25a
Gospel: Matthew 11:16–19, 25–30

43 The word of the week

'And the word of the week is …' That's what Jill heard every Monday morning from her teacher, as soon as the class had assembled and morning prayers had been said. Jill's teacher had a passion for words, and, aged eleven, Jill had already been drawn into that passion.

Why her teacher chose this word or that was a complete mystery to an eleven-year-old. But Jill had to admit, she just *loved* first thing on Monday morning when her teacher said to the class, 'And the word of the week is …' For she knew that another Aladdin's cave of immeasurable pleasure ('immeasurable' and 'pleasure' having both been the 'word of the week' in recent times …) was about to be opened and she was going to be invited inside.

The teacher involved was Miss Amelia Caruthers. The children of Class 7 weren't supposed to know that Miss Caruthers had a first name at all, far less what it was. And of course they kept this little secret to themselves. So as far as class time was concerned, and even when referring to the teacher of Class 7 outside the classroom setting, it was always 'Miss Caruthers'.

Miss Caruthers was a matronly type whose silver-grey hair was always pulled back severely from her face and tied in a tight bun. She invariably wore tweed skirts and white blouses, and her reading glasses, kept from being lost by a silver chain around her neck, were often perched precariously on the end of her nose when she was talking to the children.

There were some things Jill didn't like about Miss Caruthers. For one thing, she didn't like the way she would slam a desk-lid down to scare the living daylights out of the class – though Miss Caruthers said she did it because it was sometimes the only way she could get everyone's attention. It worked!

And Jill – and all the other children in the class, too – didn't touch her, and the look of horror on his face. She could remember … and she hated it. But it wasn't her fault.

The depression had lasted a long time, and even when the spell in hospital was over, she wasn't the same. She couldn't cope with physical contact with Dan. She couldn't be bothered with the noise of the kids. She just couldn't be bothered – period …

Dan had tried for ages. But it was no use. *She* was no use. So Dan had left with the children. He had gone up north to stay with his mother. The children would be happy there, and so would Dan, he'd told her. That had been three months ago. Mildred had been in the coffee shop many times since then, and she had been at her table for a long while again today. She looked down at her empty coffee cup and noticed for the first time that the blue napkin she'd been holding was in shreds, pulled to pieces by her nervous fingers during all the time she'd been thinking about the children.

It wasn't so much that she was worried about them. Of course she wondered about what they were up to, and whether they'd made new friends. She went over and over in her mind whether they would have settled in their new school, and whether Dan's mother was feeding them too much junk food. It was as if they were in a foreign country, with things happening to them or influencing them that she neither knew about nor could be part of. She wasn't worried, not really worried, because she told herself they would be happy with Dan, happier than they would ever have been if they'd stayed with her for much longer. That much she had convinced herself of.

What she was *really* concerned about was the damage she had done to them. There had been hurt, of course. The children couldn't have been immune from the atmosphere and the tensions. But had it harmed them for good? Would it be permanent? Had their innocence been taken away too early? Might they be damaged for ever? Could they survive? Would they turn out like her?

She left her shredded napkin on the table and went up to the counter to order another cup of coffee. It would be a while yet appreciate the tests every Friday afternoon – sums, spelling and Scripture – which determined the seating arrangements for the next week. The class positions were appropriately adjusted first thing on the Monday morning, the brightest at the top right of the class, and the not-so-bright at the bottom left, close to the draughty door and well within Miss Caruthers' admonishing reach.

But all that, and much more besides, was forgiven by Jill when she heard her favourite announcement – 'And the word of the week is …'

'And the word of the week is … AUTOMATON', and the whole class would be invited to say the word out loud, play with it on their tongues, whisper it, carry it with them as the week went on and relate it to others parts of their curriculum (yet *another* recent 'word of the week'!).

At some point during the week the Greek or Latin or other derivation of the word would be explored – a suffix noted, a root discovered, a prefix explained. Other words would be looked at – antonyms, synonyms, and words that just sounded the same – to explore the connectedness of language. For a quiet time, the children would be invited to put the word in a mini-crossword, tie other words to it, and compose a cryptic clue. And there were always encyclopaedias to be looked through, pictures to be drawn, and endless tracts of imagination to be explored.

'And the word of the week is … BRAGGART', and they were off again.

'And the word of the week is … MISANTHROPE,' and another adventure began.

'And the word of the week is … HOVERCRAFT,' and a week of explorations commenced.

'And the word of the week is … WURLITZER,' and a new treasure-trove was discovered.

And of course, at some time in the week, Miss Caruthers would gather the children around her – usually as a reward for something they'd done particularly well – and read a passage to them which contained their 'word of the week'. That way, when SLOUGH was the 'word of the week', Jill was introduced to *The Pilgrim's Progress*, when 'The Slough of Despond' was the centre of their attention; and when RECESSIONAL was explained as the title of one of Rudyard Kipling's poems, a whole vista of poetry was opened up; and when she heard that TOTTERING appeared in the first page of Robert Louis Stevenson's *Treasure Island*, she just couldn't wait to read the whole thing.

'The word of the week' had a lot to answer for, not least because it actually made learning fun, and of course because it made Miss Caruthers very special indeed. Miss Caruthers, if only she knew it, had planted many seeds for Jill with her 'word of the week' …

That's why, many years later, when Jill was being interviewed for a new job and she was asked about the important influences on her life, she spoke first and foremost of a fairly stern teacher she remembered from Class 7 in her local school when Jill was eleven years old. 'Miss Amelia Caruthers she was called …' and Jill went on to explain the importance of 'the word of the week' for an impressionable child.

Jill got the job! And she wonders what Miss Caruthers would make of this little lass from one of her Primary 7 classes ending up in the English Faculty of an Oxford college as a specialist in English Literature, where the word of the week for the newly appointed member of staff was none other than PROFESSOR.

The seed I have scattered
Words & Music: William A. Spencer (1886)

The seed I have scattered in springtime with weeping,
And watered with tears and with dews from on high;
Another may shout when the harvester's reaping,
Shall gather my grain in the 'sweet by and by'.

Refrain

Over and over, yes, deeper and deeper
My heart is pierced through with life's sorrowing cry,
But the tears of the sower and songs of the reaper
Shall mingle together in joy by and by.
By and by, by and by,
By and by, by and by,
Yes, the tears of the sower and songs of the reaper
Shall mingle together in joy by and by.

Another may reap what in springtime I've planted,
Another rejoice in the fruit of my pain,
Not knowing my tears when in summer I fainted
While toiling sad-hearted in the sunshine and rain.

Refrain

The thorns will have choked and the summer's suns blasted
The most of the seed which in springtime I've sown;
But the Lord Who has watched while my weary toil lasted
Will give me a harvest for what I have done.

Refrain

(Accessible at www.cyberhymnal.org/htm/s/o/n/songreap.htm*)*

Eleventh after Easter

Old Testament: Genesis 25:19-34
Epistle: Romans 8:1-11
Gospel: Matthew 13:1-9, 18-23

44 Sorting things out

No one knew that Jeanie Kennedy kept her old black-and-white photographs in a biscuit tin at the bottom of her bedroom cupboard. But, there again, no one *needed* to know, as no one was ever invited into the privacy of Jeanie's bedroom, far less given the opportunity to rake around in bottom of a cupboard.

All of that changed, of course, when Jeanie moved out of her retirement flat in the complex next to the church and into the nursing home on the other side of the town. It was a good move and one that Jeanie had been planning for a time. Life without Jim, her husband of fifty-eight years, was tolerable but devoid of real pleasure. Jim had left Jeanie comfortably well off and there was enough money for the nursing home fees. So it was all a matter of judgement and timing, when the balance of independent living swung towards worries about coping on your own. That balance had shifted and, with good grace and a resignation to the inevitable, Jeanie's place in the nursing home was secured.

Jeanie had lived a simple and unostentatious life, and as a consequence her retirement flat wasn't cluttered with too much 'stuff'. So when it came time for Harriet, her only niece, to clear the house in preparation for its sale, there really wasn't too much to do. Jeanie issued instructions and Harriet carried them out. Bit by bit, papers were sorted through, furniture was disposed of, usable utensils were passed on to local charities, and old and unusable things were taken to the Council's recycling centre.

That's when Harriet came across the biscuit tin of black-and-white photographs in the bottom of Jeanie's bedroom cupboard. For a moment Harriet thought it could be an exciting find, and that she might come across a photograph of a long-lost relative or a picture of Auntie Jeanie in her younger years. But no such luck. Harriet didn't recognise anyone, or any view, or any event. The old black–and–white photographs in the biscuit tin at the bottom of Jeanie Kennedy's bedroom cupboard were a mystery.

Not even Jeanie could cast light on the collection of pictures. She didn't know any of the people or places or events either. In fact, she confessed to Harriet that she didn't even know the biscuit tin had been there. 'It must have been some of the stuff your uncle Jim collected. I promised myself I'd sort it all out, but I never got round to it. No use to anyone now. Just gather them all together and bin them, dear. Take them to the skip with the rest of the rubbish. They're no use at all.'

That's why a collection of old black–and–white photographs in a biscuit tin from the bottom of Jeanie Kennedy's bedroom cupboard was dumped in a black bag ready to be taken to the Council's recycling centre on Harriet's next trip.

★★★

Betty and Anne were always the ones who sorted through the bags and boxes which were regularly delivered to the church and community's charity shop on the town hall square. 'Nearly New – Just For You', it was called, and as charity shops go it was a thriving and profitable enterprise. Harriet had been a regular visitor to the shop in recent weeks, and the volunteers were well aware of the source of her donations. They were pleased, too, that Jeanie Kennedy approved of her bits and pieces being put to good use, as in her own better years Jeanie had been one of the shop's original volunteers.

Betty and Anne were sorting through what they had been informed by Harriet would be her final donation of things from Jeanie's flat. They were on their last black plastic bag when they found a biscuit tin full of old black–and–white photographs stuffed in the top.

'Strange thing for someone to donate,' said Betty.

'Better off being dumped, I would have thought,' agreed Anne, 'as the rest of the stuff is clearly rubbish. I'm sure this bag shouldn't have come here at all.'

'Best throw it in the corner with the other rubbish, then,' suggested Betty. But as Anne did as she was instructed the biscuit tin slipped from her hands and dropped at her feet, dislodging its lid and scattering its contents all over the floor. 'Clumsy,' muttered Betty and bent down to help her friend retrieve the contents of the box.

It was Anne who stopped first. Picking up one of the photographs and holding it at arm's length, she announced, 'I know I don't have my glasses on, but that looks awfully like Tam McGlinn's fishmonger's shop before it was knocked down for the extension to the bus station. And I'll bet that's old McGlinn himself. That'll be in the 1920s, eh?'

Betty was next, retrieving another picture and announcing, 'And that looks like a class posing outside the old school. Goodness, would you look at their clothes! That could be the 1920s too, or even earlier.'

And that's the way it continued – two ladies, soon to be joined by other volunteers, identifying this place and that, working out who people might be and when a picture was taken and puzzling over what had happened to a view or a building in the background.

By the time the afternoon was finished there were photographs spread out all over the back room table. There were many to be kept, researched and pondered on further. And the ones that were no use to anyone were put back in the biscuit tin and placed on a shelf 'for future reference'.

'Just as well we didn't bin them all,' Betty said to Anne as they were closing the shop at the end of the day.

'It would have been sad if the good had been chucked out with the bad, eh?' offered Anne. And Betty nodded in agreement.

★★★

Just last week, a new display board appeared in the town hall's foyer, as part of the 'All Your Yesterdays' exhibition. A photograph of Tam McGlinn and his newly opened fishmonger's from 1922 is there, along with other fascinating photographs from the same era, all enlarged, digitally doctored and neatly labelled. And at the centre there is a photograph of a school class from 1905, with a cheeky face at the end of the front row identified as one 'Robert Kennedy'.

When Jeanie Kennedy was taken from her nursing home to see the display – as a thank-you for being the source of some of the pictures – she was delighted to remark that the Jim Kennedy who'd been her beloved husband for fifty-eight years clearly got his good looks from his grandfather.

Weeding

'What's a weed,' Grampa?' the little one asked.
There was weeding to be done,
and Grampa needed an apprentice weeder.
And the enthusiastic helper wanted to get it right,
and please her grampa.
'What's a weed, Grampa?' the little one asked.
'A weed's a plant that's growing in the wrong place,
at the wrong time,
for the wrong purpose,' Grampa replied.
And an apprentice weeder was none the wiser …

Twelfth after Easter

Old Testament: Genesis 28:10-19a
Epistle: Romans 8:12-25
Gospel: Matthew 13:24-30, 36-43

45 CC

Chic Chandler was a character, and during his time in St Jerome's Seminary, the city's theological training college, he'd become a firm favourite with students and staff alike, and in so doing had become one of James Thompson's best friends. Chic – known universally as CC – was an American postgraduate student doing a year's research in St Jerome's as part of his Doctorate thesis. James was in his final year of training for the priesthood, and it would be fair to say that CC had a greater influence on James Thompson's theological thinking than anything else in recent times.

For a start, CC was a bit of a clown. With his long hair tied in a ponytail, his wispy goatee beard, his flamboyant shirts, and his strong – and often loud – New York accent, CC was hard to miss. James first came across this extraordinary character on the first day of the year's opening semester. They'd been sitting next to each other at the 'welcome event' in the Seminary chapel, exchanged 'hellos' casually before the gathering began, and settled back to take in the welcome speech by the Dean of the Seminary. It was much the same as usual, and familiar in style to the ones James had listened to in his previous two years. It always had a theme. This year it was the initial letters of the esteemed seminary, and so the Dean droned on through: 'Now, let's look at the meaning of St Jerome's. To begin with, S reminds us that this is a place of study …' and he went on for ages on the merits of learning; 'and T points us to theology …' and off he went on a treatise on the value of theological thinking; J gave him scope to explore the theme of journeys, as staff and students learned together, and so on, and so on.

By the time the Dean had got to E for excellence, James was losing the will to live. Just then, CC tapped him on the leg and, in a barley concealed whisper, suggested, 'It's just as well we didn't enrol in the Massachusetts Institute of Technology or we'd be here for ever.'

James was a touch embarrassed that he was part of the group of those who responded to the jibe with a muffled titter, but decided, there and then, that he liked this guy.

During a particularly stressful winter term, when the weather and the workload were to nobody's liking, CC brought a ray of sunshine into the student common room when he announced that he was ill. Not that CC being ill was itself a thing of amusement, but when concerned colleagues enquired as to the nature of his illness, CC informed them that he was suffering from a dose of The Februaries. 'What on earth is that?' James and the others enquired. 'Oh,' CC replied, 'The Februaries are a creeping depression that starts sometime around the first week in January and doesn't begin to lift till about the end of March. It's my name for the winter blues.' And a common room full of weighed-down students smiled and nodded in agreement.

CC was full of stories, like the time he'd spilled a glass of water over his prayer book, rendering it useless, and having to conduct half a worship service making it up as he went along, 'Winging it …' to use his own phrase. Or the time he had to announce 'Smoke gets in your eyes …' as the closing music at a crematorium funeral service and couldn't pronounce the Benediction for muffling his giggles with his handkerchief. Yes indeed, CC was a character, and James and the whole of St Jerome's were the better for his company.

But it was CC's passion for raising money for the Seminary's anti-landmine project that had the greatest influence on James Thompson. Each year the Seminary Council chose a charity which was to be the focus of the St Jerome community's fundraising efforts. This year it was centred on the work of various organisations working in different parts of the world to alleviate the suffering of the innocent victims of landmine explosions. Millions of landmines had been left behind after various conflicts. Many, many people were being maimed or killed as a result.

CC threw himself into fundraising for the project like no one had ever known before and was at the forefront of the campaign to stop the use of such devastating devices. Who but the extraordinary CC could persuade the college to have a 'movie fancy-dress day' so that even the Dean could be seen sporting a Stetson and walking with a suspiciously familiar John Wayne roll? What contacts did CC have when he could organise a well known TV presenter to chair a charity auction attended by a host of local and national celebrities? Had there ever been a more moving presentation in the Seminary chapel as project workers and community leaders from a charity project in Rwanda shared with the students and staff the need for money for food and clothes, educational and employment programmes, medical personnel, and supplies of painkilling drugs?

How CC fitted in any time for his studies, James never knew. For it seemed as if, for a whole year, the anti-landmine project was CC's life and work. Not surprisingly, the money for the project that year was more than the Seminary had ever raised before. That was all down to CC.

Not long before the end of the Seminary's year, James and CC were in the pub together, sharing what CC – gently mocking the politeness of James and his friends – was pleased to call 'a small refreshment', when James decided to ask CC, 'Why?'

'Why what?' CC asked in response.

'Why the passion for the anti-landmine project? I've never seen anyone as committed to anything in my whole life. So, why?'

CC took a sip of his beer, placed his glass carefully on the table, and sat silent for what seemed to James to be an awfully long time. Then, turning to his friend, CC announced, 'My older brother was in the US military and had his legs blown off by a landmine during the first Gulf war. He never recovered and died of his wounds. He was my only brother. It wasn't his fault. And I know there are many like him, all over the world, who are victims, just as he was. It's not their fault either. There's no point in being bitter. It won't bring my brother back. So I do what I can to help those I'll never meet to have a chance my brother never had. All those who are the innocent victims of landmines have become my brothers and sisters. I don't know why. It's just happened. What can I do but play my part in helping them?'

James Thompson didn't have to reply. But he knows it was that conversation that confirmed the influence a renegade, extraordinary New Yorker had on his theology. And he knows it was the beginning of a journey that led him to his present ministry – as an administrator with a national charity in a countrywide project in the Sudan among the landmine victims.

So small

It's so small, this faith of mine,
too frail, too basic
to be called a 'faith';
too unformed, too inadequate
to make a difference.
But here it is;
it's all I have –
even though it still looks so small,
this faith of mine.

It's so small, this commitment of mine,
too gentle, too diffident
to have the name of 'commitment';
too uncertain, too incomplete
to make a difference.
But here it is;
it's all I have –
even if it sounds so small,
this commitment of mine.

It's so small, this passion of mine,
too weak, too tentative
to have the label 'passion';

too unglamorous; too unsure
to make a difference.
But here it is;
it's all I have —
even if it feels so small,
this passion of mine.

OK, but doesn't the mustard seed
grow into a fruitful bush?
And your tiny faith …?

And can't the smallest shoot
develop into a blossoming shrub?
And your smallness of commitment …?

And can't the tiny bud
burst into a glorious bloom?
And your little passion …?

So bring your little faith
and see it bear fruit;
bring your little commitment
and see it blossom;
bring your little passion
and see it bloom.

Remember the mustard seed?
Even such smallness has potential.

Thirteenth after Easter

Old Testament: Genesis 29:15-28
Epistle: Romans 8:26-39
Gospel: Matthew 13:31-33, 44-52

46 The impersonator

Benny Cargill had prepared well for the talent competition. Not that he needed much preparation, it has to be said, for Benny was considered a master of his art by those who knew him well. Indeed, he considered himself to be pretty hot stuff. Benny – if he was old enough to know what it meant – might have said that he could walk on water …

Mind you, complacency wasn't what was needed on the night of the annual talent competition, so Benny gave himself to one final rehearsal. Because he was only eight years of age, the rehearsal was organised by Benny's mum – his manager, mentor, driver and all-round support network. The rehearsal took place in Benny's front room where Benny had strutted his stuff for as long as he could remember. For despite his tender years Benny was a seasoned trouper and, for his age, a bit of a star turn. He was an Elvis Presley look-alike, an impersonator *par excellence* of the king of rock and roll!

Benny adored performing – 'a wee natural', his mum never tired of saying – and with his sequinned jumpsuit, his swivelling hips, his amazing renditions of 'Hound dog' and 'Love me tender' among other Elvis classics, he was, some had said, destined for stardom.

The rehearsal went well, Benny's mum pronouncing herself well pleased, and Benny – confirming his belief that he'd been well enough prepared already – was satisfied that everything was in place for the 'big night'.

For years the annual talent show had been the biggest night in the town's social and entertainment calendar. Sponsored by the local newspaper, 'The Big Talent Show' was the showcase for budding local talent of all ages, styles and quality. Having just turned eight – the lower end of the age-range for the show – this was Benny's first go at the competition. He was looking forward to it immensely. Apparently devoid of such a thing as nerves, he was amply endowed with self-confidence. He could walk on water, his mother had said. Even The Big Talent Show held no fear for the young Elvis Presley himself.

Excitement was in the air as the crowds gathered on the night of the show. The judges took their places at the long table set out at the front of the hall, the audience taking up every available seat behind them and filling the town hall to its maximum capacity. The judges were important people – Mrs Clifton, head of the music department in the High School, was first to arrive; Johnny Banana (*aka* Mr John Hopkirk) well known local magician and children's entertainer (a professional, and therefore excluded from this amateur parade of talent) came in next; he was followed by Digby Middleton, owner and editor-in-chief of the local newspaper, and chairman of the judges; Matilda Desmond (*aka* 'Mrs Descant'), lead soprano in the church choir was the fourth judge; and finally Joe Reid, local MP, completed the talent competition's judging panel.

At the appointed hour the lights dimmed, the stage was lit, and after a mercifully brief word of welcome from the chairman of the judges, the competition commenced. The crowd and the judging panel were not to be disappointed, for the array of talent on the hall stage over the next hour and a half was as impressive as it had ever been. 'The Duval Duo', a brother-and-sister acoustic-guitar act, wowed the audience with their Cilla Black medley; Chris Carnie, one of the staff in Benny's school, was well received for his stand-up comedy routine; a retro skiffle band, 'Murray and the Megatones' – the competition favourites – almost brought the house down; a trio of matronly ladies did surprisingly well with their 'Three little maids from school' performance, ably doing justice to the Gilbert and Sullivan classic; and, of course, there was Benny.

Benny's turn went very well indeed. The crowd cheered him to the echo. His mum pronounced herself well pleased. And in time, when the show was over, she and Benny took their places – and their fair share of free cakes – in the room at the back of the hall to await the judges' verdict. The atmosphere was tense. Everyone knew that with such a high standard the choice of a winner was going to be hard. Benny wasn't too bothered. This walking-on-water business was easy …

Eventually Benny and the other contestants were called back on stage for the announcement of that year's winner. 'In reverse order …' Digby Middleton intoned, 'and in third place … The Duval Duo'. Appropriate and heartfelt applause. 'And the runner up is … Murray and the Megatones.' Gasps, then loud and appreciative cheering. 'So this is it … what you've all been waiting for … this year's rising talent and winner of The Big Talent Show …' Benny could see his mum, fit to burst, and grinning at him from the front row. Benny had worked out who he was up against. The bookie's favourite having gone, he only had three old ladies and a not-very-funny comedian to contend with. 'This year's winner is … ' Anticipation … much holding of breath … horrible pause … '… your cheeky comic, Chris Carnie.'

Benny was told later by his mum that there were some boos and hisses before they were drowned out by deserved applause. But Benny never heard them. He was too devastated to notice. He'd let everyone down. His mum would be *so* upset.

That was thirty years ago. Benny swivel-hips Cargill now runs his own taxi business in the town. But he also makes a passable living as an Elvis Presley tribute act in the pubs and clubs of the district. It's the only thing he does that he really enjoys. He's done OK at it. But he doesn't try to be too clever any more, because he remembers a night in his local town hall when a young Elvis impersonator tried to impersonate someone who was able to walk on water but almost sank without trace.

Come on!

It's OK, honest. Come on.
   But it looks too hard.
No, it's fine. Come on.
   But it's not for me.
Look, it's not that hard. Come on.
   That's OK for you to say.
Get real. If I can do it ... Come on.
   But I'm scared.
I know. But you can do it. Come on.
   OK. I'll try.
Well then, what's keeping you? Come on.
   I'm off – look – I'm doing it!
Well done. I knew you could. Come on.
   Oh no! Oh no!
What? What's the matter now? Come on ...
   Oh God! I'm falling.
You'll be OK. Come on.
   No, it's all going wrong.
No it isn't. It's your imagination. Come on.
   I'm sinking, I'm going under.
Oh God, and you were doing so well. Come on.
   I can't! I can't!
Give me your hand, look, here. Come on.
   I can't ...
Hold on to this. Come on.
   Oh God!
See, it's OK now. Come on.
   But I was going down ...
Come on ...
   But what if ...?

Come on?
　　　　If you weren't ...
Come on ...
　　　　Could I do it again ...?
Yes! Come on!

Fourteenth after Easter

Old Testament: Genesis 32:22-31
Epistle: Romans 9:1-5
Gospel: Matthew 14:13-21

47 A miracle in Hope Street

'It wasn't a *great* miracle,' Tubby announced to no one in particular. 'In fact, I'm not sure it was a miracle at all. But my mum *insists* it was. "The miracle of Hope Street" she calls it. But, as miracles go, it wasn't *that* amazing. Not like getting a smile out of the barman in this place, or you getting off with my sister, or Mac paying for a round … Now, that *would* be a miracle, eh?' Tubby chuckled at his own joke. Mac pretended he hadn't heard, preferring instead to keep his eyes glued to the TV in the corner. But Ginger looked up with a start from the sports' section of the evening paper.

'Did someone mention another round? Mine's a pint of bitter,' he announced.

'No, not a round. I was talking about miracles, you dozy clown.'

'It'd be a miracle if *that* one offered to get a round in,' Ginger replied, pointing at Mac.

'I've done that joke,' Tubby protested. Mac still didn't pay any attention.

'So, what's this about miracles, then?' Ginger enquired.

The three mates were in the pub as usual after work. 'A swift half' on the way home usually meant a couple of pints in The Red Lion and an hour or so together at the end of the day. It was an opportunity to wind down, sort out the troubles of the world, and have inconsequential conversations about nothing in particular. However, Tubby was delighted he now had the attention of 50% of his pals.

'My mum says it was a miracle.'

'What was?'

'The do at the Fairleys' house.'

'The Fairleys? Wasn't it Big Jim Fairley's funeral yesterday? Bad so-and-so, I reckon. Just out after a ten-year stretch, wasn't he? Got what was coming to him.'

'I know all that,' Tubby protested. 'But that's the point. You'd never have expected a miracle at the Fairleys', eh?'

'What miracle? The priest didn't manage to turn the water into vodka or Barney the Baker's sausage rolls into something edible, did he?'

'No, but that's the point.'

'What point?'

'The miracle.'

'The "Miracle of Hope Street"?'

'Exactly!' Tubby went quiet. But Ginger was having none of it.

'Well?' he exclaimed. 'Let's have the story.'

'OK, then, but I'm still not sure I've got it right. It's my mum's story anyway.'

'So, since she isn't here, you'll just have to do the Jackanory bit. So, come on!'

'Well, my mum figured that it wasn't the Fairleys' fault that the old man was a rogue, and she felt really sorry for the rest of them, especially Ella, his old woman, who'd been through the mill. And then he goes and dies. Well, anyway, my mum said it was a shame that Ella Fairley would have all those mouths to feed after the funeral – you know, the meat pies and curled-up-ham sandwiches do, back at the house. And what with all her kids and her sister's lot, and Big Jim's tribe, and the neighbours, she reckoned there would be *hundreds* of people back after the funeral, and what with Ella Fairley not having two brass farthings to rub together, there was going to be nowt to eat.'

Tubby paused to draw breath, and then, after a gap that allowed his one-man audience to capture the scene, he ploughed on with his tale.

'Well … so my mum decided to make a loaf of sandwiches, cheese and chutney and stuff, and take it round. And my dad said she was off her napper as a half a dozen loaves of sandwiches wasn't going to make a blind bit of difference and she'd be better having nothing to do with such a useless bunch anyway. But my mum always wins those kinds of arguments, and so in a nanosecond she's got the sandwiches made and she's off round the Fairleys' with the goodies in a poly bag.' Tubby paused again. But his audience was restless.

'Aye? So?' Ginger offered encouragingly, clearly feeling this story of Tubby's mother's wasn't turning out the way he'd hoped. 'So?' he exclaimed again.

'Well, it was a miracle.'

'What was?'

'At the Fairleys', eh? When my mum got there, the whole of Hope Street was like the shopping precinct on a busy Saturday.'

'With all the Fairleys' lot, right enough.'

'No. The Fairleys' crowd were all *inside*. It was the neighbours. They were all there. The whole street. There were folk with bags of cakes, and sandwiches of all sorts. Tam Althorpe from the top of the road had a crate of lager, and even old Mrs Wilson had bought half-a-dozen pies from the corner shop. By the time my mum got inside with her cheese-and-chutney offering, the place was full of food. Ella Fairley was speechless. There was more food at the Fairleys' than anyone had ever seen. And, my God, everyone was getting stuck in good and proper. No one went hungry.'

'Who would have believed it?' Ginger responded. 'And for the Fairleys too. But where's the miracle in all of that?'

'Well, that's where I'm not sure. But my mum says it's a miracle that her loaf of sandwiches meant everyone was fed. No, not just *hers*. But when everyone chipped in … well, there you are. And my mum reckons that if she'd not given her contribution, because it was the Fairleys or because she didn't feel it would do much good, other people might have done the same. And the Fairleys would have gone hungry. So, it was a *kind* of miracle, eh, don't you think? It started with a loaf of sandwiches and ended up with more than enough to go round.'

Ginger nodded. Tubby joined his audience in a pondering silence.

And just then, Mac, having had a sufficiency of the TV in the corner, swung back to rejoin his mates.

'Did someone mention a round? Mine's a pint, lads.'

Miracles

It was a miracle when someone was kind to Tommy,
when no one else was,
and Tommy managed a smile –
wasn't it?

It was a miracle that Emily made something of her life,
even after a bad start,
and had her own kids –
wasn't it?

It was a miracle that Andy stayed off the drink,
when he was going down the tube
very fast indeed –
wasn't it?

It was a miracle that Jenny died peacefully,
when the illness had been so bad
for so long –
wasn't it?

It was a miracle when Sally hugged,
and Tony laughed,
and Evelyn cared,
and Brian walked,
and Jimmy coped,
and Mandy cried,
and Bobby fell in love –
wasn't it?

No?

Well,
if you don't open your eyes and see *these* miracles
what will miracles *ever* mean, eh?

Fifteenth after Easter

Old Testament: Genesis 37:1-4, 12-28
Epistle: Romans 10:5-15
Gospel: Matthew 14:22-33, 14:13-21

48 Only a little part of me

'Has my sister told you?' Monica and Terry were sitting in the back garden of Monica's whitewashed bungalow set in the leafy suburbs at the edge of the town. The day was warm and the garden, as ever, a haven of peace and tranquillity which Terry always enjoyed. Today, as usual, he'd been ushered through the house to the garden beyond by Monica's sister, Anne, to find Monica comfortable in her lounger and sipping her familiar iced lemonade. Anne, with whom Monica had shared a home in recent years, had bustled back indoors with the promise of a replenished supply of lemonade and some cream scones. And as soon as she'd gone Monica's question came like a cold blast on a balmy afternoon. 'Well, has she told you I've got cancer?'

Terry didn't know how to respond. Of course he'd been told. It was why he'd come to visit, after all. And Monica was no fool. Why else would Terry come calling on the afternoon of a working day? Not that he wouldn't have been visiting at some time in the week, for his visits to Monica were as regular as they were pleasurable. But this visit was different.

Monica was one of Terry's favourite people. They'd been colleagues on the teaching staff of the local junior school for many years before Monica had retired early on the grounds of ill-health. A deep friendship mattered to them both. 'Fellow travellers,' Monica had once described their relationship. And so when Anne had phoned Terry in tears to tell him that her sister had been diagnosed with pancreatic cancer, Terry had gone round right away.

He'd tried to be cool, of course – as you do – kissing Monica on the cheek as he always did, before he sat beside her to await the delivery of fresh iced lemonade. But Monica was clearly having none of his pretence. 'Has my sister told you I've got cancer?' had been her opening and dramatic gambit.

Terry had no idea what to say. On the way to see his friend he'd been trying to figure out what kind of conversation they might have and how he might cope with the twists and turns of their discussion. But he just wasn't prepared for such an up-front opening before he'd settled down.

The imperceptible nod of his head gave away the truth. Monica let out an exasperated sigh. 'I knew it! I just knew it,' she exclaimed. 'Telling all and sundry, just to elicit sympathy. Oh bother! Oh *bother*! Not what I wanted at all. I wanted to tell you myself when you came round, and in my own way and in my own time. Now it's been spoiled …'

Not usually lost for words, Terry still didn't know what to say. In his mind he was shifting between thoughts of 'I shouldn't have come' and 'It'll be good to let her have a rant' when the tension was broken by Anne returning with a tray of fresh lemonade, along with Terry's glass and three cream scones on a delicate patterned plate. Monica had lapsed into silence. Terry was still tongue-tied. Anne was busying herself being a taciturn hostess. Silent companionship was embraced by the warm summer air, and the chirping and whistling of the birds seemed enough for now.

Eventually it was Monica who broke the silence. 'OK,' she said, 'it looks like it's all out in the open – thanks to Anne.' Anne reddened and stared down at the plate of scones, studying them intently. 'I know that Terry knows. I suppose that's OK. So let's get it all clarified. Terry, it's true. I got the diagnosis confirmed yesterday. I've to start chemotherapy next week – with all that entails, hair-loss and the like,' she continued, running her fingers through her auburn locks. 'It's going to a long haul.'

She paused. Terry wondered if he should try to say something. He needn't have bothered. Monica wasn't finished. Stretching over to take his hand in hers and squeezing it tightly, she looked him straight in the eye and went on, 'So, let me lay down the ground-rules from here on in. I've got cancer in my pancreas. It may spread. But for now, that's where it is. And I know from the doctors that the tumour is the size of a golf ball. So here's the deal.'

She let go of Terry's hand and raised her own hand to eye level, midway between the two of them. She opened her thumb and fore-finger so there was just about a golf-ball-sized space between them. 'That,' she offered boldly, 'is the size of my cancer. Take a good look. And remember how big it is.' Then, dramatically, she took both her hands and stretched them out to either side as far as she could reach – nearly knocking the pitcher of lemonade from the table in the process. And with her frail arms widely flung, she announced, 'And *that,* and bigger even than that, is the whole of me. See the difference?'

Monica dropped one hand on her lap and with the other hand held up her imaginary golf ball once more. 'So this cancer is very small compared to the whole of me. It's a part – and it's going to be a damned difficult part. But it's only a part of me, not the whole thing. So when you come to visit, Terry Pollock, ask about this little part, and I'll tell you how it is. But keep on asking about the rest too, all of this' – and her arms were flung wide again – 'for all of this is still the same Monica Morrison you've always known and loved. I'm the same as I ever was. I am not defined by my cancer. I'm still all of me.'

Terry was never lost for words again when he visited Monica. For when he parted from his friend that warm summer afternoon and gave her a huge hug as he always did, he felt he was embracing the whole of Monica Morrison, cancer and all. But the 'golf ball' in the pancreas remained only a part of the whole – 'only a little part of me' – for that's the way it was, and that's the way Monica always wanted it to be.

Defined

I once went to visit an elderly lady in hospital.
She was one of my favourite people –
loving,
dignified,
prayerful,
sharp-witted.
It did me no end of good when I was with her.
So I went to visit her in hospital,
to see how she was,
for her good – and for mine.

But I didn't know what bed she was in,
so I asked a nurse at a desk –
professional,
efficient,
pleasant,
available –
if she could tell me where I could find
Miss Elizabeth Pinkerton,
so that I could visit her –
for her good and for mine.

The nurse was busy, her mind on other things –
bedpans,
admissions,
medicines,
coffee-breaks –
so she looked up her list on her clipboard.
'Oh, yes, I remember now.
That's the fractured hip in the end bed' –
for her good and for mine.

So I went to see the hip in the end bed –
and much more besides –
a smiling face,
a tender touch,
a lively mind,
a questioning faith –
all of Miss Elizabeth Pinkerton –
including a hip that wasn't working right –
a whole person,
for her good and for mine!

Sixteenth after Easter

Old Testament: Genesis 45:1-15
Epistle: Romans 11:1-2a, 29-32
Gospel: Matthew 15:10-28

49 What's in a name?

Ever since Millicent had got herself a dog, she'd become part of the fraternity of local dog-walkers. There was no joining fee, no constitution, no rules of behaviour, no organising committee, no membership card. You just appeared with a dog, met other dog-walkers, and you were in. All you needed was an ability to walk, and to be accompanied by some kind of four-footed animal that could pass as a dog, and you were a *bona fide* member of the dog-walkers' club.

Dog-walkers were nice people. They stopped and had a chat as your dog and their dog sniffed around each other. They greeted you with a smile on a wet morning. They compared notes with you about your respective dogs – how old, what breed, quirky temperaments, feeding regimes, and the like. They enquired after your dog's welfare when you were negotiating your trolley past theirs in the supermarket. They even recognised you when you were out walking without your dog and greeted you with a nod or a wave or a cheery hello.

But the thing that surprised Millicent the most about the dog-walkers was that none of them seemed to know – or care about – each other's names. You would meet a new dog-walker – just as Millicent had been some months before – and without saying, 'Hello, I'm Millicent,' or, 'I'm sorry, I don't know your name,' you would immediately launch into dog-related chat, and of course enquire as to the name of the animal.

Such conversations ran something like: 'Hello. Lovely animal. Had her long?'

'Oh, she's a he, and he's just under a year.'

'Oh, lovely, still a puppy really.'

'And yours? Springer Spaniel, isn't it?'

'Yes. Pure bred. Full of energy she is. She's just over seven. Second one I've had.'

'What's her name?'

'Oh, she's Corrie. We're from the Highlands, you know. It was the children's choice. And it kind of stuck. She's got a fancy kennel name too – Michelle Corrour of Corrour – but she'll always be Corrie to us. And yours?'

'Oh, a rescue-dog from the RSPCA. Fifty-seven varieties, but a lovely temperament. Mad as a brush! He's called Scooby Doo, after that daft cartoon dog. But he's just Scooby to me.'

'Oh, lovely. Good boy. Good boy. Well, must be off. Bye then. Bye, Scooby. Let's go, Corrie. Walkies! Come on, girl …'

'Bye-bye. Cheerio, Corrie. Good dog … Well Scooby, wasn't that a lovely dog? Eh? Nice friend for you. C'mon then. Race you to the park …'

So henceforth Millicent knew another dog-walker as 'Corrie's dad,' for she had no earthly idea what the owner's name really was. And of course Millicent was known in the dog-walking club as 'Scooby's mum' and she was pretty sure no one knew her real name either.

Scooby had been Millicent's salvation both during and after her bout of depression. It wasn't really that bad, but the menopause and a redundancy from work had combined to send her into a bit of a tail-spin. She'd not experienced depression before, so she didn't know what she was supposed to think or feel. Not that she was bothered at the time. She just wanted to curl up and hide, pull the duvet over her head and never see another living soul.

But she couldn't. Well, there was Scooby, wasn't there? Not that he demanded much, just feeding a couple of times a day – and, of course, regular walking.

At the start, when the depression set in, it was all Millicent could do to drag herself out of bed and take Scooby for his walk in the morning. He didn't seem to mind and was always ready to go, tail wagging, as soon as Millicent had her coat on and his leash in her hand. It was the same at lunchtime. There he was, waiting patiently at the bottom of the stair, eyes bright, twitching to get out – while Millicent felt like hell.

But what did a mad mongrel know about depression? All *he* was bothered about was that Millicent appeared at all, and that he got fed, and that walks were a regular part of his day, and that he knew who looked after him.

Millicent chooses not to think too much or too often about her bout of depression. Scooby gets longer walks now, and gets off the leash in the park too. He's still as mad as ever, and still thinks that the world is totally, fabulously, excitingly, beautifully wonderful every time Millicent puts her coat on and has his leash in her hand …

Now's she's more on top of things, Millicent chooses not to think much about her period of depression. But she does give Scooby a big hug sometimes when she remembers how important he's been for her during and since her bad spell.

And she remembers how important *that* was when, on the worst of days, she'd dragged herself to the shops to be greeted by the shopkeeper with a cheery hello. Millicent had barely enough energy to reply, but as she was leaving she heard another customer remark that 'Yon one's a bit of a grumpy so-and-so.'

'No,' the shopkeeper protested, 'she's a lovely lady.'

'Oh, d'you know her then?' the customer enquired.

'Yes, very well indeed. We're great pals. That's Scooby's mum …'

Who am I?

Who am I?
The carpenter's son from Nazareth …
Mary and Joseph's boy …
A wandering teacher …
Right?

Who am I?
Your mother was the local nurse ...
You're the double of your older sister ...
Ah kent yer faither ...
Right?

Who am I?
You ask awkward questions ...
You challenge authority ...
You're always putting your oar in ...
Right?

Who am I?
You went with the wrong crowd ...
You had it made, but now ...
You're no use any more ...
Right?

Who am I?
You took it to the end ...
You loved me for ever ...
You always kept your promises ...
Right?

Who am I?
You never gave up on me ...
You always seemed to do it right ...
You were there when others weren't ...
Right?

Who am I?
I am what I am —
Right?

Who am I?
You're all right.

Seventeenth after Easter

Old Testament: Exodus 1:8-2:10
Epistle: Romans 12:1-18
Gospel: Matthew 16:13-20

50 An invitation

'You are not, under any circumstances whatsoever, to set foot inside
Mrs Cunningham's garden' had been a clear instruction Harry could
remember for as long as he could remember anything at all. In later
childhood years, when he was able to understand instructions a little
better, the rule was expanded into 'Even if your football is to go over
the fence, you're not to go looking for it, OK?' and 'If I catch you
even *thinking* about going into Mrs Cunningham's garden, you're for
the high jump, understand?' And, of course, Harry *did* understand,
especially when his dad's instructions had put the fear of death into
him – for as long as he could remember anything at all.

When Harry was old enough he actually plucked up enough
courage to ask his dad 'Why?' After all, as far as he knew, Mrs Cunningham was quite a *nice* lady, and there were no funny stories about
her that Harry had heard. Harry's dad was surprisingly forthcoming.

'Dahlias …' he said with a grunt.

'Dahlias?' Harry replied, as politely as he could, never having
heard the word before and hoping it wasn't rude.

'Dahlias,' his dad responded, 'dahlias, prize dahlias. Don't you have
eyes? Those big flowers that she guards as if they were gold dust. And
if you set foot in yon garden, even before they start to bloom, she
goes mental. MENTAL, so she does. It's the dahlias. She's got dahlias
on the brain, so she has. No one's to go near Mrs Cunningham's
dahlias – ever. As far as Mrs Cunningham's concerned, her garden and
her dahlias are *holy ground*. OK?'

Of course it was OK, 'cause Harry's dad knew best. And Harry
had kept his eyes open. Well, Mrs Cunningham's garden was hard to
miss. It was a blaze of colour all through the summer, and even when
there were no plants growing, Mrs Cunningham was out there in all
weathers, pruning this and digging that, turning over mulch and

clearing weeds, watering beds and tidying edges. 'So these big, round, colourful flowers must be the dahlias, then,' thought Harry, and made very sure, every day, that his ball didn't stray over the fence.

One Saturday Harry was sitting on his front step reading a comic when he heard a voice. 'Harry,' it said. Harry ignored it, figuring it must be from the TV in the living room and returned to his comic. 'Harry, young Harry,' the voice persisted, and Harry realised it was coming from *outside* the house and not from the inside. He looked up from his comic, listened for a bit, heard no more, and got on with his reading. 'Harry! Coo-eee! Harry, over here.' This time, the voice couldn't be ignored.

So, laying his comic on the step beside him, Harry stood up and took a tentative step in the direction he thought the voice was coming from – the fence between his garden and Mrs Cunningham's. He was peering and wondering … when he was almost scared out of his wits by the large figure of Mrs Cunningham, complete with green overalls and wearing a fetching straw hat, jumping up from behind her border-display of vibrant blooms. Seeing Harry's surprise and obvious discomfort, Mrs Cunningham let out a roar of laughter such as Harry had never heard before. 'Ah ha! Gotcha! You never expected that, eh?' she guffawed. She was right! Harry *hadn't* expected that at all! But he didn't know how to say so. All he knew was that Mrs Cunningham was talking … from her garden … behind her prize dahlias …

When Mrs Cunningham's laughter had subsided to a gentle chuckle, she leant on her rake and smiled at Harry. 'Hello, young man. Nothing to do? Well, I need an extra pair of hands with my dahlias today. D'you want to come over?' she offered. Harry couldn't believe his ears – or his eyes, for that matter. Here was Mrs Cunningham … from behind her prize dahlias … asking him over.

'But my dad …' Harry stammered.

'Uh huh?' encouraged Mrs Cunningham.

'He says I've not …' he stuttered.

'What?' the gardener asked.

'Not to … dahlias …' was all that Harry could get out. Mrs Cunningham smiled.

'Oh, I know that,' she said reassuringly. 'And I would *chase* you if you set foot in here uninvited.' Harry nodded, not knowing what else to do. 'But I've had a word with your dad and it's OK if I *invite* you, because I'll know what you're up to, for you'll be with me all the time, never out of my sight, young man.' Harry nodded some more. 'So, what's it to be? Want to come over?' Another speechless nod from Harry. Mrs Cunningham smiled again. 'Well then, come round to the back gate. Wait there and I'll let you in. Just for a while, mind, because I don't want your family to think you've got lost. Come on then, quick as you like …'

Harry spent half an hour with Mrs Cunningham and her dahlias. He'd thought they were pretty good and bright enough when he could see them from across the fence. But up close … Wow! And he learned how the dahlia had been named after a Swedish botanist and why they were called 'Georgia' in Germany; he was asked to repeat names such as 'Davenport Sunrise' and 'Aurora's Kiss'; he heard about Mrs Cunningham's success at the local flower show with her Waterlily and Cactus varieties. And all the time Mrs Cunningham made Harry feel very special indeed.

When Harry's dad came home later in the afternoon, Harry was back sitting on the front step reading his comic. 'You're looking pretty pleased with yourself,' his dad remarked. 'Good comic, then?'

'Oh it's OK,' Harry replied.

'So why the grin, then, eh?' his dad persisted.

'No reason,' Harry replied. But as his dad shrugged and slipped past him into the hallway, Harry added in a voice barely above a whisper, 'apart from the fact that today I've been standing on holy ground.'

Holy ground

If Moses stood before a bush that never burned away,
And knew he was on holier ground than any other day,
And heard a voice that called for him to be what he could be ...
I wonder – what is holy ground for me?

Perhaps it's when I go to church and holy thoughts ascend;
Or maybe in the presence of a very special friend;
Or taking in a sunset far across a glassy sea ...
Pray tell me – where is holy ground for me?

And when I'm lost in music, and my mind's on higher things;
Or when I read of saints of old, and know my spirit sings;
Where peace has been established, and harmony's the key ...
I ask you – is this holy ground for me?

It is! And when you doubt yourself and wonder what's going on,
Just live within the moment, and know new truth will dawn.
This wonder, peace and beauty are the gifts I guarantee.
You're standing here, on holy ground, for me!

Eighteenth after Easter

Old Testament: Exodus 3:1-15
Epistle: Romans 12:9-21
Gospel: Matthew 16:21-28

51 A red-letter day

The day the Queen came to visit the factory was a red-letter day for everyone – apart, that is, from the boys in the Labs who'd decided they wanted nothing to do with the whole affair.

After all, the Labs were stuck in the basement of the factory complex, and there was no intention of the Queen being invited to visit *there*. And when the Lab-boys heard that everywhere the Queen was to visit in the factory was to be done up with a fresh coat of paint, new pictures on the walls and replacement carpet-treads on the stairs, and that *their* pleas for new equipment and some redecoration for their Labs would fall on deaf ears once again, 'boycott the Queen's visit' was the order of the day in the factory Labs.

Not that there was much boycotting to be done. For the boys in the Labs it was just another ordinary working day – samples to be tested, reports to be written, quality assurance to be sorted. The Queen and her entourage would come and go while their work went on uninterrupted. Or so they hoped ...

For the rest of the factory, however, the day of the Queen's visit was far from being just another ordinary working day. The Queen was officially to open the new production area. The new wing of the factory had been in use for some weeks and was, therefore, still in fairly pristine condition. But that wasn't to stop the place being spruced up to ensure that the Queen saw it at its best. (Who was it that said the Queen probably thinks that the whole world smells of fresh paint, because that's always what's around her when she visits anywhere?)

But the sprucing up of the new wing was nothing to the make-over given to the other areas the Queen was going to walk through. The whole of the front foyer was redecorated and the floor tiles replaced. The square of grass outside the front door, which had a brown track diagonally across it where the workmen who were clocking in would take a short-cut rather than follow the path, was completely dug up and re-laid with fresh turf. The passageway from the foyer to the factory floor was redecorated and hung with fancy paintings. The lift which was to take the Queen from the factory floor to the next level up for the short walk to the new wing was carpeted and wallpapered. And, in the lift, over the '2' button for the second floor, had been fitted a white button with red lettering stuck on – well, it was to be a 'red-letter day 'wasn't it? – which boldly proclaimed that this was the 'UP' direction for the Queen's visit.

All was well. When the Queen arrived, the boys in the Labs – who were having nothing to do with the whole affair, remember – just got on with their work, only remarking when the given time of ten o' clock arrived and they could hear the faint cheers of the crowd outside, 'That'll be her, then,' and got on with their jobs.

All was well – or, at least, all *should* have been well if the managing director had *really* understood what a 'red-letter' day was, or had been properly briefed, or was able to work out that red lettering on one of the lift buttons had some significance to the overall success of the royal occasion. But he was either stupid, or couldn't read, or was overcome with nerves … for it was in the lift that things went disastrously wrong.

The royal party had moved as planned through the foyer – did the Queen notice the new turf on her way in? – along the corridor to the factory floor – any remarks about the nice paintings? – arriving at the lift at other end of the factory floor, the door wide open to welcome the dignitaries. Now, the managing director will *probably* tell you he was distracted, but the truth of the matter is that no one had told him they'd put a new red-lettered sticker on the '2' button in the lift. So when he looked at the buttons, he couldn't find the '2' for the second floor. What did 'UP' mean? Was that all the way to the top? Where had the '2' gone? There was a '1', but did that mean they'd changed to American numbering in deference to the US ownership of the factory?

Why the MD pressed 'B', therefore, no one but he can tell you. But press 'B' he did, and the lift, unsurprisingly, went 'down' and not 'up'. And down, of course, was to the basement – and the Labs.

The boys in the Labs insisted later that this was just a devious way of the factory ensuring that they couldn't boycott the Queen's visit altogether. The MD would insist it was nothing of the sort, and that it was just an honest mistake. And the Queen? Well, what she made of the scene that confronted her when the lift reached 'B' and the doors opened has never been recorded. She *must* have seen Johnny sitting in the corner with his feet up having a mug of tea and reading his paper. She *must* have heard Bill's 'Oh, bugger' as a beaker slipped out of his hands and smashed on the floor. She *must* have noticed Raymond wiping his hands on what had once been a white lab-coat and adding to the multicoloured stains down the front. She *must* have smelled the pungent stench of the chemicals in the vat Wally was carrying to the sink. But she never said.

She was probably too busy wondering why the MD was frantically pressing the red-letter-day button on the lift panel and hoping against hope that the doors would close quickly and the royal entourage could be taken away from a scene of such chaos and mess.

'That'll be the Queen, then,' Wally commented after the lift had gone.

'Probably wanted to see some *real* people at work,' Raymond chirped.

'Maybe we can get some new equipment out of them if we promise not to tell the story,' Bill exclaimed.

'There's a horse running in the 2.30 at Haydock Park this afternoon that might be worth a few quid. It's called "Red Letter Day",' Johnny offered, as he chucked his paper on the table and got back to work with the rest of the boys in the Labs.

Special

I always knew it was a special day
when my neighbour baked a cake.
I knew she'd baked a cake
because she always brought me a piece –
well, living alone,
and never having baked anything in my life,
she knew I appreciated home baking.
And I would always ask her,
'What's the cake for this time?
What's the special day?'
And, over the years,
I'd had a share in family occasions,
and anniversaries,
and homecomings,
and leavings,
and celebrations for coming back again,
and big birthdays,
and little birthdays,
and retirements,
and babies being born,
and Scotland winning the grand-slam at rugby,
and Labour winning an election.
I would always ask her.
And I always got my share.
And I always enjoyed my cake.

Then, one day, my neighbour baked a cake
and brought me a piece,
and I asked her, as usual,
'What's the cake for this time?
What's the special day?'

And she said, 'Nothing.'
And I asked, 'Nothing?'
And she said, 'Well, nothing *really* ...'
And I said she'd have to explain.
And she said that she'd just felt
she should bake a cake and share it with me,
because she liked being my friend –
and it was good to be alive!
And I said, 'Oh!'
So we shared my neighbour's cake –
and we both agreed it was a very nice cake,
because it was shared by friends
on a *very* special day.

Nineteenth after Easter

Old Testament: Exodus 12:1-14
Epistle: Romans 13:8-14
Gospel: Matthew 18:15-20

52 Revenge

Andrea was planning revenge. On the third afternoon of end-of-school detention, various devilish plots were being hatched in her mind. After all, revenge was *necessary*. Nearly a week's worth of detentions deserved the very worst revenge.

She knew she hadn't broken the nursery class window. It wasn't her fault that she'd come round the corner of the playground just in time to hear the breaking of glass and to see all the other kids scarper as if their lives depended on it. Andrea wasn't quick enough to take stock of the situation. She was just standing there when she heard The Voice. 'Andrea Jackson! FREEZE, girl. Don't you dare move a muscle. I want to know what all this is about.'

The Voice belonged to the Head. And when Mrs Wallace, head-teacher of Andrea's primary school, used The Voice you certainly knew it. Andrea froze as The Voice had commanded. What else could she do? And anyway, she had nothing to be frightened of. *She* knew she hadn't broken the nursery class window, and it was just her bad luck that she'd come round the corner of the playground in time to hear the breaking of glass and to see all the other kids scarper as if their lives depended on it.

And that's what she told Mrs Wallace when she was interrogated in The Voice's office a few minutes later. But in between an angry head-teacher's rantings about 'There was no one else there …', 'Just as well the wee ones had gone home …', 'You're just trouble, you are …', and the like, Andrea's protests fell on deaf ears.

Things got worse the following day when she was 'grassed up' – falsely, as Andrea knew well enough – by all the previous day's scarpering kids. Lies such as, 'It wisnae me, Miss …', 'On my way home, Mrs Wallace …', 'Must have been Andrea Jackson …', and 'Couldn't have been anyone else, Miss …', had stitched her up good and proper. She'd tried to protest her innocence, of course. But then she'd had a 'record of misdemeanours' – so The Voice reminded her when sentence was being passed. It was clearly a case of 'give a dog a bad name'. So it was four days' worth of detentions. And that was plenty time to plan a devilish revenge.

In the midst of her rantings Mrs Wallace had let slip that chief among Andrea's accusers was Patsy Sherwin. 'I might have guessed,' Andrea had thought darkly. And so an unsuspecting Patsy Sherwin became the focus of Andrea's plotting.

Taking the path through the corner of the wood was always the quickest way home. If 'home time' had been as per normal, the path would have been filled with talkative, excited kids on their way back from school. But this was the third night Andrea had walked home alone after her detention – all the more time to plot the necessary retribution.

She almost missed seeing the dog. It was the whimpering that attracted her attention. If she'd been with the other kids, no one would have noticed. But, faint though the whimpering was, and being on her own with no other distractions, it made Andrea stop in her tracks. Following the distressing sounds, Andrea quickly located the source of the cries as she came across a little scruffy grey mongrel dog all tangled up in the thorn bushes. The more the little dog struggled to free itself, the more trapped it became and the more distressed were its cries.

It wasn't easy for Andrea to free the unfortunate beast. Pretty soon there were scratches across the backs of her hands, both her knees were muddy and there was a snag in the sleeve of her jumper. But, the rescue job done, Andrea gathered the scruffy dog in her arms and tried to work out what to do next. She was sure she recognised the animal, but she couldn't remember from where. Given that the little mite was trembling in her arms and still whimpering – though not so loudly as before – she decided to take it home and ask her mother's advice.

Her mother, of course, was all over the sad specimen with kindness when Andrea arrived home. Carefully checking the dog for major injuries and finding none, she sat with the animal on her knee for a while, stroking it gently, until its shivering stopped and the whimpering died away.

It was only then that Andrea's mother dropped the bombshell. 'D'you know, I think this is the Sherwins' dog, from over the back, in The Terrace, Patsy Sherwin's family, you know, that big girl who's in your class. I think we should take it round. C'mon. We'll go together. After all, you're the one who should get thanked.'

It was the second time that week that Andrea Jackson tried to protest. And it was the second time that week when someone refused to listen. So when Andrea and her mum were standing in the Sherwins' kitchen a few minutes later, and Patsy Sherwin was crying because she'd got her dog back safely, Andrea didn't know where to look or what to think.

On the Friday, the final afternoon of her detention, Andrea was still planning revenge. Various devilish plots were being hatched in her mind. After all, revenge was *necessary*. A week's worth of detentions deserved the very worst revenge. *She* knew she hadn't broken the nursery class window. It wasn't her fault that she'd come round the corner of the playground just in time to hear the breaking of glass and to see all the other kids scarper as if their lives depended on it.

But, somehow, a whimpering dog and an insistent mother and Patsy Sherwin in tears kept working their way into her thoughts as well. Revenge was *necessary*, after all. After all ... after all ... revenge was *necessary* ... or was it?

Sweetness

'Revenge is sweet' the wise have often said.
But not as sweet,
And not as neat
As it would be,
For them and me
If they had found forgiving words instead.

Twentieth after Easter

Old Testament: Exodus 14:19-31
Epistle: Romans 14:1-12
Gospel: Matthew 18:21-35

53 Bernie and the chores

Bernie was slow. There was no getting away from it, he was slow in everything – he thought slowly, for watching him work something out was like waiting for the mechanisms of Big Ben to come slowly round to the chiming stage; he spoke slowly, and occasionally listening to Bernie was like hearing a record playing slightly slower than it was meant to; and he walked slowly, his lumbering gait causing great frustration for anyone with him who was in the tiniest bit of a hurry. For Bernie was not to be hurried – in anything.

The group in the Adventure Camp that week understood Bernie. In fact, there were others there too who were not that much different. It was a week for different people with different needs learning from each other as they shared community together. Bernie had been before. He knew the form. He was delighted to be back, and the others were pleased to have him around too.

That's why the camp leaders were taken aback on the second day to hear a great rumpus in the common room, and even more surprised to find Bernie in the middle of it all – for Bernie and rumpus simply didn't go together. But here he was, up to high-doh, ranting and raving with the best of them. When the leaders got closer, they could see that the rumpus centred on Bernie and Rachel, one of the other kids from Bernie's Day Centre. And the focus of their attention appeared to be a sweeping brush. They both had a firm grip on the brush, Bernie with the handle and Rachel with the sweeping end, and neither was going to let go. 'Give it to me. It's mine,' Bernie was yelling. 'No it's not, it's my turn for the brush,' Rachel was screaming even louder.

Eventually the leaders managed to separate the feuding pair and a semblance of order was restored. It took ages to figure out what had happened – Rachel was as slow as Bernie – and there was still a fair bit of name-calling thrown in. But it became clear that the argument was over chores. Bernie had been on sweeping-the-common-room chore the day before, and now it was Rachel's turn. Bernie was to be peeling spuds, and he didn't fancy that, so he wanted to do the sweeping again.

'Why do you want to do the sweeping so much?' one of the leaders asked Bernie once he'd calmed down. 'Because I *always* do the sweeping,' Bernie replied. 'It's my job at the Day Centre. Everyone knows that. Mrs Buchanan says I'm good at it, so I do it every day. Sweeping's my job, not Rachel's … And I'm no good at peeling spuds.'

So, after much explaining and compromising, a deal was struck – Bernie would do the sweeping every day and Rachel would be a temporary 'Mrs Buchanan' and make sure it was done right. And that's the way the week continued, with Rachel and Bernie working together, and there was never another rumpus.

On the final night at the camp there was a tradition of thank-yous and presentations to be worked through – like 'appetite of the week' for the camper who enjoyed their food the most – and there were any number of contenders for that award; 'snorer of the camp' – one really noisy sleeper walked away with that one; and a few more. When it was done, the leaders were about to suggest to the whole crew that it was time for bed because there was an early start in the morning, when they noticed that Rachel and a few of the other kids had disappeared – into the kitchen area they discovered. But within minutes they'd returned and announced that they had a final award to present – it was 'common-room-sweeper-upper-of-the-decade'. The award was a sweeping-brush wrapped in tin foil with a big rosette at the top, and it was to go to – Bernie.

Bernie – now *aka* 'sweeper-upper-of-the-decade' – carried his silver brush all the way home the following day. It never left his side. Bernie was slow, but he knew what he was good at, and thankfully all the others knew that too. 'Sweeper-upper-of-the-decade'? The leaders weren't so sure. They reckoned they would have made Bernie 'sweeper-upper-of-the-century'!

I am what I am

'I am what I am'
God said once.
I never really understood that –
too obscure for me, I'm afraid.

Until I met a man who was slow,
and I wanted to define him,
to label him on my terms,
within my understanding;
for it would be much easier for me that way.

One day he said to me,
in his frustration and my confusion,
'I am what I am,'
and went on with his sweeping –
slowly and deliberately,
being what he was and what he had to be.

So now I understand a little clearer
who he is and how he sees himself.

'I am what I am.'
Isn't that me too?

Oh … and thanks to a man
who stopped me labelling him as slow,
I'm beginning to understand a little more clearly
what God was on about.

Twenty-first after Easter

Old Testament: Exodus 16:2–15
Epistle: Phillippians 1:21–30
Gospel: Matthew 20:1–16

54 A good clear-out

Sylvia's flat was always tidy. It was a first home for her and Rodney since their marriage the previous year, and she took great pride in their little pad.

Sylvia's flat was always tidy, and slowly but surely she was getting Rodney into her way of working – no socks left on the bedroom floor; supper dishes washed and put away after the meal; newspapers and magazines tidied away in the rack by the sofa – and Rodney actually seemed to be genuinely delighted.

Sylvia's flat was always tidy, just in case her mother-in-law called unexpectedly. It wasn't that Rodney's mum was difficult – not at all. She was lovely, and always seemed happy to visit, and never *appeared* to be looking around in a critical fashion … not like her friend Ruth's mother-in-law who *always* ran her finger along the window-sill of her house in the suburbs to check for dust before she sat down. Yeuch! But, nonetheless, Sylvia did like to make a good impression, and though she knew it was all in her head, she liked it when her mother-in-law seemed pleased at the way a new wife was looking after her son.

Yes, Sylvia's flat was always tidy – apart, that is, from the drawer in her bedside cabinet … That, she would confess only to herself, was her guilty secret, for it was the place in her tidy flat where she stuffed things that had no other place of their own. When she was tidying, she'd come across something that just seemed out of place, making a room look cluttered. So it was tucked into a jeans' pocket or laid in the hall and, if it was small enough, would find its way into the drawer of Sylvia's bedside cabinet until a permanent place for it could be found. The trouble was, a permanent place seldom appeared, and with lots of things largely forgotten about once they'd been put away, the drawer in the bedside cabinet became more and more jammed full of stuff.

Sylvia knew that well enough, for on the two occasions she'd been to the drawer recently she was surprised – and not a little disturbed – to discover how much stuff was there. The first occasion had been the previous Wednesday when she needed some drawing-pins to fix on the kitchen pin-board a picture her nephew had painted in his nursery class. She *knew* the packet of drawing-pins was in the drawer in her bedside cabinet, because she distinctly remembered stuffing it in there a week or so ago. But the more she rummaged in her drawer, the more untidy it became; and the more untidy it became, the more frustrated she got; and the more frustrated she got, the less patience she had to search for the drawing-pins. So her nephew's cherished painting never made the pin-board, and ended up being jammed into the space between the frame of the kitchen door and the wall.

The second occasion was just that morning when she was tidying away the cards from Rodney's birthday. She didn't want to throw them out – after all, it was the first birthday they'd shared together in their new home. But there was no place for the cards, except … but when she opened the drawer of her bedside cabinet, there was no *way* there was space for even a leaf of writing paper far less a bundle of precious cards.

Sylvia had sat down on the bed and cried. She was angry with herself. What kind of wife was she? Could she not keep a proper home? Surely she could be better organised than this? By the time her tears were over, Sylvia had made a decision. The drawer in her bedside cabinet had to have a good clear-out!

And that's why, with newspaper spread over the kitchen table, Sylvia was sorting through a mountain of stuff for most of the afternoon. There were things there she'd forgotten she had – like the packet of post-it notes all in different colours; the letter opener she'd got from Auntie Vi; the phone number of an old friend she'd promised she'd call and never had; the medal from the 10K charity run she'd taken part in just after her wedding. Each one was carefully laid aside, grouped with other things that seemed to go together and, finally, carefully returned to the drawer. Each one now had its own place, and she'd know where to find it the next time. And, of course, she found the drawing-pins as well, and it wasn't long before a child's colourful painting was properly displayed on the pin-board for all to see.

There were also things she put to one side to be looked at more carefully later – the little white Bible she'd got as a gift at her christening, with her name in italic script inside; the invitation-card to a Royal Garden Party that Rodney had got through his work, with its memories of a very special day; the Order of Service from her grandmother's funeral.

But it was the things Sylvia threw out that made the exercise most worthwhile – the menu from her last work's Christmas night out (not a good memory at all!) – into the bin bag it went; a bag of rubber bands that were so perished with age they were no use to anyone – into the rubbish bag as well; and the letter from Jackie … *that* letter, that *horrible* letter from someone Sylvia had always thought of as a friend, with its criticism and nastiness. Sylvia cried when she read it again, recalling the unfairness and the unfounded allegations, the way she'd written back to defend herself, hoping for an apology that had never come. Why had she kept such a bad thing? Why would she want to keep it any longer? So, with passion, anger, and an overwhelming sense of relief, Sylvia tore up the letter into tiny pieces, and sprinkled them with relish into the bag with the rest of the rubbish. The letter was gone, thrown away. There was no more damage it could do!

After a while, the clear-out was done. What had its place, had its place; what was to be looked at later would have its time; and what needed to be thrown out was chucked away. And, quite remarkably, the drawer had *much* more space in it than it had had before, for, with the sorting and the discarding, there was room for lots more – and Rodney's birthday cards were tucked away safely too …

Sylvia's flat was always tidy. And now that the drawer in her bedside cabinet was tidy too, she'd decided that every now and again she'd have another clear-out – and maybe it wouldn't be as much of a chore next time around.

Angry

I get angry with myself
for making all those wonderful promises
about doing things right,
and sorting things out,
and being better than I've been before.
I need to get angry with myself sometimes,
provided it helps me focus,
and keeps me on my toes,
and doesn't destroy me altogether.

I get angry with other people
for not being what I think they should be,
and doing things right,
and sorting themselves out,
and making things better than they've been before.
I need to get angry with folk sometimes.
It makes me feel better for one thing,
But I hope I don't stand on too many toes
and destroy people altogether.

I get angry with God,
for not being the God I need him to be,
and doing things right,
and sorting things the way I want them to be,
and being better for me than he's been before.

I need to get angry with God sometimes.
And God, it helps me with my focus,
and helps me sort out my faith,
and, thankfully, doesn't destroy what God and I do together.

Twenty-second after Easter

Old Testament: Exodus 17:1-7
Epistle: Philippians 2:1-13
Gospel: Matthew 21:23-32

55 Thou shalt not

Uncle John was an expert on the Bible – or so he was always telling Edward when the subject came up. Uncle John always had Sunday lunch at Edward's house and so he was always there when Edward and his parents came home from church. Uncle John never went to church himself, Edward had noticed, so he must have learned all about the Bible long, *long* ago. But, no matter. Edward enjoyed his chats with his uncle John before lunch each week, because, as Uncle John said himself, he was an expert on the Bible.

'Did you know that King David rode a motorbike? It says so in the Bible,' Edward's uncle had announced when Edward had been telling him that his Sunday-school class had been learning about King David and his exploits.

'Did he, Uncle John?' Edward had responded. 'And where does it say that?'

'Oh, didn't you know that the Bible says, "And the sound of David's Triumph was heard in all the land."?'

'Oh,' had been Edward's only response. He *presumed* that a Triumph must be a type of motorbike and took a mental note to check this out later – as well as the truth of Uncle John's statement.

'Did you know that Moses was tough on his employees? It says so in the Bible,' Edward had been informed when he'd been telling his uncle John about the Children of Israel crossing the Red Sea.

'How was that, Uncle John?' Edward asked, not remembering any reference to Moses being a hard task-master at all.

'Oh, didn't you know that the Bible says, "And Moses stretched out his staff."?' And Edward decided some day to call his uncle John's bluff and get him to say which part of the Bible he was *actually* quoting from.

Sometimes Uncle John would volunteer information before

258 Welcoming each wonder

Edward asked for it. 'Did you know there are no bees in the Bible?'

'No bees, Uncle John? And how did you find *that* out?'

'Well,' came the reply, 'it must be true, because there's a book in the Bible called "nae-hum", got it? Nahum! OK? And if you're not *sure* it's true, you'll find it's confirmed by another book called "nae-hum-either"? Nehemiah! No? Oh, well, never mind ...' But Edward *did* mind because he wasn't exactly sure that his uncle John's knowledge of the Bible was for real.

The chance came one Sunday when Edward's Sunday-school class had been hearing about the Ten Commandments. And so Edward had a BIG question for his uncle John. 'Uncle John,' he began, 'do you know about the Ten Commandments?'

'Certainly do,' was the immediate response. And laying down his Sunday paper Uncle John continued, 'But did you know there were originally thirteen?' This wasn't what Edward had expected *at all*.

'Thirteen?' he muttered, his animation quickly draining away.

'Yes, thirteen,' responded the erudite biblical scholar. 'You see, Moses and God had a debate about what was going to be kept in and what might be left out. "Thou shalt not covet" was only kept in because Moses made a deal with God to drop another three.'

'Did he?' Edward was now wide-eyed. 'So what ones were left out, then?'

'Well, God decided that "Thou shalt not moan about school" could go, and then he agreed to leave out "Thou shalt not leave thy bedroom in a terrible mess", and Moses got him to ditch "Thou shalt not complain when thou art told to eat thy greens" – because he reckoned that mums could usually deal with all of these anyway and so they didn't really need to take up room in the commandments – so there were only ten left, the Ten Commandments we have today.'

That was enough for Edward. This couldn't *possibly* be true. And anyway, how could Uncle John *know* all this if it wasn't actually IN THE BIBLE ... So Edward decided this was the time ... And, without even responding to his uncle's thirteen-to-ten story of

Moses and the Commandments, he blurted out, 'Well then … what's … what's "covet" mean if it's so important to God? Eh? What does "covet" mean, Uncle John?'

It was Uncle John's time for silence. He'd detected that his young nephew might actually be seeing through his jokes and his bluff and bluster – *and* the fact that he was not the biblical expert he made himself out to be. This seemed like a serious question, and maybe for once it needed a more serious answer …

'Covet, eh? Covet,' he mused. 'Now, let's see. OK, sit down while I tell you.' And with Edward cross-legged on the floor, his uncle John began. 'Now, d'you remember King David?'

'Yes, Uncle John, the one with the motorbike,' Edward replied.

'Yes, that's the one. Well, David was very fond of his Triumph. Indeed, it was the most important thing he had. It was just the best ever. No one had ever had a Triumph like his in all the land. But, you see, it was *so* special, and there wasn't another one like it, that other people got jealous, very jealous indeed. Green-eyed with jealousy, they were. *They* wanted a Triumph motorbike too. So they plotted and schemed. They planned and organised. And one night, they broke into David's shed and they stole his Triumph. And when David woke up in the morning and found that his Triumph had gone, he was furious. And he ranted and raved and shouted and swore. Not very nice behaviour for a king at all …'

Edward was transfixed. 'What happened next, Uncle John,' he asked encouragingly, desperate to hear the rest of the story.

'Well, nothing,' was the reply. 'You see, the plotters couldn't use David's motorbike, because if the sound of the Triumph was heard in the land again then David would know it was *his* Triumph and there would be a big fight while he got it back. So the plotters had to keep the Triumph hidden away in a garage. And the sound of the Triumph was never heard at all. And, d'you see, it's all about "covet". If they hadn't coveted the motorbike in the first place, all this would never have happened. D'you see? Being jealous isn't a good thing. So God told Moses that one of the Ten Commandments had to be "Thou shalt not covet", d'you see? Thou shalt not covet a king's motorbike, or *anything*, d'you see?'

Edward wasn't sure that he saw at all … But at least he knew that this coveting business wasn't good, and that the ten – or thirteen – commandments were important. But he wondered, just for a moment, if it might be OK – just a little bit – to covet his uncle John's knowledge of the Bible … Because Uncle John was an expert in the Bible after all, wasn't he? And Edward would *very* much like to be the same.

The almost-commandments

And God got himself organised,
and pulled his thoughts together,
and said, 'Now listen.
I am the Lord your God, and I know best.
I sorted things out for you, didn't I?
so that you could escape the clutches of the dastardly Pharaoh.
So the least you can do is to pay attention when I'm talking, OK?
So, listen up!
Here's the deal.
Write this down.
You shall have no other gods before me, OK?'
And Moses nodded, and wrote down,
You shall have no other gods before me.
'You got that?
So, number two,
You shall not make any thing at all into a god you can worship,
because you're for it if you do, OK?'
You shall not make any thing at all into a god you can worship,
or you're in trouble.

Note to self: check out whether large-screen TV is included,
or else try to watch in secret.
'That took too long to write down.

Quicker next time, please.

So, number three ... Ready?

You shall not take the name of the Lord your God in vain, OK?'
You shall not take the name of the Lord your God in vain ...
Oh fiddle.
That means that everyone's going to have to be on their toes
with their language and dubious jokes, and stuff.
Note to self: Is it OK if something is just blurted out
in the heat of the moment?
'Come on man, keep up.

I haven't got all day.

There's a long one to write down now:

Honour the Sabbath day and keep it holy, OK?'
Honour the Sabbath day and keep it holy ...
Goodness, he's going on a bit, isn't he?
I'll just keep it simple.
As long as people feel holy enough, that'll do.
The explanation stuff he's going on about doesn't really matter.
You can't have too many rules or make them too wordy ...
'That's better.

You finished that one quickly enough.

OK, we're getting on fine.

Now, number five:

Honour your father and your mother – that way, you live longer,
OK?'
Honour your father and your mother eh?
Even when your dad's a right sod – like mine, eh?
Mmmm, I'm not so sure ...
Note to self: check it out with Aaron

to get his take on this parent business …
'Now, four short ones.
But don't assume that because they're short
they're any less important.
Six: Don't kill, OK?'
Don't kill …
But what about Afghanistan and stuff, eh?
'Seven: Don't commit adultery, OK?'
Don't commit adultery …
Damn!
'Eight: Don't steal, OK?'
Don't steal …
I wonder if that's a blanket ban, or can we get away with little things,
like paperclips, and mileage allowances, and photocopying,
or does everything have to count?
'And, nine: No fibbing about your neighbour, OK?'
No fibbing …
But my neighbour next-door-but-one
did the dirty on me, only last week …
Is it not OK to get my own back, eh?
'Now, you'll be pleased that I'm keeping it to ten,
so, if you've been counting,
you'll know I'm nearly done.
But this one matters a lot, right?
So, last but not least:
Don't give in to jealousy, OK?
Now, I've got a long list of possibilities here …'
No jealousy …
Piffle! Who's he kidding? Jealousy's natural, isn't it?
He's asking the impossible …
Maybe I can miss this one, or maybe one of the others.
It'll be hard keeping them all, eh?

OK, maybe he'll be happy enough with nine out of ten,
or a 50% pass-mark,
That would do, wouldn't it?
'So, got all of that?
I'll get you to read them back so I know you've got them all down.
So now I've got myself organised,
and pulled my thoughts together,
it's up to you.
Now listen.
I'm the Lord your God and I know best.
I sorted things out for you.
So the least you can do is to listen to me, OK?
There's no wriggling out of this stuff, believe me.'
Oh?
'No deciding which ones matter more than the others, OK?'
Damn!
'Now, scoot.
And make sure the people know what I've got you to write down.'

Twenty-third after Easter

Old Testament: Exodus 20:1-4, 7-9, 12-20
Epistle: Philippians 3:4b-14
Gospel: Matthew 21:33-46

56 A reasonably high score

Philip liked weddings. He hadn't been in the ministry long, but he'd come to realise that it wasn't all going to be a bed of roses. He was coping well enough and, of course, learning all the time. And he'd worked out pretty early on that he needed some good things to compensate for some of the more difficult circumstances he had to deal with. Weddings were good things, and while he didn't have all that many planned for the year ahead, there were enough to give him some good events to look forward to.

Philip already had a few weddings 'under his belt' and, barring the odd nervous moment, they'd all been completed without any major hitches. He almost always went along to the wedding meal after the ceremony. He was a single man and, to be frank, a nice sit-down meal on a Friday or Saturday evening was a meal he didn't have to prepare himself. He wasn't much of a cook and a good, substantial spread wasn't to be laughed at. He didn't stay for the dancing afterwards, though he usually hung about long enough so that the people didn't think he'd just come for the meal and nothing else – though, as he knew well enough, that was *exactly* the truth of things.

There were things about going to the wedding receptions that Philip didn't like much (though even those could be tolerated if the wedding meal was worth it!). There always seemed to be a loud uncle who would try to ply him with drink, or a bride's father who would compliment him on the wedding service and announce that 'if all the ministers were like you, son, the churches would be packed – and I might even go myself. (*'Aye, right!' Philip would muse, and smile benignly …*) There was occasionally a maudlin aunt who got all sentimental and wanted to pour out her troubles. There was always the necessary polite conversation which had to be coped with at the top table – trying to chat with a giggly bridesmaid, or the groom's mother, or the like, when anything approaching meaningful dialogue was clearly limited.

None of that, however, could diminish Philip's enjoyment of weddings. And apart from the church service and the free meal, the part he enjoyed most was when he was invited to 'say a few words'. Such invitations were seldom pre-planned, and it was often over the coffee at the end of the meal that the bride's father would lean across and ask if he would offer a few closing remarks. Philip was always up for that and, like most of those in his profession, always had a few well chosen jokes or funny stories with which to amuse the company. And anyway, the 'company' was usually drunk enough by that time that Philip could have recited the phonebook in a moderately amusing way and got a good laugh out of it.

There was always a lot of hanging about at weddings. Philip usually knew very few people – often just the bride and groom – and apart from the occasional drunk uncle or maudlin aunt bending his ear, he usually spent a lot of time on his own. That's when he would seek out the function manager, or the head waitress, or the piper, or the photographer's assistant, and enjoy a few minutes engaged in reasonable conversation with reasonable people. Philip liked that.

The function manager at the Crown Hotel was good value. The first wedding Philip was involved with there was a fairly typical affair, and Philip enjoyed his conversation with Bob Valentine, who was clearly a wedding aficionado *extraordinaire*. Pretty soon they were swapping stories of this wedding and that, Bob Valentine enjoying offering the young clergyman some hints and tips about what to watch out for at future events.

In time, with the meal about to start, Bob Valentine had to see to his managerial duties, and Philip resigned himself to the good (the chicken breast in a white wine sauce) and the bad (a taciturn bridesmaid sitting next to him) of the wedding meal. But Philip was feeling good and so, when Bob Valentine whispered to him over coffee that the bride's father would like him to say something at the end of the speeches, and that Bob would give him the signal, Philip scribbled down a few notes on the back of the wedding menu in preparation for his turn. And when his time came, it was, 'Ladies and gentlemen. Pray silence for the Reverend, who will offer us a few words.' There was muted applause. Philip was undaunted. He knew what he could do.

The short speech went OK. With a few well chosen words, Philip's best joke, a quality of delivery which was vastly superior to the mumbling of the Best Man and the blue stories of the bride's father, Philip knew he had rounded off the proceedings in excellent style. He only spoke for a few minutes, but when he sat down he was greeted with – well, it was what could only be described as *thunderous* applause. There were cheers and whistles, some folk were standing and applauding loudly. The people at the nearest table were doubled over with laughter. Philip was chuffed, *very* chuffed. He veritably *glowed* with pride. He knew his speech had been good – not *that* good, but he was prepared to take any accolades that were going. This was *exactly* why Philip enjoyed weddings.

The applause and cheering went on and on, and Philip decided he should get to his feet again and take a bow. This was going to be a moment to remember. So he stood up and smiled broadly at the assembled company. It was then he realised that people weren't actually looking at *him,* but were directing their gaze, and therefore the focus of their applause, somewhere over his left shoulder. Philip slowly turned round, and there he saw Bob Valentine, who'd obviously gone unnoticed round the tables at some point during the meal and removed some of the table numbers, and who was now standing behind the minister, his arms above his head, and scoring Philip's speech at 5.6!

When the meal was over, Philip had a word with Bob Valentine. Resisting the temptation to enquire why he hadn't got 'a perfect six' for his speech, Philip asked the grinning function manager whether he did this for *all* the ministers and priests at all the receptions. 'Of course not,' Bob Valentine replied. 'It's only for those who can take it, Reverend, only those who can take it!' Philip smiled back, and he knew he had yet another reason why he enjoyed weddings, and was more than happy with his reasonably high score.

All right?

So, how did I do today?
Did I get it right?
Was my score high enough for you?
Was I close to perfection this time?

You did fine, just fine …

No, really, you can be honest …
How did I do?
Pretty good, no?
Better than last time, eh?

No, really, you did all right …

All right?
Is that all?
Come on, you can't be serious.
All right?
I tried *so* hard.
Surely …
Surely, more than that …

OK, more than that … you did really well.

Really well? Really, really well?

Yes, really, really, really well,
You did REALLY well …

So, I did really well, then …

Enough!
You want me to be honest?
You did really, really, really well.
But now you're beginning to annoy me.
It's all about you, isn't it?
It's all about, 'Look at me. Didn't I do well?'
It's all about, 'I'm the centre of things …' Eh?

What?
That's not what I meant at all.

I know that.
I know!
But look at you.
You want me to say you're wonderful?
OK … 'You're wonderful …'
See, I can say that.
But you're not perfect.
If you think you are, then you get people to worship you.
If that's your motivation, then I'm out of here.
Just be yourself.
You do fine.
You get it right.
You even get better.
But don't take it too far …

OK. OK!
I get it.
Don't go on …

Fine ...

Fine ...

Happy now?

I guess so ...
But, did I ask you how I did today?

You did fine ...
You did just fine ...

Twenty-fourth after Easter

Old Testament: Exodus 32:1-14
Epistle: Philippians 4:1-9
Gospel: Matthew 22:1-14

57 Reds under the bed

Raving Lefties were ten-a-penny on the estate. The MP was Labour. All the Councillors of the day were socialists, and the area was a hot-bed of political activity. It was more than 'Reds under the bed'... It was Reds everywhere you looked! But, thankfully, the local people were very straight and honest and were not backward in holding their political representatives to account. And that was especially true if any one of them, including the local MP, started getting above themselves and even more the case if money was involved. Scandals with expenses were to be nipped in the bud ...

Rumour had got round that one of the Councillors for the area had claimed council expenses for attending a church service on Remembrance Sunday, and the gathering at the war memorial, the previous year. An example of 'getting above themselves' it seemed, and certainly not paying proper respect to the Fallen. So it had been decided that this was 'not on', and some of the more militant political activists were determined to challenge the guilty party at the following year's Armistice service.

The minister, not being particularly politically aware, knew nothing of this, and found herself at the door of the church on the next Remembrance Sunday ready, as was the custom, to welcome invited visitors. She was about to shake hands with the local Councillor who'd just arrived, when she was elbowed aside by none other than the bold Mrs Carmichael. Auntie Bessie, as she was also known, was *El Presidente* of the local Pensioners' Action Group, and a fiery, militant Red! Accosting the unsuspecting Councillor and gripping him by the sleeve, she started, 'Hoi, you, are you here on official business or not?'

'I'm here for the service,' he replied with as much dignity as he could muster.

'Aye, I know that fine. That's why we're all here. Why would we be coming to church on Armistice Sunday if it wasn't for the service, eh? But are you "official" or are you one of us?'

'I'm representing the Council,' the bewildered man replied.

'Aye, right enough,' the rant went on, Mrs Carmichael now obviously warming to her task. 'But are you being *paid*, eh, paid for being here, eh, taking expenses for coming to our church, eh, eh, just like you did last year, eh?'

By this time, other members of the militant-Trotsky wing of the local congregation were closing in. The local Councillor was on a hiding to nothing. Whatever his normal expenses' allocation, he knew he was on a loser on this particular morning. His face was reddening. He was beginning to perspire. His dignity was long gone. The cornered prey had no escape. 'Yes, yes, it's true,' he blurted out. 'But it's the system.'

Auntie Bessie and her entourage were now ready to go in for the kill. By now the trembling minister could imagine the headlines in the local *Argus & Advertiser* – 'Riot at Church Service' – 'War Not Peace at Armistice Worship' – 'Seventy-six-year-old Pensioner Arrested for Assaulting Councillor'. But the Councillor, wily politician as he was, was not yet finished. The cornered animal had obviously been cornered before – and survived. You don't continue to make it in the messy jungle of local politics without learning how to get yourself out of a dangerous situation.

So he played his master card – 'But, you see, I've decided this year to give my expenses for today to charity, or the church, whatever's best – and last year's expenses as well. It's only right, don't you think?' The hunting pack was held at bay.

'To the *church*?' Bessie asked.

'Yes, to the church, if that's best, as soon as they come through,' came the reply. Glances were exchanged. And with imperceptible nods the knot of people parted, and a relieved Councillor was allowed access to the sanctuary.

The minister confessed to friends later that she didn't remember much about that particular Remembrance Sunday Service. But she *does* remember that a couple of weeks later she got a cheque in the post from the Councillor in question along with a scribbled note that this was a donation to the church for its valuable work, to be used as the minister saw fit.

What it really should have said, if he was honest, was that it was to keep Mrs Carmichael and her marauding hordes off his back. But then honesty can sometimes be in short supply in politics, can't it? And when money is involved, well …

The minister didn't know whether the cheque was the full amount of his expenses or whether it included a back payment for last year. But she made sure that Bessie Carmichael was the first one to be told about the donation, and Auntie Bessie went around for days sporting the biggest smile you could imagine.

Politics

Don't talk about politics and religion, they say,
because it just causes trouble.
But what else is there to talk about?
What else matters?

'Politics, pacifism and personal pep,'
George MacLeod would say,
because that's what it's all about.
It all has to hang together.

Society, peace and faith, God says,
all tied in with one another.
What else is there?
What else matters?

Twenty-fifth after Easter

Old Testament: Exodus 33:12-23
Epistle: 1 Thessalonians 1:1-10
Gospel: Matthew 22:15-22

58 Mrs Garrity's box

It was 'show and tell' time for Mrs Garrity's class on the Friday after-noon. It didn't happen every Friday, but about once a month or so it was a fun way to round off a week. This Friday afternoon it was the turn of Benny, Yvonne and Megan to 'show and tell', and at the appointed time twenty-four excited children sat cross-legged in the reading area at the back of the room. Mrs Garrity sat on a high stool and introduced the three stars who had brought along their prize items to show the others.

Benny had brought his grandad's World War Two medals, and the children were fascinated as he pinned them on his school sweatshirt and told his story about his grandad's time with the RAF from 1941 to 1945. The applause for Benny's 'show and tell' was loud and enthu-siastic. There was equal enthusiasm for Yvonne's red begonia, which she'd planted herself from a seedling she'd been given by her next-door neighbour, and which she clearly knew a *great deal* about. After such excellent presentations, Megan didn't disappoint. Her story about the two little dolls with their traditional outfits which her big sister had brought back from a business trip to Estonia had the chil-dren wide-eyed with amazement. A third period of applause was loud and long.

Mrs Garrity was delighted. But as she glanced at her watch she realised that 'show and tell' this week had been completed more quickly than usual. There were still seven or eight minutes to go before bell-time. She had to think quickly. But Mrs Garrity was a smart cookie!

'Well, children,' she began, 'since we have a few minutes left, let me show you something *I've* brought to tell you about today.' The children gasped. Mrs Garrity smiled. 'Now sit quietly while I show you what I've got hidden back here.' She moved behind the book-table and returned with – nothing! But the 'nothing' was grasped between her two outstretched hands which she held in front of her about a metre apart. 'You see what I've brought? This is very, *very* special to me.' There were puzzled frowns all round. Some of the children started to fidget. One or two were whispering to their neighbour. But Benny couldn't stand it any longer.

'But, Miss,' he blurted out, 'you've got nothing, nothing at all!' Everyone in the class nodded in agreement.

Mrs Garrity had them – and she knew it. 'Ah, but you're wrong, children, quite wrong. For you see what I've brought is ... well, let me show you ...' Slowly she bent forward and placed her 'nothing' on the floor in front of the children. The class followed her every movement. 'This, children, is my special box. You see it? No? Well, let's see what this special box has inside.' The children looked puzzled. A few were shaking their heads. Benny surreptitiously tapped his temple with his finger and mouthed 'she's gone loopy' to Yvonne and Megan. Mrs Garrity didn't bother. For with great ceremony she was taking the lid off her special box and laying it carefully to one side. She tipped her imaginary box forward. 'Can you see what's inside, children?'

'But there's nothing there, Miss,' chirped Megan.

'Ah, that's what *you* think. But I know this box is *full* of all kinds of interesting things. Let me show you ...'

She leant forward and dipped a hand into the box, and straightening up she held out her hand to show the children. 'You see this?'

'No, Miss,' the children chorused.

'Oh, of course, I forgot to tell you. My special box is special because it's full of things you can only see if you do them. So this is ...?' Shaking of heads all round ... 'This is ...?' Worried frowns ... 'This is ...' and gently Mrs Garrity waved her hand at the children. 'You see? I told you there would be interesting things in my box. Look! A wave, from me to all of you – but you can't see it till you do it. Do you have a wave for me?' And, as one, the children waved at Mrs Garrity and their teacher continued to wave back. 'Now,' she said, 'what else can we find?' She leant forward and pulled something new out of the box and held it in her other hand for the children to see. 'What's this, then?'

'Another wave?' someone suggested.

'No, silly, can't you see this is *different* from the last one?' And, with that, she bent forward and shook hands with Yvonne. 'See, it's a handshake, and because it's from my special box, you can't see it until you do it. Have you got a handshake you can share with someone?' And in an instant there were handshakes all round.

'Now then, what's next?' The children were wide-eyed. Mrs Garrity delved into her box once more and unearthed ... Well, she stood with her arms in front of her. 'I need two hands for this, but can you see what it is?' Silence... 'Come, now. Remember the wave and the handshake? You couldn't see them until ...'

'I know, Miss, I know,' squealed Megan, bouncing up and down with excitement. 'I know, Miss!'

'What is it then?' Mrs Garrity asked.

'It's a hug, Miss, because you can't see that till you do it either.' Everyone laughed.

'Well, then, have you got a hug you can show?' And spontaneously a whole class of children were hugging each other with unbounded enthusiasm.

'So then, one final thing from my box ...' Everyone went quiet and all eyes were on Mrs Garrity as she retrieved from the box something small which was tiny enough to be held between the thumb and forefinger of her right hand. 'And what's this?' The children were way ahead of her.

'It's a kiss, Miss,' a number of them shouted in chorus.

'Yes!' a smiling teacher replied. 'So, have you got a kiss for someone?'

'Yeuch!' murmured Benny – on behalf of the whole class it seemed.

'OK, then, but why not blow a kiss to each other?' And once Mrs Garrity had blown her kiss to all her children, lots of children's kisses of all shapes and sizes were being blown all over the room.

The bell rang for the end of the day. Surprisingly, no one moved, for Mrs Garrity wasn't quite finished. Very carefully she took her 'invisible' box, put its lid back on, and returned it behind the book table. 'There,' she announced. 'My special box, ready to be opened some other time, to share all the loving things inside that you can't see until you do them. So when you get home, children, go and find your own box, open it carefully, and share the things that are inside with the people you love. You've got lots of things in *your* box — but you can't see them until you do them.'

The children spilled out of the classroom for the weekend, chatting excitedly to one another. Another show-and-tell session that would always be remembered … And as Mrs Garrity watched the last of the children leave, she was delighted to see Benny, with his arms out in front of him, obviously struggling with the weight of his own special box.

To love

'Hello, I said. Nice to see you.'
And I shook his hand –
confirmation of my cheery greeting.
And in his firm grip,
I felt the acceptance of my friendly words.
The saying and the doing;
the words and the action,
bound up together.

'I forgive you.
It's all right now …'

as a 'sorry' is accepted,
and a relationship is healed.
But what then?
The embrace of forgiving love;
the hug of wholeness;
the open arms offering a new beginning.
Words are OK.
But the action?
How much more is shown
in the healing embrace of love's redemption.

'To love and to cherish …
To have and to hold …
Till death us do part …'
You've heard it said,
maybe even in your own or your partner's words.
But then,
'With this ring, I thee wed.'
And a ring is given,
placed on a finger,
a token of all that is given
a sign of absolute commitment.
You've heard it said;
you've seen it done.
Words and actions going together
to make the promise true.

'I love,
with all my heart,
with all my mind,
with all my strength.
I love,
I love,

I love ...'

Great!
I hear you.
Your words are good ...
But where are the actions
to confirm the words are true?

Twenty-sixth after Easter

Old Testament: Deuteronomy 34:1-12
Epistle: 1 Thessalonians 2:1-8
Gospel: Matthew 22:34-46

59 The letter

Ellen always wrote to her gran, and her gran always wrote back. It had started when Ellen went off to college. Waiting for her in her new room in Halls of Residence was a handwritten letter. 'Dear Ellen,' it ran, 'this is to wish you well for your new beginning. I've been too poorly to go out to buy a card, and if I were to ask the home-help to buy one, she'd probably get the wrong one anyway. You'd end up being congratulated on your retirement rather than being welcomed to your college. And you know I don't have a computer so I can't do that e-mailing stuff you talk about. And as for texting, well, that's quite beyond me. So I'm writing to make it more personal, with the notepaper I always keep beside me. And that's my promise to you, my dear. I'll write regularly, and with a proper fountain-pen too, the one your grandad bought me all these years ago. So, for now, this is just a note from me to wish you well. Much love, Gran.'

Ellen had written back, on one of the little notelets that had been a Christmas present from her sister, and in the spirit of her grand-mother's communication she'd handwritten the letter – though with a ball-point pen, as she'd never mastered writing with a fountain-pen. And that had been the start of it, Ellen and her gran, exchanging letters once a week or so, sharing news, offering encouragement, keeping in touch.

Gran would write about who she liked in a reality TV show, and Ellen would explain why she liked someone else. Ellen would share some feelings about a new boyfriend, and Gran would tell a story about a young soldier she'd dated before she married John. Gran would moan about her arthritis and the variable quality of her home-helps, and Ellen would moan about her college workload and the variable quality of her lecturers. Ellen would encourage her gran when she was low in spirits, and Gran would offer Ellen some insights into coping with life's problems. Always personal; always welcomed; always handwritten. Ellen always wrote to her gran and her gran always wrote back.

Of course there were visits during vacation-time and family gatherings at Christmas and the like. But it was the letters that were special for Ellen and her grandmother, something just for them.

When Ellen finished college, her gran was the star guest at the graduation ceremony. It was very special and everyone was so buoyant, not least Ellen herself. The letter of congratulation from her grandmother will always remain precious to her.

Problems arose when Ellen couldn't find work. Not that any kind of work wasn't available. There was always bar work and the waitressing Ellen had done to supplement her cash-flow during her years in college. But there weren't many opportunities in Ellen's chosen field, and the opportunities that did come up always required the completing of long application forms, the adjustment of a CV, the composing of an appropriate 'personal statement' and the checking out of references. Pretty soon Ellen had a veritable pile of rejection letters – 'thank you, but …', 'not enough experience …', 'many suitable applicants …', 'hope things work out …', and the like. She'd had one unsuccessful interview that had taken a lot out of her and had left her really deflated. Simply put, from the excitement of graduation to the reality of finding a job, Ellen was getting really down. So she did what she often did in these circumstances – she wrote to her gran.

It was the longest – and hardest – letter she'd written in a while. But it was also the most honest. All her struggles, self-doubt and despondency were poured out in a long epistle. Halfway through she wondered whether she should be burdening her grandmother with all her woes. But by the end of the letter she was glad she had. Gran's reply came a few days later – on the best notepaper, in a firm hand, written with a fountain-pen:

My dear Ellen

Thank you for your kind letter. You know I always enjoy hearing from you. You write so well.

It is a struggle, my dear, to know what the future might hold. I remember when I was your age I wanted to work as a nurse. But no one seemed to want me. There always seemed to be someone who got there before me, or who was better qualified, or who presented themselves better than me. I remember thinking I was in a corridor, trying a door that was half-open. I wanted to go through it, but it wouldn't open far enough. Sometimes I felt I might be able to squeeze through, but the gap was never wide enough. And sometimes the door would actually close while I was trying to open it. And sometimes it would close even before I got there. So I moved to another door, and tried that, and failed to find one that would even budge.

Then I came to realise that I was never promised success. I had many disappointments before I found a door that would open. But, then, I had a very long corridor, and there were many doors beyond the ones I already knew. There would be one that would open, of that I was convinced. I just had to keep trying before it became clear.

No experience in life is ever wasted, my dear – even the rejections and the closed doors. Each one is an encouragement to move on to the next one. And when we do, we are better equipped than we were before.

Keep your spirits up. Keep trying the doors. There will be one that's yours.

Every good wish.
Gran

Ellen still has that letter. She's older now and has a grandson who has just finished college. He's struggling to find work. Last week she wrote to him.

Dear Ian

Your mum tells me things are hard for you just now. I can't write as well as I used to as my fingers get sore so quickly. But come to see me soon, and I'll

*read you a letter I got a long time ago from a very wise woman. I think you
might find it helpful.*

God bless you.
Granny

and she wrote the letter with a fountain-pen she'd inherited from her
Gran.

*I know of no better way to celebrate the Communion of Saints than to offer the
words of this lovely Scottish song. It's one of only two poetic pieces in this book
which I've not written myself. But for me it has always beautifully encapsulated
the assurance of faith, that in the letting go of this life there is the assurance that
we are gathered together with the saints and angels in the land of the 'leal', the
land of the faithful – where our loved ones are waiting to be 'fain' – loving and
affectionate – when it comes our time to join their Communion.*

The Land o' the Leal
Lady Carolina Nairne (1766-1845)

I'm wearin' awa', John	*awa' = away*
Like snaw-wreaths in thaw, John,	*snaw = snow*
I'm wearin' awa'	
To the land o' the leal	*leal = faithful*
There's nae sorrow there, John,	*nae = no*
There's neither cauld nor care, John,	*cauld = cold*
The day is aye fair	*aye = always*
In the land o' the leal.	
Our bonnie bairn's there, John,	*bairn = child*
She was baith gude and fair, John;	*baith = both; gude = good*
And O! we grudged her sair	*sair = sore*
To the land o' the leal.	

But sorrow's sel' wears past, John,   *sel' = self*
And joy's a-coming fast, John,
The joy that's aye to last
In the land o' the leal.

Sae dear's the joy was bought, John,   *sae = so*
Sae free the battle fought, John,
That sinfu' man e'er brought   *sinfu' = sinful*
To the land o' the leal.
O, dry your glistening e'e, John!   *e'e = eye*
My saul langs to be free, John,   *saul = soul; langs = longs*
And angels beckon me
To the land o' the leal.

O, haud ye leal and true, John!   *haud = hold*
Your day it's wearin' through, John,
And I'll welcome you
To the land o' the leal.
Now fare-ye-weel, my ain John,   *fare-ye-weel = farewell*
This warld's cares are vain, John,   *warld = world*
We'll meet, and we'll be fain,   *fain = loving, affectionate*
In the land o' the leal.

All Saints

Old Testament: Psalm 34:1-10, 22:1
Epistle: Revelation 7:9-17 and 1 John 3:1-3
Gospel: Matthew 5:1-12

60 The greatest

'My mobile phone's better than your mobile phone.'

'No chance! My mobile can do *everything*, and it's even got a recording of my baby sister giggling as one of its ring-tones ... So *there!*'

'That's nothing! Our TV's bigger than *your* TV. My dad just bought it last week and it's *massive*. It fills the whole of one wall of our living room. And my dad says it was dead expensive, and was the biggest in the shop, and cost *thousands* ...'

Jake, he of the baby-sister-giggling-ring-tone, was not to be deterred. 'Huh,' he shrugged, 'we've got a TV twice as big. But anyway, who's bothered about TVs when my dad's got the snazziest car in our street. It's *fantastic* and it's silver and it's got alloy wheels and massive speakers. And me and my sister have a TV in the back and we can watch cartoons while my dad goes well fast on our way to town.'

'Who cares,' massive-TV-along-the-whole-of-one-wall Charlie retorted, his eyes opening wider and his voice getting louder. 'Anyone can get a silver car with all that stuff. But my brother's bigger than your brother. He's just well tall and my mum says he's going to be nine feet high and the biggest man in the *whole* world ... way bigger than *your* brother. Nyaahh!'

Jake was on his feet now, getting red in the face. 'Brothers are nothing compared to ... my bedroom! My bedroom's way better than your bedroom. It's huge, and I don't share it with *anyone*, and it's got a PlayStation, *and* cable TV, *and* an iPod docking station, *and* I've got a signed picture of Man United ...'

He never got the chance to finish. Charlie was well riled. '*Everyone's* got that. But we go on better holidays than you, in a *ginormous* plane that holds hundreds of people, and we fly *millions* of miles to the other side of the world, and play on beaches that go on for ever and *ever* and there's nothing but sand and our family owns the *whole thing*.'

Charlie and Jake were now facing each other, nose to nose, and Jake was about to suggest that his father owned half of Africa when Mrs Hamilton, the lower-school head, strode boldly across the playground towards the two competing lads. 'Goodness me, boys,' she gasped. 'I could hear you from the far side of the yard. You look as though you're about to do damage to each other. And I thought you were best friends. What on *earth* are you arguing about?'

Jake and Charlie looked suitably sheepish. 'Nothing, Miss,' Charlie offered.

'*Nothing?*' Mrs Hamilton replied. 'That didn't seem like nothing to me. Come on, tell me the truth.' Jake looked at his feet. 'We were arguing about who is the greatest, Miss,' he confessed.

'Greatest?' Mrs Hamilton responded, incredulously. 'Greatest! Between you two? Now that's a laugh!' And she was about to give two little boys a lecture on humility when she stopped herself. 'C'm'on, both of you. Inside with me. I'll show you who's the greatest.'

'But, Miss,' Charlie whined, clearly scared that this indoors-march was going to lead to some horrible punishment. Mrs Hamilton read his mind. 'Now don't worry, there's no punishment coming. Just a wee lesson in who's the greatest …'

Within minutes, a relieved Jake and Charlie were sitting in Mrs Hamilton's classroom while she was putting a DVD into the machine under the TV. 'Watch this,' was all she said.

The pictures were of a small black boy filling a dirty water-container from a little stream. The battered container was almost as big as he was, and he was having to carry it along a rutted track. 'This is Djuma,' the commentary said. 'He's the only one in his family in the Sudan who isn't sick. So he has to walk a mile and a half to get water, and a mile and a half back to bring it to his mother and sister.

Djuma has to do this every day.'

The scene changed to a small hut, with a sick mother lying on the floor, and a skinny young girl sitting cross-legged by her side. Djuma is pouring water from the container into a small bowl. 'Djuma's mother and sister have malaria,' the commentary continued, 'and Djuma has no one to help him ...'

Charlie and Jake were wide-eyed at what they were watching. But their focus on the TV was interrupted by Mrs Hamilton's gently admonishing voice. 'Well, boys, do you see Djuma arguing about who's the greatest?'

'No, Miss,' two suitably humbled lads replied in chorus.

'Does he have a TV and a big bedroom and a fancy holiday to boast about?'

'No, Mrs Hamilton.'

'Isn't it better to care for someone than to argue about who's the greatest?'

'Yes, Miss.'

'Well then, off you go, and let that be a lesson to you.'

Charlie and Jake rose quietly from their seats and headed out of the classroom. Mrs Hamilton smiled. And as they were going through the classroom door, Jake turned to Charlie and whispered, 'My mum's younger than your mum.'

'No she isn't,' an offended Charlie replied indignantly. 'My mum's totally cool and she still listens to Radio 1 and *everything* ...' Jake cast a glance over his shoulder, fearful that Mrs Hamilton might be listening. But she wasn't. For she was too engrossed in watching a little lad called Djuma giving his dying mother a drink of water he'd walked three miles to fetch.

Blessed

You're blessed when you love,
and you're loved when you're blessed.

You're healed when you're blessed,
and you bless when you heal.

You're blessed when you serve,
and you're served when you're blessed.

You're forgiven when you're blessed,
and you bless when you forgive.

You're blessed when you seek peace,
and you know peace when you're blessed.

You're made new when you're blessed,
and your blessings make things new.

You're blessed when you're great,
and you're the greatest when you're blessed.

Twenty-seventh after Easter

Old Testament: Joshua 3:7-17
Epistle: 1 Thessalonians 2:9-13
Gospel: Matthew 23:1-12

61 Ready or not?

Jennifer and her team had been ready since the crack of dawn. Actually, they'd been getting ready for the big day for weeks, ever since Jennifer had received the invitation. But on the morning of the special event, everyone had been ready for *ages*, and all that was to be done now was to wait.

The 'waiting room' for Jennifer and her team was the church hall where they had their weekly practice. Gymnastics was Jennifer's life, and having the opportunity to work with youngsters and help them progress from stage to stage with their BSGA badges was a real delight. But the group of girls she'd selected from this year's class were the best ones she'd ever worked with. They'd achieved what Jennifer had always hoped for – they'd become a skilled, popular and much-sought-after Junior Gymnastics Display Team.

And that's why Jennifer and her team had got the grant from the Royal Trust – for new tumbling mats, hoops, balls and ribbons for the team's displays; to cover accommodation and travelling costs; to help them develop their skills, share them with the wider community and test them in various competitions. And it was the grant that had led to the special day.

The Royal Trust had arranged for a gathering of recipients of grants to meet the Prince, the Trust's patron, so that he could see first-hand the beneficial effects of the Trust's work. It was to take place in a huge sports' hall on the edge of town. Lots of people from all over the county were to be there. And when Jennifer told her team about the invitation for them to be part of the gathering, there was more excitement than you could ever measure.

So Jennifer and her team had been getting ready for the big day for weeks. They'd spent hours perfecting their routines. They'd made sure every team member had her costume in pristine condition and that all

290 Welcoming each wonder

the BSGA badges were up-to-date and sewn on properly. Jennifer had to submit the names and photographs of all the team to the organisers so that they could all be issued with appropriate security badges – and how chuffed the children were when *they* arrived. And on the morning of the special event, the children were well scrubbed, got to the church rendezvous in good time, made sure they had their security badges safely with them, and waited with crackling excitement for the time to come round when they would go to meet the Prince.

Jennifer had hired a minibus for the day – no public transport or being squeezed into private cars for *this* special occasion. They'd been instructed – so Jennifer had assured the children – to be at the sports' hall car-park an hour before the event was due to start. So, with the starting time at 2 o'clock, Jennifer made sure they had plenty of time to be there for 1pm, get the minibus parked, make sure the team knew where they were going, get things organised in the appropriate display area, and be ready in good time for the arrival of the Prince and his entourage at 2pm. She had it all worked out in her head. They were ready. Nothing could go wrong.

So it was an excited gymnastics display team who piled into the minibus ready to leave the church in good time. The journey across town was uneventful. The conversation in the back of the bus was animated and constant. Jennifer was pleased. Everything was going to plan. This was going to be a very special day indeed.

They arrived at the sports' hall car park just before 1 o'clock. As they turned in through the main gates, Jennifer was surprised to see how quiet the car-park was, expecting there to be much more activity than was apparent. As she pulled the bus into a vacant space she was even more surprised to see groups of people coming *out* of the building – three boys carrying unicycles, several St John's Ambu- lance people, four policemen, and a camera-crew with two trolleys piled high with equipment.

Jennifer's team didn't notice. They were too excited to be aware of anything else. But Jennifer knew something was amiss. 'Wait here,' she said to her team, 'while I go and check things out.'

There was lots of activity in the foyer of the sports' hall. Two policewomen were standing by the main door. Seeing Jennifer looking somewhat lost, and knowing that they'd not seen her before, one of them asked, 'Can I help you, miss?'

'Oh, sorry,' Jennifer replied, presenting her security pass as she had been instructed, 'I've come for the Prince's visit.'

'Oh, I'm sorry, miss,' the policewoman responded, 'you're too late. It's all over. It started at 12. People had to be here at 11. The Prince stayed for just under an hour. He's just gone, and now we're just clearing up. I'm awfully sorry. But you've missed it.'

Jennifer went cold. Mumbling an inadequate 'thank you' she turned on her heel and headed out of the building. As she did so, she retrieved the instruction sheet from her back pocket. Sure enough, what she'd read as 2 really was 12. And what she was sure had said 'be in the building by 1', actually said 11. In her excitement, she hadn't read the instructions properly. She and her team were ready. But they weren't ready for the right time.

Jennifer slipped the instruction sheet back into her pocket and headed to the minibus. She could see the faces of the excited gymnasts through the windows of the bus. She had no idea what she was going to tell them …

Ready?

I can't be ready for everything, now, can I?
I can be ready for what I need to be ready for,
for what I know about.
That's hard enough, and, to be honest,
it takes up enough time and energy.
But how can I be ready for what I don't know about,
the unexpected, the unplanned event?
If I was to be ready for everything,

I'd spend all my life getting ready,
and never have any time to do anything useful at all.
I'd just be hanging about all the time, ready and waiting.
So, I'll just be as ready as I can be,
and hope that the unexpected can be coped with as well.
Maybe I can't be ready for everything.
So I'll just have to try to be ready for some things at least –
at least some of the time.

Twenty-eighth after Easter

Old Testament: Joshua 24:1-3a, 14-25
Epistle: 1 Thessalonians 4:13-18
Gospel: Matthew 25:1-13

62 Good dog! Good dog!

Mrs Rumbelow had a dog. The dog was called Oddjob. And Oddjob was dangerous. Not that Mrs Rumbelow's dog was a danger to Mrs Rumbelow, for she had him well trained. But Oddjob was dangerous to any other unsuspecting person who would dare to venture within ten yards of the ferocious beast.

Mrs Rumbelow's ten-year-old mongrel had been her constant companion since it had been a puppy. She had named it Oddjob because, before she had him properly house-trained, he was inclined to leave little odd deposits in different parts of the house. But as the loveable puppy transmogrified into the full-grown adult beast which now ruled the Rumbelow flat, it was clear that Oddjob was more than aptly named, for with his black coat, white collar and black head, and the flat, pug-nose that had appeared as one part of the fifty-seven varieties in its mongrel genes, it looked remarkably similar to the Oddjob villain of James Bond movie fame.

And this canine version of Oddjob was equally dangerous. For if Mrs Rumbelow's flatmate and minder could have had a steel-rimmed bowler hat with which to inflict major injury on unprepared antagonists, it might have been his weapon of choice. But without it Oddjob had to make do with a well-practised low growl, vicious-looking teeth, dripping jowls, and the occasional attempt to take a chunk out of the nearest available thigh.

Dr Thompson knew all about Oddjob. In recent years Mrs Rumbelow had become largely confined to her flat. Severe arthritis and a right-sided weakness following a slight stroke had combined to restrict Mrs Rumbelow's out-of-doors forays. So, though she had done remarkably well to stay in her own home, all the caring services had to visit her in situ. Dr Thompson was no exception. Through his routine visits and emergency call-outs, he had got to know Mrs Rumbelow very well.

Dr Thompson and Oddjob knew each other well too, or at least as well as Dr Thompson had chosen to get acquainted with Mrs Rumbelow's companion and bodyguard. The first time Dr Thompson had encountered Oddjob, dripping jowls and vicious fangs had been evident as soon as he'd entered Mrs Rumbelow's living room – from Oddjob, that is, not Dr Thompson – and Mrs Rumbelow had just about managed to haul the dangerous Oddjob away from feasting on Dr Thompson's thigh and shut him in the kitchen – Oddjob, that is, not Dr Thompson. Ever since then, Dr Thompson, whenever possible, had phoned Mrs Rumbelow to give her ample warning of when he would visit, and he was always relieved to find that Oddjob was in the kitchen when he called, even though the low growl and the scraping at the kitchen door was a clear indication that Dr Thompson's thigh would still have been Oddjob's preferred snack.

It was a Friday afternoon when Dr Thompson was walking past the front of Mrs Rumbelow's flat. He was relieved that she wasn't on his house-call list, and delighted indeed that, as far as he knew, she was doing pretty well at the moment. He glanced towards Mrs Rumbelow's abode and was about to hurry on his way when he heard Oddjob. But this was no low growl. This was full-fledged, ferocious, I'll-take-much-more-than-your-thigh, all-out, incredible, scary barking. Dr Thompson jumped, expecting to see a mad and angry Oddjob ready to attack him right there in the street. But there was no dog to be seen. There was only the continual sound of Oddjob's unmistakable barking.

Dr Thompson went to investigate. Tentatively, he peered in through Mrs Rumbelow's front-room window. No sign of Oddjob, but still the continual noise. He went into the stair to Mrs Rumbelow's front door, first on the right. He flipped up the letterbox. No Oddjob, just more and louder barking. He proceeded through the stair, out through the door to the back yard and round to the rear of the flat. He squinted through the net curtains of what he knew was Mrs Rumbelow's bedroom, and almost jumped out of his skin when he encountered a clearly enraged Oddjob peering at him through the window, inches from his nose. He hoped the window was made of toughened glass, for Oddjob's demeanour was clearly not a happy one.

It was then that Dr Thompson saw why. For stretched across the bed, fully-clothed but not moving, was the prostrate figure of Mrs Rumbelow. Something bad had happened. And Oddjob was trying to get someone's attention.

Things moved pretty quickly after that. The police were first to arrive. Brave though they were, they decided not to enter the house without back-up. The dog-wardens were summoned. The door was broken down before the ambulance got there. Oddjob was hauled off at the end of a long pole, secured by the metal noose ten feet from the quivering hands of two dog wardens. The paramedics took care of Mrs Rumbelow. Dr Thompson reckoned it was another stroke. The house was made secure. All went quiet.

That was three months ago. Oddjob wasn't happy in the Council kennels, and was delighted to be reunited with Mrs Rumbelow when she was discharged from hospital – at least, that's what she told Dr Thompson when he came to visit, though the growling of Oddjob behind the kitchen door seemed much the same as before. But in Mrs Rumbelow's eyes, Oddjob was a hero, for without him she might have lain undiscovered for ages. And who knows what might have happened then? At least, that's what she recounted to Dr Thompson when Oddjob's loud bark could be heard again in response to Mrs Rumbelow's frail old voice shouting affectionately, 'Good dog! Good dog!'

Talents

What can I offer? What can I give?
What can I bring you today?
What can I do now? What do you need?
What do you want me to say?

What can I help with? What's to be done?
What are my skills to prepare?
What am I good at? What's any use?
What are my offerings to share?

Bring me your tenderness; offer your touch;
Give me your comfort again;
Hold out your hopefulness; stay when I cry;
Be by my side through my pain.

Hold me and help me; for that's what I need.
Be a companion that's true.
You have the talent; you have the skill.
All that I'm wanting is you.

Twenty-ninth Sunday after Easter

Old Testament: Judges 4:1-7
Epistle: 1 Thessalonians 5:1-11
Gospel: Matthew 25:14-30

63 Home

Don Anderson was on his way home. He'd taken a long time to get round to it, though the delay wasn't of his own making. But now, home was where he was heading, and that was all that mattered.

For many years, home for Don, as far as living, working, family and culture were concerned, had been in Washington DC in the USA. Work with the UK Admiralty had taken Don to the States as a liaison officer with the US Navy, and several promotions found him in a senior administrative position with the military in the Pentagon. That, combined with expanding family life, had contrived to bind Don to the west side of the Atlantic for longer than he would really have wanted.

There was no doubt about it that, as far as everyone who knew him was concerned, home for Don Anderson was in the good old US of A. But home in Don's heart was three thousand miles away across the pond. Home for Don Anderson, as far as nationality, belonging, roots and history were concerned, was in the village of Netherton, in the wilds of Northumberland, just south of the Scotland-England Border. Home was in the village where, till the age of thirteen, Don and his younger sister, Caroline, had spent their idyllic childhood.

Netherton – where their mother had been teacher in the village school, teaching the children of the farmers and the shepherds from along the valley, and caring for Don and Caroline as two-parents-in-one since their father had been killed on the beaches of Normandy at the D-Day landings.

Netherton – with Mrs McAllister's village post office and telephone exchange, the centre of the village's economy and social life and a resource for lots of local knowledge and titbits of gossip, mostly because all the phones in the valley were on one party line.

Netherton – where Don had spent endless fascinating hours at Bill Watson's Smiddy, watching him beat out metal shoes on his anvil for the farms' shire-horses, repair the blades of a broken plough, and turn red-hot metal into wrought-iron gates, and where an invitation to pump the bellows for the forge was the highlight of Don's school holidays.

Netherton – where Don was welcome in every home; where every garden was a playground; where every resident was a friend.

Netherton – with its dangerous 90° bend in the road right in the middle of the village, with the ever-increasing risk of accidents, especially when the traffic on the road north became busier and busier, culminating in the bakery lorry's momentous crash into the school railings.

Netherton – with its little church at the edge of the village, surrounded by its higgledy-piggledy graveyard, with his mother's grave marked by a grey granite headstone in the far corner.

And it was to this Netherton – this home of his heart – that Don was heading, on a much-awaited, long-promised, early retirement homecoming.

The drive from Prestwick airport was much like any other journey, and it wasn't until Don had passed through the Ayrshire, Galloway and Dumfriesshire countryside heading to the Scottish Borders, and was over the border at Gretna, that he began to feel close to home. But it was when he turned into the top of the valley of his childhood that Don Anderson's heart really began to sing. For there were the low, craggy cliffs above the three-acre field, from which two sheep had famously jumped onto the roof of his mother's car, causing great damage to the vehicle and no apparent damage to the sheep. There was Johnstone's meadow, which had served as the school football pitch and the venue for the village fairs and local agricultural shows. There was the church and the higgledy-piggledy graveyard, which was to be Don's ultimate place of pilgrimage, so that he could lay flowers on his mother's grave.

And there, as he turned the bend past the church was … nothing – no village, no cherished childhood place, no Netherton. Instead what Don was gazing on was a flattened, expansive wasteland, the centre of earth-moving activity, as bulldozers and trucks, diggers and asphalt-lorries busied themselves on the creation of a new road.

It was, Don discovered later, the much-awaited 'road-improvement scheme', to take out the dangerous 90° corner in the middle of a run-down village, to allow the busy traffic on an increasingly important trunk road to speed on its way. A better road – but at the expense of a village school, and Mrs McAllister's post office, and Watson's Smiddy, and the homes of his friends …

Don pulled his car over. And as he sat and gazed at the scene, he was confused, angry and disappointed. A new road had taken away his childhood home. He didn't know what to think. It wasn't what he'd expected at all. Was this the way it had to be?

So Don did what he always did, what he'd always done when he needed to work things out. He went and had a chat with his mother. And sitting on the low wall at the far corner of a higgledy-piggledy graveyard, Don and his mother duly worked things out. Of course there had to be progress. Good roads couldn't have dangerous 90° corners. Busy travellers needed a clear way ahead. Run-down villages had had their day. Progress always meant change. The old had to give way to the new.

Don's mother was always wise. Her reflections were as good as ever. But this time there was more. Can a new road really take away an idyllic childhood? Could a flattened construction site erase the vibrancy of formative memories? Would progress remove memories of home?

As Don drove back north – the beginning of another journey – his disappointment had gone. His journey home hadn't been wasted. Whatever the future would contain, he would take Netherton with him. No fancy road could remove what was part of him for ever. If home was where the heart is, Don Anderson's heart would always carry the memories of his childhood village.

In 1989, I spent three months of sabbatical leave in Washington DC, nurtured and changed by the remarkable people of 'The Church of the Saviour'. I stayed in the home of John and Sarah Levering. John had terminal cancer, and while I was there he died peacefully at home. His funeral service was a celebration of life, a gathering of memories, and an affirmation of faith. I'd written a poem for John, which I had the privilege of sharing with him before he died. I wrote it when he came home from his final visit to the hospital. Sarah invited me to share it at the funeral. It was one of the hardest and most positive things I've ever been asked to do. But it was a privilege and a joy. John had gone home.

Home

Home is where the heart is.
Home is where the love is.
Home is where I really want to be.
Home is where I rest now.
Home is where I'm blessed now.
Home is where the welcome's wide and free.

Home is what I aim for.
Home is what I yearn for.
Home is what defines my journey's goal.
Home is what fulfils me.
Home is what sustains me.
Home is what gives healing to my soul.

Home, giving a sign here;
Home, promising hope here;
Home, without condition, offering grace.
Home, where I can wait now;
Home, where I find peace now;
Home, forever held in love's embrace.

Last Sunday of the year

Old Testament: Ezekiel 34:11-16, 20-24
Epistle: Ephesians 1:15-23
Gospel: Matthew 25:31-46

Also by Tom Gordon:

A Blessing to Follow

Contemporary parables for living

A companion volume to Welcoming Each Wonder, with stories relating to lectionary cycle C.

A Need for Living

Signposts on the journey of life and beyond

Everyone has a need for meaning in life. For most of us, it is only when we are facing a life crisis, or the loss of a loved one, or the reality of our own death that the search for meaning becomes real. How then do we express what really matters?

Facing this in his work as a hospice chaplain, Tom Gordon has created a book for people facing a life crisis and for those who care for the dying. Ultimately it is for everyone, especially those for whom traditional words and symbols have failed, and who need new images to help them live again.

New Journeys Now Begin

Learning on the path of grief and loss

Bereavement is a journey to be travelled, not an illness to be treated or a problem to be solved. Tom Gordon writes with sensitivity and clarity about real people as they begin to understand their journeys of bereavement, helping us understand the unplanned and often frightening twists and turns grief forces the bereaved to face.

The Iona Community is:

- An ecumenical movement of men and women from different walks of life and different traditions in the Christian church
- Committed to the gospel of Jesus Christ, and to following where that leads, even into the unknown
- Engaged together, and with people of goodwill across the world, in acting, reflecting and praying for justice, peace and the integrity of creation
- Convinced that the inclusive community we seek must be embodied in the community we practise

Together with our staff, we are responsible for:

- Our islands residential centres of Iona Abbey, the MacLeod Centre on Iona, and Camas Adventure Centre on the Ross of Mull

and in Glasgow:

- The administration of the Community
- Our work with young people
- Our publishing house, Wild Goose Publications
- Our association in the revitalising of worship with the Wild Goose Resource Group

The Iona Community was founded in Glasgow in 1938 by George MacLeod, minister, visionary and prophetic witness for peace, in the context of the poverty and despair of the Depression. Its original task of rebuilding the monastic ruins of Iona Abbey became a sign of hopeful rebuilding of community in Scotland and beyond. Today, we are about 250 Members, mostly in Britain, and 1500 Associate Members, with 1400 Friends worldwide. Together and apart, 'we follow the light we have, and pray for more light'.

For information on the Iona Community contact:
The Iona Community, Fourth Floor, Savoy House, 140 Sauchiehall Street,
Glasgow G2 3DH, UK. Phone: 0141 332 6343
e-mail: admin@iona.org.uk; web: www.iona.org.uk

For enquiries about visiting Iona, please contact:
Iona Abbey, Isle of Iona, Argyll PA76 6SN, UK. Phone: 01681 700404
e-mail: ionacomm@iona.org.uk